HOME IS WHERE THE HEART IS

GERALDINE COX

For ~~████~~,

Love,

Geraldine

MACMILLAN

Pan Macmillan Australia

Geraldine Cox can be contacted on geraldine.cox@bigpond.com.kh

First published 2000 in Macmillan by Pan Macmillan Australia Pty Ltd
St Martins Tower, 31 Market Street, Sydney

Copyright © Geraldine Cox 2000

National Library of Australia
Cataloguing-in-Publication Data:

Cox, Geraldine.
Home is where the heart is.

ISBN 0 7329 1034 X.

1. Cox, Geraldine. 2. Child welfare workers – Cambodia –
Phnom Penh – Biography. I. Title.

362.73092

Typeset in 11/15 Proforma by Midland Typesetters
Printed in Australia by McPherson's Printing Group

Dedication

Dedicated, not only to the millions of Cambodians who perished during the years of war and genocide, but to those who survived the killing fields and to their children who live on, striving every day to put their personal sorrows behind them, to make Cambodia the land of plenty, peace and harmony that is, for many, only a distant memory.

Acknowledgments

While writing this book I have delved into works of distinguished authors for hard facts, especially *Sideshow: Kissinger, Nixon and the Destruction of Cambodia* by William Shawcross, Hogarth, London, 1986; *Khmers Stand Up!: A History of the Cambodian Government 1970-1975* by Justin J. Corfield, Centre of Southeast Asian Studies, Monash University, 1994; and *Cambodia – From Red to Blue: Australia's Initiative For Peace* by Kenneth Berry (my old colleague and friend), Allen & Unwin in association with the Department of International Relations, RSPAS, Australian National University, 1997.

Tributes

Thanks are due to the many friends and lovers who have agreed to their real names and stories being part of *Home Is Where the Heart Is*. But special gratitude goes to those wonderful Cambodians who were willing to open old emotional wounds to make this book more real. Thanks to my nurturing friends in Phnom Penh who are not mentioned in this book, such as Rosemary Chan, Saleha Hamsan, Gerald Trevor, Pascal Brandt-Gagnon, Thierry de Roland Peel, Dawn and Peter Booth, the Harper family, Chanta Sandford, Charles Cooper, and many others who comforted me when I cried, listened to me when I screamed, wined and dined me when I had no money, and were simply always there for me. Thank you to my family and friends in Australia, such as Cherie and John Woolven, Lyn and Neil Stagg, Carolyn Ashmore, Barbara Zuegg and Gloria Scott, Barbara Whiteman, Shamim Mohamed-Khawaja, Johanna van der Spek, Andy Baker, Jan and John Munro, the much missed Tim, and Teresa Atkinson, and Curly and Joy Templeton, who greeted me with open arms every time I returned, as though I had never left. Thanks to Dory Taraghi, Pam Jeremy and Dr Daniel Sussott, who opened their homes to me when they saw my need. Thanks to Jack Brooker, the sweetest stepfather in the world. I thank Marcia Puhl, who nominated me and did all the hard work that eventuated in my being awarded a Member of the Order of Australia in 2000. Thanks to Adriana Volona for her prayers, generosity and artistic creativity. Thanks to all the other very special volunteers who gave of their time and varied skills to live and work with the children in Cambodia – Lara Francis, Gill Fryer, Michael Hartley-Smith, Rebekah Grindlay, Andrew Newdick, Anthea Barrington, Tracey Shelton, Dr Tania James, Ronelle Owen, Stephanie Hewitt, Brigid McKay, Simon Taylor, James Reynolds, Peter Salerno, Sue and Allen Laverton, The Family, Patty Zenonos, James Montagu, Chris Franckel and the Soapbox Organisation. Special thanks go to Janine Hosking and Leonie Lowe, who were so touched when they first visited the orphanage that they personally invested in the filming of *My Khmer Heart*, a sensitive documentary which portrays the hopes and dreams of the orphans of Cambodia. And on behalf of the children, thank you to all the sponsors, every one of you who gives so that the children at The Australia Cambodia Foundation's orphanage know they are loved.

Contents

B.C. – Before Cambodia

Canberra, December 1970 – May 1971

Today was the day. After a gruelling training period in Canberra I was finally going to be told my first posting with the Department of Foreign Affairs. I checked my make-up and hair for the tenth time. I knew that I was regarded in the grey world of the public service as a tad too colourful, but refused to make any concessions.

I was definitely the only woman in the department flaunting false eyelashes. But this was the beginning of the seventies – and at least they were real mink. Miniskirts were still in, but as soon as I saw the long maxi dresses in fashion magazines, I jumped at the chance to hide my sturdy legs under them. I went to work wearing long boots and dresses down to my ankles, which was quite a contrast to all the mini-clad secretaries with whom I was working. It only took a few days for personnel to tell me that my style of dress was 'too modern' and to advise me to 'conform more'.

So I did.

I dressed for work the next day in a short dress, and when I looked in the mirror I knew it was not a good look. But they wanted me to conform, and this was what all the other slim, young things were wearing to work. In the hallway on the way to the typing pool, I passed the woman who had counselled me about my dress the day before. I twirled in front of her, giving her a good view of my tree-trunk thighs, and said, 'Is this more like it?'

That was the one and only day I wore a miniskirt to work. After that there were no more complaints.

⌒

I had thrown myself into many training courses and worked hard to reach the standard required of secretaries to be posted overseas. I felt at a disadvantage because I had left school at the age of fifteen, before the end-of-year intermediate exams. I felt I wasn't as well educated or qualified as many of the other young women I was training with.

I had prepared a very eloquent letter in answer to the advertisement for secretaries to undertake overseas service. I was twenty-five and had been employed for ten years in responsible positions, and pointed out to them in my letter that this was surely worth a miserly pass at the intermediate standard. The recruitment officer succumbed and interviewed me. Then I sat an IQ test, and a typing and shorthand test, and answered a questionnaire on international affairs.

I was in.

I knew it was going to take months for ASIO to give me the necessary security clearance, and I decided to do something really different while I was waiting. I went to work as a miner in the opal mines at Coober Pedy in South Australia. My aim was to try to pay off the debts I had acquired while working for an Adelaide stockbroker. He had advised me, at the worst possible time, to invest in the Poseidon venture, which brought many Australian stock market players to their knees.

Mining was backbreaking work, and I think that at the time – 1969 – I was the only unaccompanied woman working as a miner and not as a prostitute. A more appropriate name for Coober Pedy in those days would have been Dodge City. The opal fields were a haven for a large part of Australia's criminal society, who were either just out of jail or running away to avoid being put there. There was no bank at all, probably because no financial institution was game enough to establish a branch in a city populated by a large proportion of criminals and misfits. I like to think of myself as being in the latter category.

It was not possible to stay unmolested without a recognised boyfriend to play the role of protector. After a thorough look around at the possibilities, things looked pretty grim. Then I met Pasquale Esposito, a very respectable, unmarried, quiet and gentle Italian man who lived with his parents. When he wasn't mining he was helping out in the Italian restaurant run by his mother, undisputedly the best cook in town. He was exactly what I needed.

During the months I spent with Pasquale he gave me all the respect and affection I wanted, as well as keeping all the other undesirable men at bay very effectively. Our relationship ended naturally and without drama when I left Coober Pedy, and it was with disbelief that thirty years later I heard he had murdered his wife and mother-in-law and had been sentenced to life imprisonment.

One night, sitting in the pub after a long day's mining, I received a letter from Foreign Affairs saying I had got my security clearance. The mail was always handed out in the pub because everyone gathered there to sink a few gallons of beer before turning in for the night. (A glass of water was actually more expensive than a beer as all the drinking water was trucked up daily from Adelaide.) Everyone wanted to know what the letter contained.

'Struth, love! Are you going to be one of those stuck-up diplomatic toffs and not want to speak to us again?' one of my mining mates asked. I answered by challenging him to an arm-wrestling match, which I knew he would enjoy winning.

I spent the next day trying to find some suitable writing paper and a decent pen so I could write a letter of acceptance. No one wrote letters in Coober Pedy. Many of the miners were hiding from the police or their wives. There wasn't one lined writing pad in the whole place, or anything other than a cheap biro to write with. The best I could do was to ask the Italian butcher to cut me a piece of paper from the roll he wrapped the meat in. He made three attempts before slicing me a sheet that didn't have bloodstains on it from his carving knife. And that was what I wrote on to accept the offer to join the Australian Government Department of Foreign Affairs. The letter is probably still in my file.

But that was all behind me. Now I was just minutes away from being told where I was going to live for the next couple of years of my life, serving my country in an Australian embassy somewhere in the world. I was so excited!

To keep my mind off the looming interview, I thought about what had led me to this point. I knew my life was changing forever, and that I was charting a course for myself. None of this fate bullshit. I was going to be the mistress of my own destiny. I got into Foreign Affairs through sheer determination, telling a few tiny lies, exaggerating a little bit, and just not letting life hand me a fair share of misery before I had even reached my twenty-fifth birthday.

I had travelled more than most of my friends, and had my taste for distant lands well and truly titillated during a trip to Europe in 1963 when I was eighteen. I sailed out of Port Adelaide on the old P&O liner, *Himalaya*, and as I watched the coastline of Australia disappear, my instincts told me from then on it would be hard for me to settle for the quiet life that Adelaide had to offer. I remember that my mother stayed on the wharf long after all my other family and friends had left. She positioned herself right at the end of it and tied a large white handkerchief to the end of her umbrella, waving it in a slow arc back and forth until the ship sailed out of sight. That's the kind of mother she is. I am her youngest, and the one who had caused her most pain and worry, and she must have known that in a sense I was leaving home forever that day.

My parents married during the Depression. My dad, Norm, had to work hard so that my mother, Dot, could stay at home to care for their three daughters. This she did with great dedication. Mum loved making our clothes and we always looked special in her dresses. But I was a real challenge; Mum would kneel, frowning, as she tried with a tape measure to find my waist for the dress she was making. She would usually have to guess and the dress would be made with the required waist somewhere around my middle. She also had a gift for interior decoration. Her husband, her daughters and her home were her life. But the tragic death of a baby girl before I was born had triggered a depression that was to revisit Mum many times. She struggles valiantly even now to conquer these sudden bouts.

My dad was a milkman who delivered milk 365 days a year. He was proud of being a blue-collar worker and voted Labor to his dying day. He died of lung cancer, caused by being a thirty-a-day roll-your-own cigarette smoker. In one of his conversations with me during his last week of life, when he was struggling to breathe, he rasped, 'If you ever vote anything else than Labor, I'll come back and haunt you!'

I grew up with little respect for, or understanding of, how to manage money. Most of the people to whom Dad delivered milk knocked on our door and paid their bills in cash. Whoever answered the door – Dad, Mum, my sisters or me – just tossed the notes and coins into a huge china salad bowl on the kitchen table. From this my mother took what she needed to buy food and pay other bills; and we girls dipped into it whenever we wanted to buy something, without being made to account for what we took. Money was always just there for whatever we needed.

Just before I left school all this changed when Dad was struck down in his earning prime by a cartel which took over his wholesale milk business, more than halving our income overnight. He fought back, and morally he should have won his court battle. But I learned early that justice is not always on the side of the good. Dad never recovered from this blow to his livelihood; he turned his suffering in on himself and soon developed asthma, and the lung cancer which would eventually kill him. He had always been proud of being able to give his family everything, and now the bowl on the kitchen table was often near empty.

He turned more and more towards the horses he loved so much. We always had at least three young racehorses in the stables at the bottom of the garden, and this was where we would find him when we wanted him. We watched helplessly as big Norm's burly physique shrank year by year after his business failed. He never allowed us to comfort him and carried his bitterness and disappointment alone.

After I turned fifteen my behaviour could only be described as delinquent, and my parents hoped that I might change while I was away. Sex discovered me when I was only fifteen, in stark contrast to my two older sisters who were virgins when they married. My carefree attitude in this area was a constant source of concern for my conservative, and always suspicious, parents. I devised all sorts of schemes to get out at night. I would kiss my parents goodnight and go off to my bedroom, where I would go to bed fully clothed and wait to hear Mum and Dad go to bed. At around 10.00 p.m., when I was sure they were asleep, I would leave a note on the kitchen table saying that I had got up early to take our dog, Skip, for a walk and would be back for breakfast. I knew that Skip would bark like crazy if he heard footsteps outside, so I crept out of the house carrying him with me. I would walk to the phone box on the corner and call a taxi to take Skip and me to my Yugoslav boyfriend's boarding house in the city, booking it to come back and collect us in time for me to walk nonchalantly in the door in the morning for breakfast. Almost every taxi driver in Adelaide knew what I was up to, but it was regular business for them. And Skip wasn't going to tell anyone. I got away with this for months.

When I returned after a year of working and flitting around England and Europe, my parents discovered I was more trouble than I'd been before I left. I found it impossible to settle down and was bored to death with the parochial nature of Adelaide. I quite arrogantly considered myself a real woman of the world.

⌒

Theo was the person I blamed for my unhappiness in Adelaide. We had been having as torrid an affair as one could have in the sleepy little town since I had met him when I was twenty-three and fell madly in love. He was certainly no Adonis or Rudolph Valentino. He had a typically large Greek nose and bad teeth, and was shorter than I generally wanted in a man. But whatever it took to make a woman feel good, Theo had it.

My family hated the relationship. They had just sighed with relief after I stopped seeing Andreas. He was a perfectly respectable and clean-living bank teller, but Andreas was a Cypriot, and Mum and Dad were never comfortable with any man I brought home who didn't have an Anglo-Saxon name. So far, men with Anglo-Saxon names had been few and far between.

Mum and Dad had had to cope with Miroslav, the Yugoslav Red Cross refugee who had been my first lover and by far the most disastrous thing to happen to the Cox family in living memory; Yakob, the Israeli freedom fighter; Ibrahim, the Turkish merchant sailor; Meho, the Lithuanian drummer; Bruno, the Hungarian forklift driver; Hassan, the Lebanese dry-cleaner; and Karl, the German wine maker. And all this before I took off for greener pastures overseas. Mum and Dad were at least spared from seeing what I got up to in Europe where there was no-one to restrain me.

When Andreas stopped coming around, they were praying for a Bruce, Roger or Barry. So they were less than impressed when Theo turned up on the doorstep and introduced himself as, 'Theodorakis Palaxides, from Piraeus, Athens'. He was charming and he was polite, and by then Mum and Dad had practically given up on being surprised by the nationality of the men I brought home.

Theo began to turn up more and more often to take me out. One night, Dad, in his dry, sardonic way, asked, 'Where's quarter-to-twelve tonight?'

'What do you mean, Dad?' I asked. I had no idea what he was talking about.

'That Theo of yours. He's not quite black enough to call "Midnight", but he's damn close to quarter-to-twelve.'

From then on Theo was known as 'Quarter-to-Twelve'.

My mother took a bit of a beating from our neighbours. One night, my sister, Sandra, told me how proud I would've been of Mum that day. Sandra was with her at the local grocer's when a woman who lived across the road commented: 'Dear, oh dear, Dot. I am so sorry for you. You must be dreadfully upset about Geraldine seeing so much of that Greek.' Sandra said that Mum gathered up her onions and potatoes, pocketed her change, and walked out of the shop with her head held high, saying loudly: 'I don't know about that. If it's good enough for Queen Elizabeth, it's good enough for Geraldine.'

⌒

Theo was a steadfast, if not often successful, gambler, and I never knew if Saturday night would be spent in bed with a lap full of fish and chips watching television, or at the most expensive restaurant in town if he'd had a good afternoon at the card table at the Greek club. And I didn't care one way or the other.

He worked in a pharmacy in the part of town that was named 'Little Italy' by those who couldn't tell the difference between a Greek and an Italian. Theo's most sought-after skill was his ability just to stand in the doorway of the chemist shop in his crisp, white medical coat, always with the top buttons undone, giving a tantalising glimpse of his smooth, olive-skinned neck. Women from fifteen to ninety years old would swarm in to buy unnecessary items just to enjoy the flattering compliments he would shower upon them, deserved or not. Watching him at work was better than going to the theatre. He could sell ice cream to an Eskimo, wrinkle-removing cream to an eighty-year-old woman, and a fine-tooth comb to a bald man.

I loved walking in that neighbourhood, where no really 'nice' Adelaide-born girl would ever dream of going. I heard Greek music for the first time. Spicy aromas wafted out of the European delicatessens, pulling me inside for a closer look at the trays of mouth-watering sweets made of honeyed pastry, dripping with crushed pistachios. There were buckets of green and black olives, containers of pickled eggplant and garlic, wedges of succulent moussaka and capsicums stuffed with seasoned rice and meat. It was another world.

I would pass restaurants where men gathered to eat and play cards. Many of them came to Australia ahead of their families and worked several jobs to make enough money to send for their women and children. They missed their wives and were very much ostracised by most Australian women, who seemed to find foreign men repugnant.

Not me. I lapped up the attention they gave me when I walked past. Australian men hardly gave me a second look. I was fat by their stan-dards, and not at all what they were looking for. But in Little Italy, the men practically drooled when I sashayed down the street. They seemed to prefer a little meat on the bones of their women, and perhaps I reminded some of them of their loved ones. I never felt dirty when they called out to me or whistled. Nor did I think they were perverts. They were simply reacting to the sight of something that pleased them.

This was my first taste of the power a woman could have, just by enjoying being female. And I revelled in it.

Theo made me think about the world. After making love, we would spend hours in the dark. Him smoking and talking, and me listening and learning. He spoke about how unhappy he was with the way life was changing in Greece. He talked about communism, fascism, socialism and democracy until my head swam. I learnt more from Theo in his shabby, rented room on the wrong side of town, in the dark, early hours of the morning, than I ever did at school.

He challenged the way I thought and made me thirst to find out what was going on in the world beyond Australia. It was now 1967 and I was following the Six Day War between Israel and Egypt, Jordan and Syria. I felt strongly about this tiny nation surrounded by enemies intent on pushing the Jews into the sea. As a teenager I had devoured every book I could get my hands on about World War Two and was emotionally disturbed by what had happened to the Jews.

One day I came home and announced to my mother that I had signed up to go to Tel Aviv to help the war effort. I never knew what a can of worms I was opening. Australian Jewish organisations were advertising for secretaries to take over jobs in Tel Aviv so that young *sabra* girls who had been trained as soldiers could go and fight for Israel. I was angry because when I signed up I was told they were taking people with full Jewish parentage first and people with partial Jewish parentage second, and would only accept non-Jews if things got desperate. I felt that my offer to do something to help had been thrown back in my face.

Mum was furious and blamed Theo for influencing me. But he had nothing to do with my desire to go to Israel. My Nana on my mother's side was at home when I broke this news, and was emotionally moved out of all proportion when I spoke about wanting to help the Jews. I couldn't understand her response. Eventually, she told us that her mother's family were German Jews, but when settling in Australia had hidden their

Jewish background because of racism. Their family name was Vogel, but more probably was Vogelstein. She barely remembered her Jewish traditions, and had gone so far as to send my mother to a Catholic boarding school as a child.

I was deeply affected by discovering this family history that had been lost to us for so many years, and was proud to have come from such a lineage. I pondered what might have happened to us if my Nana's family had remained in Germany in World War Two. It didn't bear thinking about.

⌒

Theo wanted children and so did I. While many others were terrified of unwanted pregnancy and never left home without enough condoms to get them through the night, Theo and I agreed to carry out our affair without using contraception. We secretly longed for a situation to arise that would push us into marriage. He was a devout procrastinator by nature, but I knew without a doubt that he would be delighted if I became pregnant, and that a wedding would be just around the corner. Often, when we made love, we whispered to each other, 'Maybe tonight it will happen.' 'Perhaps this time, darling.' But nothing ever happened.

After a couple of years of copious, unbridled, healthy sex, Theo hinted that maybe I should have a checkup. I agreed, and didn't really feel threatened. Perhaps all that was required was a minor adjustment to my plumbing and, bingo, I would be producing babies at the speed of light. It did occur to me that it was strange that Theo didn't consider having *his* fertility status checked out while I was in hospital. But then, he was a Greek.

When the medical reports revealed that my fallopian tubes were so blocked that my chances of ever having children were remote, Theo tried to hide his disappointment. He was even more loving and attentive for a time. But he was one of the most transparent liars I have ever known, and I knew that his love would never be strong enough to survive a childless marriage with me.

I subjected myself to weeks of excruciating treatment. I lay with my legs in stirrups while water was pumped into me, which was supposed to burst my fallopian tubes open. I am sure the pain was equal to childbirth. After a few water treatments I thought they had finished with me. But they came up with more torture. Gas was sure to flush out my tubes, they said. So I lay down and bit my lips until they bled, as they pumped gas into my vagina. I still cross my legs whenever I recall this period of my life. The x-rays at the end of the course of treatment showed no change to my blocked tubes. The doctor patted my hand and said that sometimes Mother Nature remedied these situations without help from medical science, and that I should not give up. But I didn't believe him.

In my heart, I knew the writing was on the wall, but I refused to accept that the end of my affair with Theo was near. Finally, a friend was forced into telephoning me to say, 'I'm so sorry to be the one to tell you this, Geraldine, but Theo can't see you tonight, or any other night from now on, because today the ship from Athens arrived with Alekka, his mail-order bride.'

I was like a sick animal that hides in a cave to lick its wounds. I hurt. I was lost in a dark tunnel and I felt that I would never find my way out. I missed his face, his voice, his touch, his thoughts. Even Mum and Dad were quiet when they saw what I was going through. Thoughtfully, they hid their glee at the end of the 'Theo Period' and worried about me, because I was not recovering as fast as they would have liked. Previously, I had always been the one to end romances, but I was on the receiving end this time, and having a bad time of it.

It wasn't just losing Theo. I was suffering from the burden I would always carry: knowing I would never bear a child. This was something I would not be able to avoid in any future relationship. Sooner or later, I would have to tell whomever might be interested in me as a wife, that I could not have children. I hated Theo for forcing me to know this.

I spent a long time alone, thinking about a life without children. Then, one ordinary day I saw what I was looking for, without knowing I was looking for it. It was an advertisement in the newspaper for women to apply for secretarial positions with the Australian government in embassies all over the world. This was my answer. Forget about a life in the suburbs hanging nappies on the Hills Hoist. I was going to live a life of travel and glamour. I was going to be accepted if it bloody killed me. Nothing was going to stand in my way.

I jolted myself out of my reverie. The time for my meeting had arrived. I knocked on the office door.

'Come in, Geraldine. Please sit down. I know you're anxious to know where we would like you to go on your first posting.'

The postings advice officer was distantly pleasant, sterile, efficient and well versed in her patter for new recruits. She knew that whatever was suggested to a new girl would never be turned down. Officers with experience or influence always found acceptable reasons for turning down undesirable countries. At the time, no-one wanted Nigeria, Papua New Guinea or Yugoslavia. The embassy in Lagos had a hex on it, supposedly because when the embassy first opened, the Australians refused to allow the local voodoo priest to exorcise the spirits in the building. A worrying number of embassy employees had since been sick with strange illnesses (one had even jumped out of his hotel window days after arriving) and bad luck seemed to attach itself to almost everyone in one way or another. In Port Moresby, women could almost be guaranteed at least one gang rape by wild, drunk, sex-crazed locals rather inadequately referred to as 'rascals'. And it was said that the smog in Belgrade was so bad that everyone in the embassy suffered from serious respiratory tract infections, sometimes requiring them to be medically evacuated.

She told me that the department had examined all my qualifications, and that they felt I was just the person they needed in Phnom Penh. She asked me to be ready to leave in two weeks. She handed me an airline ticket and the latest posting report, which contained information on what to expect in Phnom Penh. My next meeting was to be in ten minutes with the security branch, where I would be required to sign the Australian Official Secrets Act. 'Good luck!' she said.

And that was it.

'Oh, wonderful! Thanks very much. I am so looking forward to my new career. Thank you for your time. Goodbye,' I said as I stumbled backwards out of the office.

⁓

Pompen? Or did she say Popen? Where on God's earth was this place? And how could I find an atlas without alerting someone to the fact that I had no idea even how to spell the name of the city I was going to live and work in for the next year or so? But I was saved from this predicament when I opened the envelope containing the posting report on Phnom Penh, the capital of the Kingdom of Cambodia.

I was bitterly disappointed. I was anticipating Rome, Madrid, Paris, maybe even Cairo. I wanted the glamour that these names hinted at. I envisaged love affairs with sophisticated ambassadors and diplomats from exotic countries, who would wine and dine me in an attempt to wheedle vital Australian government top secrets out of me. But I would never succumb. I was just going to lay back and enjoy what was on offer, living luxuriously in an apartment paid for by the embassy, reading clandestine reports about the politics of the country I had been sent to.

But I have always been able to take the punches when they come. Hiding my disappointment, I read the posting report avidly, hardly noticing that it had been prepared a couple of years earlier. There was only a brief reference to the war in neighbouring Vietnam. Cambodia was, after all, a completely different and neutral country. There was a lot about a Prince Norodom Sihanouk, the head of state and leading royal figure. But I was mostly interested in the living conditions and things of a more practical nature. I figured I would have plenty of time to delve into the politics of the place once I arrived.

⁓

When I had first arrived in Canberra, I lived in a public service hostel called Lawley House, which was within walking distance of the department. I've seen better jails in my lifetime. One little rectangular room with a bed, cupboard, sink, desk and chair. Shared bathrooms and meals served on the dot. It didn't matter what day of the week it was, or whether it was lunch or dinner, there was always a plate of grated carrot. I began to think that the manager must have had a carrot farm. Suicides were not uncommon, but were always kept quiet. Some people could not cope with being away from their families, and depression and suicide were often the result. It was difficult to establish friendships in the hostel, as most of the time people were just passing through.

After a few boring months of living in Lawley House, I moved into a townhouse with three other girls in Blamey Crescent. We were all public servants. These girls partied hard, and constantly gave the neighbours something to talk about. We all caught the same bus in the mornings, and the driver was so taken with the honey blonde, dark blonde, brunette and redhead who were always late and running for the bus, that often he would get out and help us put our rubbish bins out so that we could catch it!

One morning, one of the girls paid for her ticket and was about to take her seat when she almost shouted for all the passengers to hear, 'Shit! I forgot to take the pill. Hang on, I'll be right back'. The smitten bus driver ignored the requests from others to drive on and actually waited several minutes while she ran back inside to take her pill.

The townhouse was always full of laughter and friends. Knowing my behaviour was being monitored by Foreign Affairs, I had to play the virgin, but the other three girls more than made up for my chaste behaviour. More than once I had to keep a visiting father or mother delayed in conversation while their daughter's suitor slid down the drainpipe or jumped onto the lawn from an upstairs bedroom window. I was going to miss life at Blamey Crescent.

⌒

The week following the confirmation of my posting promised to be a test of all I had learned in the previous months. Sir Keith Waller, the respected Secretary of the department, had asked personnel for a reliable secretary to replace his own, who was on leave. I was chosen. I was looking forward to working in an office where most secretaries never even got to deliver a file.

Sir Keith was a kindly, stylishly dressed middle-aged man. He explained that all that week he would be planning the placements of our most senior diplomats for the next six months. This meant working out what duties each of them was to perform for the Australian government during their postings.

On Friday afternoon he was ready to dictate to me the notes that had taken him all week to scribble. He dictated from 1.00 p.m. to 5.00 p.m. almost non-stop. I had never had to take shorthand for such long periods of time, and I was straining to keep up with him. I had only just passed a test for taking shorthand at 100 words a minute, and he was dictating at around 200 words a minute, for hours on end. By the end, I had filled both sides of a whole shorthand notebook. When Sir Keith had finished, he leaned back in his chair and tore up his handwritten notes into tiny little pieces and put them in the red security rubbish bin. The guards would empty it that night, then the contents would be shredded and burnt.

He thanked me and asked me to have it all typed up by the end of the day on Monday so he could give his reports to the ambassadorial designates on Tuesday morning. My heart sank. There was no way I could just sit down and type those notes. I could barely read them. But if I couldn't transcribe my notes, no ambassadorial designate was going anywhere for the next six months!

It was time to make one of the most serious Department of Foreign Affairs security breaches imaginable.

Every employee who walked through the department's doors was told that no papers or files were ever to leave the office without high-level written permission. I never asked what the punishment was for people who broke this regulation. I imagined it to be the rack, or being sent to Chad in deepest, darkest Africa. But if I was to have a chance of finishing Sir Keith's reports on time, I had to take the shorthand book home and spend the weekend writing it out in longhand while I could still remember most of it, ready to type it up on Monday morning.

I stuffed the notebook in my shoulder bag and nonchalantly waltzed past the guards at the exit. On Friday night, everybody worth knowing in Canberra had a couple of drinks at the Wellington Hotel, affectionately referred to as the Wello, next to the National Press Club. And I needed a drink after the day's shorthand session. I also wanted to bask in the glow of being recognised as Sir Keith Waller's secretary, even if it was for only a few days.

Even if I had wanted to indulge in a relationship in Canberra, I had not seen a single man who even remotely rang my bell. They all looked the same, sounded the same, dressed the same, said the same things and did the same jobs. But I checked the room out anyway before taking my place at the bar and ordering my usual vodka gimlet – shaken, not stirred, of course. That was when I noticed the waiter behind the bar. He wasn't the same as the other men in the room. He was foreign. His name was Slobodan, and that alone was enough to arouse me. He was Serbian. I impressed him with the few Slavic words I could remember from my very first Yugoslav lover, and from then on he was my slave. He wanted to take me home but his shift didn't finish until much later, so we exchanged telephone numbers and I agreed to go out with him another time. I toddled off home a little tiddly, but in control. That is, until I went to my bag to start work on my smuggled notebook.

It wasn't there.

I panicked. I had walked home from the Wello. I'd have felt it, and heard it fall out, if I had lost it then. It had to be at the Wello somewhere. I'd only been at the bar and in the ladies' toilet. Oh my God, what was I to do?

I had two choices. Kill myself or find the bloody thing. I decided on the latter.

I had to wait till nearly midnight before Slobodan answered his phone. He was the only person I could ask for help. I would promise him anything – anything – if he would agree to open up the hotel and help me go through the rubbish bins. I begged him. I don't beg often, but when I do, I'm good. By 1.00 a.m. we were both bent over the rubbish bins, elbow deep in beer slops and cigarette butts. After an hour of searching, Slobodan held up the notebook. It was wet, and stained with beer, cigar ash and food. Some of the shorthand was smudged. But it *was* the book! I was crying with relief and willing to commit any obscene act Slobodan wanted, there and then. Luckily, he was just as tired as I was, and content with a really warm hug and promises of lots of good things to come later that week.

I did nothing else that weekend but rewrite the notes completely. I went to work at sparrow's fart on Monday morning, worked through my lunch hour, and had everything typed up and clipped onto Sir Keith's blotter by 3.00 p.m. There were a few mistakes, and he changed things around a little, but all in all he was very pleased with what I gave him. Poor Sir Keith. If he only knew that the government's secret political appointees' instructions had been in the hands of a Serb national. Only years later, when I heard that Sir Keith had died, was I relaxed enough to tell the story to anyone.

I still had a week's communications training to go. I would rather go to the dentist and have a Pap smear at the same time than repeat that week. It was then that I came to realise something about myself that would not change all my life. Machines and I don't mix well. When I was working in the communications area, photocopiers, for instance, would jam, and stop or start by themselves, when I entered the room.

Every day, at the same time, for every Australian embassy in the world, staff must change a code, or absolutely no communications can be sent or received. I was given little rectangular boxes with a lot of little numbered holes, and attached to these little black boxes were a lot of red and white plastic wires with little flags bearing corresponding numbers wrapped around them. My mission, if I chose to accept it, was to stick the right coloured wire into the right numbered hole, for the right date, for the right embassy, in the right country. There was no room for mistakes. By the end of the week I was a frazzled mass of nerves. But my trainer, Josie Wall, was in a far worse state. I doubt she has ever had a more useless communicator.

I was exhausted after each session, and at the end of a particularly bad day, I had to attend the most secret of all security briefings one gets prior to departing for a posting. I sat at the back of the room and promptly fell asleep. No one noticed. To this day, I don't know what was said, and felt far too stupid to ever ask anyone in all the years I was in Foreign Affairs. I was probably the most secure officer they had overseas, because I didn't know what it was I wasn't allowed to tell anyone.

A mortifying incident made me realise how totally unprepared I was for the diplomatic world. The then Cambodian ambassador and his wife were well known for their hospitality and interest in entertaining Foreign Affairs officers who were going to Cambodia to work in the embassy. I was invited to attend a formal dinner party at the Cambodian residence and turned up dressed to kill, looking forward to a pleasant evening. I had even learned a few words of Khmer to impress my hosts.

The ambassador and other guests, Australian and international, were ushered into the dining room. I was seated on the right of the ambassador as the guest of honour, and the waiter appeared by my side first, offering me a huge plate of food. I was twenty-five and had travelled all over Europe and dined in expensive restaurants. But in every one of these restaurants, I had always ordered from a menu, and the meal had been set before me by a waiter. I didn't have a clue what I was supposed to do, and thought it was probably a Cambodian tradition to serve a huge meal to female guests before the others. So to be polite, I took as much food as I could fit on my plate and waited for the big plates for the other guests to come out. I waited a long time. They probably had to cook a whole lot more food in the kitchen very quickly. It finally dawned on me that this was a different kind of table service than I was used to and I had probably put half the other guests' food on my plate without realising it. The milkman's daughter still had a lot to learn about dining etiquette.

⌒

I returned to Adelaide for a few hectic days of saying goodbye to family and friends. I invited many of Theo's friends to my farewell parties, and being with them brought back home to me how much I still loved him. While in Canberra, I had forced myself not to think of him being a married man with a beautiful, young and fertile bride; but when I saw the sympathy on my Greek friends' faces, I knew they understood I was still suffering. I suppressed the desire to ask what he was doing, and to pass on a tender goodbye message to him. I knew the passage of time, and living in a new country with nothing to remind me of him, would help my love and pain fade.

I was ready to take on the world.

Laughter and Tears

Phnom Penh, June – September 1971

I was a seasoned traveller, but my paltry savings had never been enough to consider flying first class. These were the good old days when every man and his dog in the Australian public service travelled first class, from prime ministers, to diplomats, even down to lowly secretaries like myself. Before that day I had never been bold enough just to look around the carefully drawn curtain that firmly separated the first class travellers from the plebeians in the economy section. Now I was on the other side of that mysterious curtain.

I don't remember much about the flight to Singapore, or the connection to Phnom Penh. I was lost in a haze of Dom Perignon, Sydney rock oysters, and Argentinean prime beef fillet mignon. I was definitely going to enjoy being a public servant.

I had read somewhere that altitude increases the effects of alcohol. But I didn't believe everything I read. In this case I should have. I drank glass after glass of champagne. And then consumed more in the first-class transit lounge in Singapore before boarding the plane for the last leg of my journey. As the plane neared its destination I began to feel decidedly queasy. I checked that my false eyelashes were on straight, and looked out the window as we glided low over the lush rice paddies of Cambodia. It was the beginning of the rainy season and I could see that in some areas flood waters had almost covered the flimsy peasants' huts; only the thatch roofs were visible.

But what were all those burnt-out fuselages by the side of the runway? I could see at least six wrecked planes, the metal all twisted and shining in the bright sunlight. Surely the pilots of Royal Air Cambodge weren't that careless.

I looked closer and saw that the carcasses were not of passenger planes, but the snub-nosed military aircraft I'd seen in war movies. Little did I know I was soon to become an expert in telling the difference between MIG fighters and B-52 bombers.

We landed, and the passengers stood up to disembark. The Cambodian head steward stood outside the aircraft on the top of the steps, his hands shielding his eyes from the glare as he peered at the land surrounding the airstrip.

'Six persons come now, please,' he said, with a sense of urgency in his voice.

And the first six in the line disembarked. This continued, with six passengers getting off at a time. I got impatient, and I couldn't fathom why he was only letting us leave in groups of six. He kept a watch on the sky in between each batch of passengers. How strange, I thought, anyone could see it wasn't going to rain. And why was he so concerned that we might get a little wet if it did suddenly start to shower?

My turn came, and I stepped off the plane and did my best to walk in a straight line to the terminal. After the air conditioning of the plane, the blast of unbelievably hot sun did nothing to help the headache I was starting to get from all the champagne I had guzzled.

Bob Devereaux, the administrative first secretary of the embassy, was waiting for me. He'd already been in Phnom Penh for some time and really knew the ropes. He diplomatically ignored my very obvious state of intoxication as I swayed from side to side with all my luggage. After he'd introduced himself, I asked him why only six passengers were allowed to get off at a time.

'Oh, there's been a little bit of rocket-bombing of the airport in recent days by the Vietnamese and we hear there might be a little more of the same some time today, so I suppose they were double-checking the area for possible enemy activity,' he said, quite casually.

A *little* bit of bombing!

Any bombing at all, no matter how little, was far too much for my liking. I nodded with what I hoped was a knowing expression. How long had the Vietnamese been rocket-bombing Cambodia, I wondered. There was nothing in the posting report about war actually *in* Cambodia. It only briefly explained the war in Vietnam between the North and the South, and how the Americans and the Australians were fighting alongside the South Vietnamese.

We walked out to the embassy car. A very strange scene was waiting for me. Moy, a quite aristocratic-looking, French-speaking embassy driver, resplendent in his neat uniform, was holding a wooden broomstick with a round mirror tied to the end. He was sweeping the broomstick under the car slowly, very intent on the image reflected in the mirror. What a strange place this was. I couldn't resist asking another stupid question.

'What on earth is he doing, Bob?'

'Oh, that's standard practice for all diplomatic, military and government vehicles,' he said. He went on to tell me that it was quite common for bombs to be placed under cars by North Vietnamese soldiers, who had infiltrated the city and were carrying out all kinds of terrorist acts and sabotage. If a driver hadn't been watching his car all the time, it was better to be safe than sorry. The bombs were very crudely made, and easily seen with the mirror.

'Don't worry about it, Geraldine. You'll get used to things like this in a short while,' he said.

I nodded doubtful agreement and was silent during the drive into town. I was beginning to sober up, fast. Once out of the airport, the drive into the capital took us along Pochentong Road, with rice paddies on each side and a few government buildings badly in need of a coat of paint. The traffic consisted mainly of bicycles and cyclos, something similar to the rickshaws I'd seen in Hong Kong. But in a cyclo, the driver sits in a seat high up behind the passenger. What was impossible to ignore was the vast number of homeless families who squatted around their meagre bundles by the side of the road. Bob explained that they were refugees from the provinces. More and more were coming in every day to escape the bombing in the countryside. They were mainly rice farmers, and there were no jobs for them. 'You'll get used to it, Geraldine,' he said.

Women were cooking food over wood fires at the side of the road; children were playing; dogs were fighting; groups of old people were gossiping avidly; hordes of children of all ages were travelling on bicycles, motorbikes or in cyclos, on their way to or from school in their crisp white shirts and blue trousers and skirts. There was no limit to how many passengers could crowd onto a motorbike or cyclo. Ox-driven carts ambled by with loads of green fodder or earthen cooking pots for sale. Homeless children and adults picked through piles of rubbish. Armed soldiers sat around in circles playing cards.

The road gradually changed into a wide avenue with fragrant frangipani trees planted along both sides. The style was distinctly French and I could almost smell the flowers, even with the windows closed. Refugee families were camped under the trees. I was horrified to notice that the next largest presence on the streets were heavily armed soldiers. They were everywhere. They were walking around with what I would later know were AK47s and M16 automatic rifles over their shoulders. Many of them had hand grenades attached to their belts. Ammunition belts criss-crossed their chests like evil necklaces. By now, I was 100 per cent sober and beginning to grasp that I'd arrived in a country well and truly at war.

We turned off Pochentong into Monivong Boulevard and swept up the driveway of the elegant, but run-down, Royal Hotel. By the time I checked in and arranged to join Bob and some of the other members of the embassy for dinner, I was in a state of shock. Why hadn't I inquired more about the region before agreeing to come to Cambodia? Why hadn't someone in the department told me more about the real situation on the ground? A person could get killed here. This wasn't what I joined Foreign Affairs for. I wanted to enjoy myself. How could I with a war raging all around me?

I opened the quaint wooden shutters of my hotel room window and looked down. It could have been the setting for a film. Beneath me was a charming garden with a swimming pool, and a small restaurant, set among palm trees and ferns. Westerners sat at the tables and chairs around the pool, enjoying the late afternoon. The women's silver and gold jewellery shimmered in the last of the day's sunlight. In spite of the war going on just outside the hotel gates, you couldn't have found a more relaxed and sophisticated bunch of people in Hollywood. A Cambodian in an immaculate white uniform with brass buttons glided unobtrusively between the tables with trays of cocktails.

A drink was the last thing I wanted. For better or worse, here I was, in Cambodia.

~

My first duty in the embassy would be to work with the defence attaché and his staff. They sent to Canberra highly classified daily situation reports, called 'Sitreps', on the military state of affairs. Who was doing what to whom, and how many were assumed dead and wounded on each side. Who planned the attacks, what weapons were used, and why they failed or succeeded. I quickly learned all I could about the country I was to call home for the next couple of years. Poor Cambodia, was all I could say.

Even before the French imposed a protectorate over the country in 1864, Cambodia had suffered many invasions by Vietnam and Thailand. They were traditional enemies, and things didn't look like changing while I was there. The French crowned Prince Norodom Sihanouk as king in 1941, but they soon discovered he wasn't the compliant person they thought he was going to be. He gained Cambodia's independence from the French in 1953. He achieved this, in part, by abdicating in favour of his father. This left him free to play a much more political role in Cambodia's new government. In 1954, the Geneva Conference on Indochina recognised Cambodia's neutrality.

Cambodia clung tenuously to its policy of neutrality, right from the beginning of the Vietnam War when America came to defend the South Vietnamese against communist North Vietnam. In 1963, when the Vietnam War was raging, Sihanouk renounced American aid, souring Cambodia's relationship with the United States. He did this to appease the Vietnamese communists. In 1966, Sihanouk was reluctantly drawn into the war – he allowed the Vietnamese communists to use the border areas adjoining South Vietnam and the Cambodian port of Sihanoukville as supply routes. This did little to please the United States. By 1967, America was making military raids along these supply routes, which in turn pleased the Cambodians even less. These attacks increased in magnitude and frequency, and in 1969, President Nixon gave approval for B-52 bombers to mount a large attack inside Cambodia. By 1970, the war had spilt over in earnest into Cambodia.

In March 1970, Sihanouk was deposed by the very men he trusted most and had put into government. Sihanouk went into exile in China and formed an alliance with his former enemies, the Khmer Rouge, to better struggle against the military government of Marshal Lon Nol, who was leading Cambodia when I arrived.

The story of the origin of the Khmer Rouge (Cambodian communists) depends on whom you talk to and what book you read. Basically, they sprung up as guerilla jungle fighters who followed the ideals of Chairman Mao. They were not given much international recognition until they took over Cambodia in 1975 under the leadership of Pol Pot. As well as presiding over genocide, he would instigate agrarian reform that forced people to work side by side with oxen, and was intent on stamping out family values, religion and education.

In 1970, Lon Nol declared a state of emergency in Cambodia, and I certainly didn't disagree with his judgment. The North Vietnamese were being supplied arms by Russia and the Cambodians were backed by the Chinese. So, in the background, lurked two huge formidable sponsors of different brands of communism, who were opposed to each other.

⟳

When I arrived, there were eighteen Australian embassy staff: the ambassador, nine supporting diplomatic, administrative, security and technical officers; the defence attaché and his backup staff; a major and a warrant officer from the Australian army; and five secretaries, including myself, to take care of these sometimes quite helpless men. We were a strange bunch of Australians from all walks of life. Ambassador Graham Feakes, and his wife, Nicola, were as classy as they come in Foreign Affairs. We all adored them and their two wickedly naughty small boys. Defence attaché Stuart Gordon and his wife, Joy, were career army types with all the breeding and discipline of most senior military staff.

Graham had a very endearing trait when he dictated his political dispatches. He would wrap the bottom of his tie around his two index fingers, and slowly wind the tie up to the knot at his neck and down again. The intensity of his concentration was measured by the number of times his tie travelled up and down. He hated public speaking with a passion, which I thought was strange for a man with a career in the public arena. Cambodia was Graham's first appointment as an ambassador and at that time he was one of our youngest ambassadors in the Foreign Service.

Michael Mann arrived shortly after me to work in the administrative area, and so began a friendship that was to last many years. He was barely twenty-one when he arrived, and I quickly became his big sister and confidante. Michael was tall, dark and fit, with the kind of curly hair depicted on the heads of ancient Roman coins. He wore sensible solid reading glasses that gave him the air of a competent television newsreader. He was posted as soon as his considerable strengths in administration were identified by the department, who sent him to the embassy when he was legally old enough to be sent abroad. Although the youngest in the embassy, he commanded respect, and it was difficult to believe he was really just a kid still wet behind the ears, compared to the rest of us.

⟜

In the beginning, I didn't enjoy having a maid at all. But diplomatic staff had no option. There were no supermarkets to buy food, so it had to be bought early in the mornings at the market. It would also have been culturally unacceptable for a white woman to be seen to be doing her own housework. So after my first few glamorous weeks at the hotel, I moved into my predecessor's apartment, taking on the maid she had employed before me. Al-aan was a Chinese/Vietnamese, who were by far the best cooks. Many foreigners employed them instead of Cambodians.

She would prepare a meal, set the table for me in the dining room, and then squat down on the kitchen floor to eat her meal. It seemed ridiculous to me that we were eating alone in separate rooms at the same time, so I often invited her to join me at the table. But this was definitely not the done thing, and she would giggle and scamper off to the kitchen.

Al-aan was somewhere between thirty and sixty years of age. Her features were classically Chinese, and she wore her thinning black hair tied at the nape of her neck. I never saw her wear anything else but a white blouse and the traditional black satin Chinese pyjama pants, worn by all ethnic Chinese/Vietnamese in Cambodia. (This was one of the little things that irked Cambodians: the Vietnamese women never donned traditional Cambodian silk.) Her English was not very good but it never really mattered, as my needs were clear. Washing, cleaning, ironing and cooking.

Her first day was as memorable for her as it was for me. I was awakened early by screams and violent banging from the bathroom. I threw a sheet around me and rushed out of my bedroom, ready to help Al-aan beat off the entire North Vietnamese Army, who were obviously mounting an attack from my bathroom.

Each night without fail I removed my eyelashes, washed them carefully and placed them on the towel hanging on the bathroom rail, fresh and ready for the next day. Al-aan had gone in to clean, and had seen what she thought was some strange kind of insect I had brought with me from Australia. She was beating my expensive mink lashes to death with a broom and they were flying around the room, bent and twisted out of shape. Laughing, I helped her flush them down the toilet. I took her into the bedroom and showed her my little boxes of lashes that were to last for years, and demonstrated what they were for. She watched in silent stupefaction while I applied them.

When I waved her goodbye as I left for work, I knew that she couldn't wait to rush to the other maids in the building and tell them what a madwoman she was working for. In my apartment building the maids lived in servants' quarters at the back of each apartment, and they simply thrived on gossip. I am sure each one knew the most intimate details of our lives. Nothing escaped them. They knew what we ate, when we shat, if we had upset stomachs, if we couldn't sleep, who our visitors were, what time we went out, and what time we came home and with whom.

Our social lives were severely restricted. It was dangerous to eat in many restaurants and if we did go, it was drummed into us never to sit by the window or with our backs to the entrance. Sitting by a window could mean that you copped the worst of a hand grenade attack and didn't live to tell the tale. It was wise to keep an eye on the door for any drunk soldiers coming in with their hand guns and automatic rifles, as often happened. Three decades later, I still automatically sit myself at the back of a restaurant and prefer a table that allows me to face the entrance. Old habits certainly die hard.

Nothing was private. At the end of each day we had to fill out a form advising the name, address and telephone number of who we would be with until the next morning. When I arrived, the security officer was an ex-policeman called Ray, who had lived in Africa for years and revelled in telling us bloodcurdling stories of the Mau Mau Uprising in the fifties. Sometimes he checked our stories and if we could not be reached where we were supposed to be, we were in for a real roasting the next day. We soon learned he was not to be trifled with. We all had army-issue radios in our homes to communicate with each other, as the phone system was more ornamental than useful. Ray checked in with security officers from other embassies all over the city to get news of where the trouble spots were, so that we could be warned away from areas where there was fighting, or demonstrations, which often turned ugly and violent.

Every Monday evening at a predetermined time, we had to check in over the radio with Ray from our homes, but very often the frequency would be full of American embassy wives looking for their errant husbands.

'If anyone sees Harry in a bar, can you tell him his dinner's ready?'

'Does anyone know if Joe is on his way home? There's a Cambodian military attaché waiting who says he has a meeting with him.'

'Can someone tell Richard that if he's not home in half an hour, our dinner party will start without him and I will leave him in the morning!'

Living like this day after day was really stressful. There was little to do after work. The radio and television were only in Khmer or French, and very little of it was entertaining anyway. There was no Western music to be heard so we all stocked up on music, spending money like drunken sailors, in Singapore or Bangkok when we 'got out' for holidays. I can remember going into Peter Chews, a well-known duty-free shop in Singapore, one day and asking them to give me the top fifty recordings of pop music. This was when I first heard Simon and Garfunkel's 'Bridge Over Troubled Waters', James Taylor's 'Handyman', Carole King's 'So Far Away' and love songs like 'Killing Me Softly', by Roberta Flack. I also bought a couple of dozen classical recordings. In Adelaide my family never listened to what Dad liked to call 'pansies' music' and it was in Cambodia that I first discovered the peace and joy of good classical music.

Music filled every night for me. It helped shut out the despair I could see in the eyes of the refugees sleeping and begging on the streets each day on my way to work, and each afternoon on my return, when I often had to step over them outside the entrance to my apartment block. Women of all ages would follow me while I was shopping in the food markets, taking off their wedding rings and earrings in the hope I would buy them, so they could buy rice for their children. Many of them had been widowed and were the sole providers for their families. But they had no skills – or if they did, there were no jobs for them.

How can one not take notice of a small boy in tattered clothes leading his blind father in a soldier's uniform, playing a haunting melody on a crude wooden flute in the hope that someone will take pity on him and give him enough money for food that day. The amputees really got to me. These soldiers, some of them no more than boys, begged for their food in the markets and streets. They still wore their uniforms, and thrust their stumps at passers-by with such an air of hopelessness that I'm ashamed to say I often crossed the road to avoid making eye contact with them. Men missing limbs were usually rejected by their families, who needed whole men to work on rice farms. Some families would have preferred their men to have died in battle rather than return disabled, as they were a great burden. In those early days I don't remember seeing wheelchairs or prothseses – just countless men hobbling along with the aid of crutches or bamboo sticks. The double amputees' lives were wretched beyond description. They could be found just dumped on the ground in market places and street corners where they might be able to solicit some sympathy.

If they were lucky, a family member or friend might visit sometimes to carry them to a toilet, but more often than not they had no choice but to hang on, or relieve themselves where they sat.

I can't count the number of times bags of bones passing as women thrust their thirsty and sick children at me, begging me to take them. Their milk had dried up and the water they were forced to give their babies was contaminated. Often the toddlers were too weak with disease to walk and the mother was too frail to carry them, so she would station herself at the side of the road until someone took pity on her and gave her enough food to help her gain strength to move on.

Move on to where? Move on to what?

Against this backdrop of human misery, I worked, dressed up, had my hair and nails done, attended dinner parties where leftover food was often thrown out, bought French champagne at the markets, haggled with shopkeepers over exquisitely worked silver antiques, and relaxed in the comfort and security of my apartment, listening to music and reading novels.

I had so much to learn, and I did so many insensitive things. In those days, a popular shopping street for Westerners was Silver Street, near the river. The whole street consisted of silver, antiques, and 'antiques'. I would often haggle with one shop and leave discontented with the price of something I wanted to buy, and go into the next shop to start all over again. It was months before I realised that all the shopkeepers in the street were related to each other, and I would never get a single item for less than the amount they had all already agreed on. How they must have been amused by my naïve antics.

Close to Silver Street, there was a line of shops that stocked supplies for the Buddhist pagodas and monks. They sold urns for the ashes of the departed, candles, incense, begging bowls, and new monks' saffron robes. I wasn't the only person who bought a bright orange robe for use as a bed-spread or tablecloth. The unrefined milkman's daughter was alive and well.

I also have to plead guilty to, one day when I was feeling a bit peckish, helping myself to a banana left as an offering to Buddha on a shrine at the hairdressers.

Looking back, I can't believe some of the cruel things I did. Every morning when I removed the cover of my typewriter I was never ready for the fright I got when a gecko, the miniature lizards that you find all over Asia, scurried out. I was sure it was always the same one, and constantly being startled like that put me in a bad mood. I wanted an end to these early morning shocks, so one day I was ready for him. I got the largest envelope I could find, opened it as wide as possible, and trapped the gecko inside it. Then I licked the flap of the envelope, sealed it, and walked over to our electric shredding machine. I dropped the envelope, gecko and all, into it and switched it on. I even boasted about it afterwards.

Kim, our Cambodian secretary, was aghast. 'That gecko might have been one of your ancestors,' she cried. 'You will be punished in your next life for this act.'

I became fascinated by Buddhist culture. Clusters of barefoot monks could be seen from dawn to around eleven in the morning, standing patiently with their heads bowed in front of homes and restaurants, silently begging for food. The devout would always give. Women would kneel in front of them, placing food or money into their bowls, careful not to touch them, as it's forbidden for women to touch a monk. All they owned were their orange robes and their begging bowls. As the war escalated it became common practice for families who simply could not feed their children to abandon young boys at pagodas, knowing that the abbot and the other monks would take the children in and do their best to feed them.

I asked my new Cambodian friend Sophea to tell me a little about Buddhism, and found myself attracted to its simplicity and uncomplicated slant on life. She explained that Buddhism is a personal journey. She strove to reject material things and do kind acts; she believed that by doing so she was coming closer to enlightenment and true inner peace.

Sophea was giving me regular French and Khmer lessons over lunch at my apartment, though it was soon clear that lunch took precedence over my language studies. Although the lessons stopped, the lunches continued and I learned a lot from her about the Cambodian people, and their beliefs and traditions. One day, she asked me if I could think of one war that has been fought over Buddhism. Muslims, Jews and Christians, even different sects like Catholics and Protestants, Sikhs and Hindus have all fought major battles in the name of their religions. Not so with Buddhism. She said Buddhists are tolerant of every man's god and it would be anathema to them to fight over religion, because Buddhism preaches peace and non-violence.

She had me there.

⌇

Michael and I were both on our first posting, and then along came Adrian Sever. Now here was a character. He could only be described as portly. Until he arrived I was the largest person in the embassy. This wasn't something that had ever worried me, but I would be lying if I didn't admit to a certain pleasure when I first met him and noticed his shirt buttons stretched to the limit over his generous belly. I warned him that, like me, he should prepare himself to be charged double when travelling in a cyclo and to have waiters in restaurants rush up with a huge wooden chair to replace the smaller ones given to other so-called 'normal-sized' people.

Adrian reported to Michael and was in charge of all the incoming and outgoing correspondence. Adrian was either very, very happy – or very, very pissed off at the world. This usually had something to do with the pressure of meeting the deadlines for diplomatic couriers. Someone was always coming in with something to put in the diplomatic pouch for Canberra at the last minute, when he had just finished filling out the contents sheet, tying the bag and securing it with a wax seal.

Like me, Adrian loved his food and was never known to turn down a drink. After a few weeks we both noticed we were putting on weight at an alarming rate, so Adrian came up with a novel idea that would encourage us both to lose some. He suggested a diet race. We would have a weigh-in party where we would strip down to our undies, be weighed, and have someone record our weights. Then, after six weeks, we'd have a weigh-out party.

'The one who loses the least weight has to pay the other's return fare to Bangkok. That will make it interesting. Are you in, kiddo?' he said.

'You're on, Adrian,' I said. 'But you'd better start saving your money. I can lose two pounds by just missing lunch,' I replied.

We shook hands on it, and a few nights later we had the weigh-in party, which was a great success, not least because of the sight of Adrian in his skimpy swimming trunks with his gut hanging over the top. I wasn't much better in a bikini two sizes too small for me.

I thought I had it made. I had a plan. The day of the weigh-in party I ate like a pig. Banana splits, soft drinks, fried rice, cookies, chocolates. I stuffed myself silly. My strategy was to put on a couple of pounds very quickly for the weigh-in, then take a handful of Ford Pills (a powerful laxative) that very night and get rid of everything in my stomach. I put on all my rings, bracelets, and my heaviest necklace and earrings, hoping this would further increase my weight for the first weigh-in. I hoped no-one would notice that I would not be wearing all this gear at the weigh-out party in six weeks.

It seemed like a good idea at the time, especially as my weight on the first weigh-in was almost three pounds more than I'd weighed the day before. My plan had worked. I watched my food as much as I could over the next six weeks and booked my seat to Bangkok for the day after the weigh-out party.

But I hadn't counted on Adrian's tenacity. Six weeks later, when we were duly weighed, he had lost five more pounds than me, and was the clear winner. When I handed over the airfare money for Adrian's holiday in Bangkok I really learned a lesson: never, ever, underestimate your opponent in anything.

Adrian had won, despite my deception. I never knew if he too had a few tricks up his sleeve as far as the diet race was concerned, but when he returned from a fun-filled week in Thailand – all at my expense – he rather sheepishly handed me a beautifully wrapped present.

'Adrian, how thoughtful. You shouldn't have. Thanks,' I said.

'Oh, it's nothing really. Just a little something I thought you could put to good use,' he said, smiling.

I unwrapped the gift in front of half the embassy. It was a very detailed, hand-carved, twelve-inch wooden penis.

It was with this kind of waggish humour and silliness that we were able to cope with all the misery just outside our doors. I remained friends with Adrian all through his career with the department. He was later to become ambassador to Nepal.

⟜⟶

Another distraction was afternoon outings with the Brits and some French friends who had houseboats along the river outside the city. They had a speedboat and some skiing gear. You had to be quite fearless, or quite mad – preferably both – willingly to put one toe in the Mekong. Quite apart from the fact that the whole country used it as their own personal toilet – and that went for the water buffaloes too – the river was full of dead dogs and bloated bodies bobbing up and down.

I only braved the water once to go skiing, and while struggling not to fall into the water, hit a bloated human corpse with the tip of my ski. It exploded and covered me with shreds of decomposing flesh. I was still screaming when I clambered back onto the houseboat. I stood under the shower for hours when I got home, and I have never tried to ski since that day.

The French who owned the houseboat all ran large rubber plantations, and they befriended me for a short time. I think they found me quaint. But their idea of a good night was to gorge themselves on the finest food and wine and then stand next to each other in the garden, men on one side and ladies on the other, sticking their fingers down their throats and regurgitating the food so that they could return to table and continue eating more. This was years before I had even heard of eating disorders like bulimia. I found this behaviour quite odd, and when they could see I wasn't enjoying myself, they stopped inviting me. So much for the French.

Although there were some pleasant people among the French I met, you could count them on one hand. The rest seemed to have forgotten that the Cambodians had had their independence since the fifties, and went on acting as though the country was still a French protectorate. It galled them that the Cambodian elite were turning towards the English language in droves and that small English schools were popping up all over the city, despite the war.

—⟜

One of the most distressing sights for me was that of women outside the locked gates of the military hospitals and the many schools that had been transformed into hospitals to cope with the huge numbers of injured soldiers coming in from the front. All day, clapped-out buses and requisitioned Coca-Cola trucks would drive to the front, only a few miles out of Phnom Penh, loaded with fresh young soldiers, some of them shorter than the rifles they held, with flowers in the barrels. Later, these same trucks would return to the hospitals with the wounded. When the trucks arrived outside the hospital gates, the women would scream and wail, and help to untangle the men's bloody limbs before lifting them out and handing them over to the hospitals' weary doctors. Some were already dead and others not far from it.

The women would shout out the names of their husbands, fathers and brothers, hoping that they might find them alive. There was no real way to know for sure if your loved one was alive or dead. Some commanders were thorough and had a list of injured and dead soldiers printed in the local newspapers. But most didn't bother.

—⟜

It wasn't long before the war began to encroach on Phnom Penh itself. The embassy chancery was right next door to the British embassy. One of the Brits lived at the back of the embassy, and there was a door in the wall between his house and the Australian chancery. Once a week we would all go to watch movies in his garden. One night, we were watching *Tora! Tora! Tora!* We had just got to the part where the Japanese were attacking Pearl Harbor, with all the kamikaze dive-bombing and explosions, when the projector broke down, leaving us in total darkness. But the sounds of explosions and shelling kept going, and it was about ten seconds before it dawned on us that we weren't listening to the film soundtrack anymore, but that the shelling was real. We stampeded towards that door in the wall to get inside and at least put a roof between the rockets and ourselves.

Rocket attacks like this were to become normal events for me. I'd read the security instructions that said the safest places to stand during rocket attacks were doorways and bathrooms. For the first few dozen attacks I followed these instructions to the letter, but after a few months I became so blasé about the attacks that I often slept through them. Yet I always remembered in the morning to gather the four corners of my bed sheet together to collect the plaster that almost always had dropped on my bed from my bedroom ceiling during an attack.

There were four apartments in the two-storey block I lived in. Michael Mann, two other secretaries and I lived there. Each apartment had a lounge room and a small balcony overlooking the street. The balconies were closed in with mosquito net so we could sit outside at night without being eaten alive. It looked like a massive birdcage, and sometimes we'd send out party invitations giving the address as The Birdcage. We all shared the long rooftop terrace. If the rocket attacks weren't too close to our part of the city we would often go to the roof with a bottle of wine, and sit and watch the war. From there we could see the planes attack the outskirts of the city; they dropped flares that lit up areas as big as a football field so they could strafe enemy troops gathered for the night. We watched and heard the tracer bullets as they were fired from planes. It sounds callous, but it was actually quite entertaining. Something reminiscent of a fireworks display on New Year's Eve.

'Last night was better,' someone would say.

'But tonight it was louder,' another would say.

'Yeah, but tonight it was closer to the city,' someone else would chime in, before we tottered down the back stairs to our apartments to sleep.

Back then I hardly gave a thought to the fact that I was actually watching and listening to the sounds of people being slaughtered. I knew it was real, yet could still get a good night's sleep.

It remains an enigma to me how this most gentle of people can smile one day and kill the next. Even King Sihanouk is quoted as saying this very same thing.

Early one morning I was enjoying a leisurely ride in a cyclo down Monivong, the main commercial street of the city. I sat relaxed, enjoying the soft wind in my hair, as I was slowly pedalled down the still quiet street. I noticed a boisterous group of boys, who were only around eight to ten years old.

There, on the footpath crowded with refugees, a wooden bar stool had been turned upside down, and jammed onto two legs of the stool were human heads bearing deathly grimaces and half-closed eyes. Their cheeks showed signs of fresh cigarette burns where they had presumably been tortured before being beheaded. There was a sign in Khmer attached to the bar stool with a nail. I later learned that the sign said these men had been collaborating with the Vietnamese, and had been caught trying to bribe children to take small cardboard boxes into the local cinemas. These boxes contained bombs which would kill the child who had been paid to carry it in, along with many others. This latest practice had closed down the Luxe Cinema in Norodom Boulevard and two other large popular public cinemas in the city. Needless to say, embassy staff were banned from even thinking of attending a local movie house.

A couple of the small children were playing with the severed heads, placing lit cigarettes between their blue lips. The street people urged them on and clapped and laughed. One child tried to poke their eyes out with a sharp stick, while another small boy busied himself by pinning the earlobes to the skin around the severed necks using a large safety pin.

How could these children ever grow up to be normal, compassionate human beings? What would become of boys like this when they became men? I shuddered and turned my eyes away, but it was a scene I knew I would play over and over again whenever I thought about the war and its consequences.

Phnom Penh was a city of contrasts. The nights when there were no rocket attacks I was often lulled to sleep by the rhythmic banging of two bamboo sticks, which signalled – almost on the dot of 10.00 p.m. every night – that the Chinese soup cart would soon be passing. Cambodians always seemed ready to eat. I often ran down the stairs in a sarong with my own bowl, to have it filled with a tasty fresh soup made on the spot over a charcoal-fired stove.

Michael loved the late-night Chinese soup too, and one night he sent the guard out to get him some. Michael's Khmer and the guard's English did not complement each other, and the next thing he knew the doorbell rang and the guard was standing there grinning, with a young Chinese prostitute.

'No! I said Chinese *soup* not girl! Get me a *soup* not a girl,' Michael said, irritated.

The guard came back three times with more girls, thinking that Michael just didn't like the others. The ambassador came down the stairs after leaving a party upstairs to see Michael arguing with the guard and the three prostitutes on the landing. He was not at all convinced by Michael's story that the guard did not understand the difference between Chinese soup and Chinese prostitutes. After that disaster, Michael always asked me to get his late-night soup for him.

⌇

One night, quite late, Michael pounded on my door, waking me up. I opened it, and he was so excited I could hardly make out his words.

'Geraldine, guess what? I'm in love! I've just met the woman I am going to marry. You can't believe how beautiful she is. I just had to tell someone. I can't wait to see her again. I feel like I've been struck by lightning!' he said.

'That's wonderful, Michael. What's her name?'

He fell into the nearest chair and leant forward, his face glowing and flushed.

'Please don't laugh. I don't even know her name yet! She doesn't speak any English and I was too shy to practise my French with her. I'm going to find out all I can about her.'

Monique. Her name was as beguiling as she was. Over the following months, Michael courted Monique relentlessly. She was the daughter of the French defence attaché and his stunning Laotian wife. In the beginning,

Monique wanted nothing to do with this crass Australian who could hardly utter one word in French. But Michael was clever and devious, and befriended her father first, getting his foot in the door that way. He was hopelessly, desperately, completely in love. Every spare second he had he spent with Monique, until she eventually caved in. When he wasn't with her he was poring over his French language books so he could communicate with her.

Monique was still attending high school. It was a standing joke at the embassy that Michael would find a way to slip out at school break times to meet her.

'Off to play-school are we, Michael? Is it morning recess time already?' we would taunt him as he tried to sneak out of the embassy unnoticed.

His determination paid off, and a few months later they announced their engagement. I was bridesmaid at their traditional Lao wedding, which took place when Monique turned eighteen. For one so young, she was calm, cool and collected on the morning of her wedding day. I watched as she sat while her mother lovingly threaded fine lacy chains, pins and delicate clips of pure gold through her long black hair. She had a serenity that was pure Asian, despite her French education and background.

Finding suitable traditional Lao clothing for me was a real quest. Michael and Monique scoured the city to find clothes that would fit me. They succeeded in borrowing a very expensive antique sarong and bodice from the very fat wife of a Lao general.

It was one of the most uncomfortable days of my life. The ceremony required the whole wedding party to sit with their legs folded sideways for what seemed like hours, while the saffron-robed monks chanted and tied white threads around the wrists of everyone for good luck. My clothes were very tight and I was afraid I was going to burst out of them at any moment. Sitting sideways with my hands clasped under my chin in the prayer position, looking reverent and holding my stomach in all at the same time was quite a challenge.

A second ceremony was needed for them to be legally married. A few days later, on the eve of their wedding in the Catholic cathedral, there was a particularly fierce attack on Phnom Penh by the Khmer Rouge, who penetrated the city to carry out suicide missions to assassinate key government leaders. The fighting went on in the streets all night. Some Khmer Rouge fighters found themselves holed up in the cathedral, and it took hours for the army to kill them all. When the last of them had been dispatched and the blood washed off the floor in front of the high altar, the military rang Michael's father-in-law, and the wedding parties set out for the church.

It was a wedding day with a difference. The organist didn't show up because he was also a surgeon and was up to his armpits in blood, operating on the wounded from the night before. But it was a good thing that the organ didn't burst forth with music at the wedding, as they later discovered a few Vietcong (North Vietnamese) who had hidden behind the organ and were there all through the service. Not the kind of gatecrashers one wants at a wedding.

Despite the previous twenty-four hours being fairly traumatic for the army, the Cambodian generals turned up at the wedding reception in full force. Cambodians hated missing a good party with free food and good wine.

At that time, no officer in the Australian diplomatic service was entitled to a double bed if they weren't married, so a double bed was the first thing on Michael and Monique's list of things to buy.

Michael went on to quickly climb the ladder in the diplomatic service, becoming ambassador to Laos, and then later ambassador to Vietnam.

⟶

I remember like it was yesterday the day my personal effects arrived from Australia. Eng – one of the local staff who we'd nicknamed 'Dusty', because a cloud of dust always seemed to follow him as he did his job cleaning the embassy – arrived at my door to help me unpack. At the end of the day, he asked me if he could have the huge wooden crate that had contained all my treasures. I agreed, and thought nothing more about it.

The next week, Dusty shyly said that he and his wife would like to invite me to their home for dinner. I had been to all the Australians' homes, but in the few weeks I had been in the country this was the first invitation I had received to a Cambodian home. I accepted with pleasure.

I ordered an embassy car and set off at the end of the day with Dusty. His home was only a few miles out of the city, but in a decidedly rural area. We stopped in front of my personal effects crate, which had been turned upside down over a dirt floor. Dusty had cut a door into the side and had covered the entrance by nailing a rice bag over it. 'G. Cox, Australian Embassy, Phnom Penh', in thick, black stencilled ink, was still clearly visible, even though it was upside down.

What I had dismissed as rubbish and was content to send away with the delivery truck, had been transformed into a home to shelter Dusty, his wife and children. The family was so grateful you would have thought I had given them a five-bedroom home with a pool and tennis court.

My God, how little these people had. I thought about how much food I consumed in any one day, and compared it to what Eng and his family ate at one meal. They ate to live where I often lived to eat.

We had a simple meal with lots of rice and vegetables, but not much meat. Dusty's young, but clearly tired, wife proudly placed the food in plastic bowls on a table which they must have borrowed, along with wooden chairs I recognised as belonging to the embassy. Rural Cambodians eat sitting on mats on the floor, but they wanted to put on a real show for me. I was deeply moved and the children were so delighted and entertained by the sight of me that they giggled all night, hiding their faces and smiles behind their little freshly scrubbed brown hands. I was made to feel so much at home. A feeling of family, love and togetherness dominated the night. There was nowhere else I wanted to be right then, than gathered with this family, eating simple food on borrowed furniture, on a mud floor inside a wooden crate in the middle of a crazy war I didn't understand.

The floor was dry, but soft from recent rain, and I could feel my chair sinking slowly but surely under my weight. The tabletop was close to my chin after a few minutes. I moved my chair slightly, into new mud. Eng went outside, and brought some slats of wood that he had left over from cutting out the door. He slid them under the bottom of the chair legs, and it seemed to take my weight better.

'Eng, may I use your toilet?' I asked. The words were out before I could stop myself. Of course, there *was* no bloody toilet. Even I am surprised by my stupidity at times. The rain was bucketing down. Eng went to the car to get an umbrella and politely held open the rice bag door which, from the gentle and graceful movement of his hand, could have been plush velvet. We walked a few metres, then he pointed to the wet and muddy ground and turned sideways from me, holding the umbrella out as far as he could, so that I could squat beneath it. I did what I needed to and we went back inside, chattering and laughing together, as though I peed outside in the rain all the time while a friend stood by holding an umbrella over me. I was coming to realise that some situations could never be covered in pre-posting briefings in the comfort of Canberra.

I slept like a baby that night because I had seen for myself that the wooden roof of Eng's home did not leak, and would keep him and his family dry all through the rainy season.

⌒

I can't think about Phnom Penh without calling up a memory of the Mekong River. It is as important to Cambodia as the Nile is to Egypt. This life-giving river has its origins in the high mountains of Tibet and meanders through southern China, between Thailand and Burma and along the border of Laos before it reaches Cambodia and flows through Vietnam into the South China Sea. In the wet season, the Mekong looks like an orange snake. It is the only river in the world that changes its course every year. In November, the flow of the Mekong reverses. This is the cause of much celebration; people from villages all over the country carry their boats, freshly painted and decorated, to take part in boat races in front of the Royal Palace. The war stopped these festivities as the Vietnamese camped on the other side of the river at the edge of the city, and rocket attacks were not uncommon. It was unnerving looking across the river and knowing that the enemy was looking back at us from the jungle on the other side.

The many-faceted and strange faces of the Mekong helped me understand the face of Cambodia and how ever-changing and unpredictable politics were from one year to the next. Just like the Mekong.

⌒

General Sirik Matak and Marshal Lon Nol were the main architects responsible for the dismissal and exile of Prince Norodom Sihanouk in 1970, which resulted in the abolition of the Cambodian monarchy, an important moment in local history. Sirik Matak lived next door to our ambassador and was a good friend of the embassy staff. One day, he invited the Australian ambassador to make a helicopter tour, and told him he could bring along some embassy staff members. I put my hand up immediately. A tour from the air of this kind during the war was certainly not to be turned down. There were six of us in a helicopter with two military soldiers, armed to the teeth, with weapons pointed down at the ground as they sat at the open doors of the helicopter. I have always hated wearing seatbelts in cars and planes, but I didn't even have to be told to belt up. I had my seatbelt on so tight I could hardly breathe. The noise of the engine was deafening with the doors open.

We flew over the province of Siem Reap, where the scenery was picturesque and peaceful. It was eerie looking down at the rice paddies with the buffaloes and farmers at work, knowing that just metres away Vietnamese soldiers were probably waiting for darkness to fall in order to mount an attack on a nearby village.

Then, like a dream, the temples of Angkor Wat were suddenly there. They simply took my breath away. The perfection of the architecture had to be seen to be believed. It was like some divine hand had reached down and designed the blueprints. There were five main towers, which had been built more than 800 years ago. I could only imagine what majestic artwork must lie hidden from view. The excitement in the helicopter was electric, and the ambassador asked the pilot to fly lower so we could see more detail.

'Your Excellency,' said General Sirik Matak, 'if we descend another 100 feet, ground-to-air missiles will be able to fire on us.' The North Vietnamese were using Cambodian temples as army barracks, and were even using ancient carved statues of Angkor kings and gods for target practice.

As the helicopter slowly turned around and flew away from the magical temples, I vowed that one day I would come back and see them close up.

I hoped fervently that they would not be completely destroyed by war and bombs. I could not understand why Angkor Wat was not listed as one of the seven wonders of the world, or at least added as the eighth wonder. No other religious monument can compare to Angkor Wat in size or artistic detail.

Apart from a few visits to the beach at Sihanoukville, the only other time I was able to travel safely outside the capital was when Colonel Chantaraingsey invited the whole embassy to the province of Kompong Speu, less than an hour's drive from Phnom Penh. Colonel Chantaraingsey was unique as far as Cambodian military people were concerned. He paid his soldiers on time and was held in high regard because he always paid for the placement of death notices out of his own pocket. Most high-level officers didn't bother with these niceties.

The colonel arranged armoured personnel carriers to guard the embassy vehicles. One in front and one behind us. We arrived at the peaceful-looking picnic spot and had our barbecue, but the ambience of the day was not enhanced by the fact that there were soldiers surrounding our group in a circle, facing the thick jungle with their machine guns at the ready.

A weekend at the seaside was not a great prospect either. The soldiers fished, but employed a much quicker method than the local fishermen. In daylight, in full view of bathers, they would take a fishing boat out, throw a grenade into a school of fish, and after the explosion would simply float around and collect with a net the dozens of fish that had died of shock.

Snorkelling was not advisable.

⟵⟶

Cambodia is where I learnt the art of giving good dinner parties, because it was so much safer than going out. I derived a wicked delight in mixing my guests with people they would never normally associate with, and enjoyed sitting back to watch the sparks fly. Without exception, the three subjects I was taught at home to avoid discussing openly – sex, religion and politics – were wildly tossed around my dinner table.

One of my favourite dinner party themes was to get Al-aan to fry up a mountain of fish and chips. And instead of serving them on plates, I would ask her to wrap them up in old Australian newspapers, so they looked just like the kind of fish and chips we would buy at home (before clean white paper became popular). Round about now Al-aan was completely certain of my insanity.

We were lucky enough to have regular RAAF flights into Phnom Penh from Butterworth in Malaysia. Strong, young, bare-chested Australian soldiers would unload tonnes of frozen legs of lamb, Balfours pies and slabs of VB and Foster's beer, as well as Australian wine for use at diplomatic receptions and dinners.

Whenever we could get our hands on some lamb, we'd have a roast dinner. Brenda, the ambassador's secretary, had once told me that she was allergic to pot and came out in a very nasty rash, which was bad enough to send her to bed for a couple of days. She knew I had no interest in smoking pot, and we often complained to each other about how widely it was used in diplomatic circles. So imagine my shock when she called me the morning after one of my lamb roasts, berating me for giving her a rash.

'Geraldine! How dare you serve grass without telling me? You know it makes me sick. I'll be in bed for days,' Brenda cried.

Of course, I denied it, but the fact was she had eaten and drunk only at my place that day, so it must have been there that she had somehow been slipped some weed. I was at my wits' end trying to figure out how this could have happened. I went into the kitchen and asked Al-aan to put out on the table everything she'd used to cook dinner the previous night. Out came oil, salt, pepper, rosemary, thyme, and mint sauce. Then she put a small crinkled brown paper bag on the table.

'What's this?' I asked, picking it up and sniffing it. Definitely first-grade stuff by the smell of it.

'Gunja, Ma'am, very good gunja. Me not buy bad gunja. Number one gunja. Cambodian people use every day in soup and food. Al-aan never buy cheap gunja. Make food very tasty. Everyone like. Everyone laughing at dinner here because Al-aan cook with best gunja. Why Ma'am angry?'

I called Brenda and told her that it happened without my knowledge and we made our peace. After that I had to keep a close eye on the contents of my kitchen cupboard. But Al-aan was right. All the Cambodian soups are laced with gunja and it is almost impossible to find a local recipe that doesn't contain at least a pinch of it. It is as normal to Cambodians as oregano is to Italians.

⌒

Phnom Penh's public utilities were not able to cope with the stresses of normal living, let alone wartime conditions. This was mainly because when the services had been set up by the French there had been a lot of corruption, and no-one had been trained in maintenance. A common joke among Westerners was that there was no word in Khmer for 'maintenance'. If something broke down, it was usually thrown away.

Consequently, with the influx of refugees, the electricity and water supplies were patchy to say the least. Everyone stored supplies of water in large plastic tubs in the bathroom, to ensure they could bathe every day. You always had to make sure you had a supply of candles, and the embassy issued us with small generators and gas-operated lanterns to use during the inevitable blackouts.

One morning I was taking a shower and washing my hair. I was thoroughly soaped from head to toe when the water stopped. My storage tub was empty. I think it was around this time in my life that I started using the 'f' word regularly. After using a towel to wipe the soap and shampoo off my body and hair, I brushed my teeth, using a can of VB beer to rinse my mouth. I went to work, after making sure that Al-aan was in no doubt that her first task was to fill the storage tub when the water came back on.

The longest I can remember going without water was ten days. Everyone in the embassy was in the same boat. We were all bad tempered and smelly, with greasy hair. I didn't wear make-up, as I couldn't wash my face at night. We might have run out of water, but no respectable Australian ever ran out of beer. We all reeked of it because it was all we had left to brush our teeth with.

The streets were always piled high with stinking, rotting rubbish. And the starving refugees, young and old, crawled through it looking for scraps to eat. Cholera, typhoid and other diseases were threatening to become rampant, but there were no rubbish trucks. The piles just got bigger and bigger, like rotting mountains by the side of the road. Thin streams of steam and smoke curled up out of the fermenting trash, and marauding dogs and feral cats fought ferociously over their spoils.

Soiled medical waste from the operating theatres in the military hospitals was emptied onto these piles in the streets. Bloody bandages with flesh still sticking to them, and body parts, could be seen being dragged away by domestic pigs and street dogs.

An animal lover would have to be sedated after seeing the sorry state of Phnom Penh's starving and disease-ridden dogs and cats. The healthy ones were whipped off to the nearest local restaurant, and I know I was probably served many a delicious meal of dog and cat soup. During the war, I never saw one healthy dog with a coat of normal hair. They were all a grey, almost dead-looking colour, and were mangy, and covered in scabs and running sores. They suffered long, slow and miserably painful deaths. Cambodians made a point of keeping their distance from street dogs at all times because rabies was common. A bite from them, or one of the bats that flew around the city after dark, and you could pretty well call it quits.

Being a monkey in Cambodia at that time was not much fun either. Although monkey restaurants were technically illegal, they thrived, mainly among the Chinese community. It was a sign of respect and a great honour to be invited to one by Cambodians.

I knew what was coming the minute I was seated at the table. There were several round holes in the tabletop. When live monkeys were brought in and fixed in place with vice-like tools under the table, I tried to hide my horror. Only the tops of the monkeys' heads were exposed. In their fear, the monkeys sprayed urine under the table, but that was stopped with one elegant, practised blow with a sharp cleaver that deftly sliced off the top of each skull, cleverly leaving the brain intact. The monkeys' bodies still shook in their death throes as my hosts delved into the brains with their spoons, urging me to do the same.

I struggled with nausea, and the bile that was rising in my throat. Again, this was something that simply never came up during the neat, sterile pre-posting briefings in Canberra. What is the correct etiquette at a monkey brain restaurant, when your hosts have paid US$100 a head for each monkey?

I imagined one of Mum's corned beef and cabbage dinners, and forced one spoonful of brain into my mouth, knowing that all the Cambodians were eagerly waiting for my opinion on what they considered a delicacy. I was the only foreigner in the room, and had somehow to not let them see how completely distasteful the whole idea of eating any animal while it is alive is to Westerners.

Other food was served but the taste of the monkey brain stayed with me for days. It was the closest I ever got to really wanting to be a vegetarian. When I got home I was able to speak to God personally as I knelt in front of my toilet and emptied my stomach of everything I had eaten.

At moments like this I wondered if overseas service, representing your country, was all it was cracked up to be.

⌒

The exchange rate in Cambodia went up and down like a toilet seat at a mixed party, as the country was in the tertiary stages of economic syphilis. The exchange rate was decided each Monday morning by the governor of the central bank and the economic boffins from the American embassy – America was, after all, bankrolling the economy and propping up the currency. Embassies were told the new exchange rate some hours before it became official.

Michael very sensibly and responsibly put it to Canberra that instead of exchanging Australian dollars for Cambodian riels to replenish the official account on a fixed day each month, as the regulations dictated, we should use this window of opportunity to make our exchanges, and save the Australian government a lot of money. Today, such a move would be expected of a good manager, but back then Michael was told to keep his nose in his account books and not dabble in foreign exchange matters. (Later, when the war had intensified, the riel was rendered valueless and we were forced to pay our Cambodian staff in rice.)

I had heard friends in the embassy whispering about the high exchange rate on the black market. Just about everybody was cashing in on the black market, but it was not openly discussed. It was another Australian government regulation that no diplomatic or official staff member was allowed to abuse the system to make personal financial gain. All very well in theory, but when you could get five times as much money on the black market, who could resist such a temptation?

So one Saturday morning I donned my Stevie Wonder dark glasses, which I stupidly thought were a good disguise, and hailed a likely looking cyclo driver. I had walked a couple of streets from my apartment building to make sure no-one followed me, but still looked furtively over my shoulder as I got in.

'Take me to the Black Market,' I said, first in Khmer, and then in French. I pulled the plastic hood on the cyclo over me to hide myself even further. I sped off in the blazing afternoon, under the delusion that the cyclo driver knew the way.

Well, I went to the New Market, the Old Market, the Olympic Market, the Bamboo Market, and markets I never knew the names of, but no-one seemed to know where this Black Market was. While passing through the streets, I kept my eyes open for a market with perhaps a black awning or something that would distinguish it as a Black Market. After two hot, sweaty, very tiring hours, my frustrated cyclo driver deposited me outside my apartment, glad to get rid of this foreigner who didn't know which market she wanted to go to.

I felt a little foolish at my failure to find the place and change my money. I had planned to spend up big in Silver Street that day with the extra cash I was sure to make thanks to the exchange rate. I had a good reason to try to financially make a killing. I had just cashed US$1000 from the bank to pay for an upcoming holiday in Bangkok. I had the cash in my hand when I took a pile of documents to the shredder at the end of the day, when we disposed of all classified material. While shredding the papers, I was gossiping with Michael, and accidentally shredded the money $100 at a time. By the time I registered what I was doing, it was too late. Easy come, easy go, I thought, remembering my childhood in Adelaide when the bottomless bowl of money was always sitting there on the kitchen table.

At the inevitable dinner party that evening, I singled out one of the handsome majors from the American embassy, as I had heard him talking about the good rate he got all the time.

'Randy,' I said (it was amazing how many of the Americans were called Randy, Hank or Junior), 'I've spent half the bloody day in a cyclo looking for the Black Market. Where the hell is it?'

'You asked a cyclo driver to take you to the Black Market!' Randy was shaking with laughter.

Randy spent the entire evening going around telling everyone how naïve I was, and I learned that no actual physical market itself existed, and that you had to find someone you trusted to make the money exchange in a back street away from watchful eyes.

Once again, the milkman's daughter was made to realise how unsophisticated she really was.

⟜

Although Nixon's statements that there were no US ground-fighting troops in Cambodia were basically correct, there were dozens of high-ranking military advisors, observers, training personnel, radio experts and communications technicians openly attached to the American embassy. One of the advisors, who became a friend, was involved in planting listening devices all over the country; these were hooked up to the Pentagon. He told me he knew when more than twenty soldiers were moving at any one time.

Although I was actually in Cambodia and could see the suffering with my own eyes, and typed up the reports of battles all over the country, I had no real concept of the wholesale slaughter that had gone on, and was going on, while I was living there.

By February 1972, the Americans would report that war and bombing had made over two million Cambodians homeless. In June 1972 the Watergate scandal would break and cause much comment in Phnom Penh diplomatic circles. The publication of the Pentagon Papers, which revealed America's secret history in the war against Vietnam, infuriated the world.

The Nixon Doctrine, which included the Henry Kissinger-inspired carpet bombing of rural Cambodia, was, in my opinion, something for which Richard Nixon's government should have hung its head in shame. Senior American military experts did advise against these bombing raids, and try to convince Nixon and Kissinger that the war could only be won by fighting on the ground, but they were ignored. By August 1973 the Americans would admit to dropping 539,129 tonnes of bombs on Cambodia (during World War Two, 160,000 tonnes were dropped on Japan, a much larger country).

The Nixon Doctrine came to pass after Nixon visited China for the first time, starting out as a policy for the defence and self-defence of Asia. History would show it to be a doctrine that led to the destruction of untold millions of lives over the years the war lasted in Indochina. Concerning Cambodia, America dabbled with the fate of an entire nation whose government and people believed it could save them from their enemies.

Considering the loss of human life by the end of the war, I wonder how Nixon and Kissinger slept at night. Nixon is dead and past any mortal punishment, but Kissinger is not. Now there's a man I'd like to be alone with in a dark room with a big stick. And I'm very sure I'm not alone in that.

⟨⟩

I spent a lot of time with the war correspondents. They were uncomplicated, and you always knew where you were with them and what they wanted, even if you didn't always want what they did. They drank hard and played hard. Most of them were stoned every waking hour of the day. I think they had to be stoned to get the courage to go down that road every morning to cover the fighting at the front.

It must have been the only war in the world where they could have breakfast at the side of the Hotel Royal pool, hire a local taxi to take them as close as possible to the shooting, and walk off the side of the road into the thick jungle of the war, while their drivers waited in their cars, out of the range of the firing. Sometimes they would drive back to Phnom Penh for lunch and head out again in the afternoon.

Neil Davis, an Australian war correspondent working for Visnews, was nothing short of a legend throughout Cambodia. Even North Vietnamese soldiers loved him. He was film-star material. He was very tall and lean, with a head of wavy blond hair and the most innocent baby-blue eyes you could ever wish to see. Neil was able to make the standard journalist's baggy safari suit with pockets stuffed with film and camera equipment look like a freshly dry-cleaned tuxedo.

Almost every woman I knew in the country – Asian, Western, old, young, married or single – secretly, or not so secretly, lusted after him. And maybe a few of the men too. He had a unique understanding of Cambodians, he loved Cambodia, and his reporting reflected an intensity that many other professionals envied.

He told me stories of boys not yet teenagers being sent to war with make-believe carved wooden guns, to face certain death. He talked of sitting around campfires with Cambodian soldiers smoking pot before they charged the front line, confident that the Buddha images they held between their teeth would save them from being killed. He told me of places on the front line where the soldiers had run out of sand for the sacks they used to make bunkers; and how they had only rice husks to fill the bags. On the front line, even during heavy shelling, he refused to wear a helmet, and stood up straight, filming as though he was at the beach!

He was fearless. I saw him once get out of a helicopter. It's a human reflex to hunch over when stepping out of a helicopter, even when common sense tells you that the flashing blades are nowhere near your head. I've seen presidents and kings automatically hunch over. But not Neil. He stood tall and walked away without even thinking about it.

He had one fault. He was a chain-smoker and no-one who smoked ever escaped without being touched for at least one cigarette. He was always trying to give up smoking, and thought that not buying any would help. Smokers would see him enter a room and immediately reach for their cigarettes, ready to hand one out.

Years later, when I saw on television that he had been killed in a senseless one-day coup in Bangkok, I cried as though I had lost a member of my family. I knew that many people all over the world were crying with me.

Dennis Cameron, another journalist, broke the cardinal rule. He got personally involved. He took a young Cambodian boy into his home. The boy had been horribly burnt by napalm and left for dead, but Dennis found him. A real professional would have taken photos of his burnt body and moved on to the next photo opportunity of the war. But Dennis had reached his limit. He put his camera down and gently gathered the broken boy in his arms, put him in his car, and took him home. He was trying to adopt him and take him out of Cambodia for medical treatment.

I knew nothing of this until I went home with Dennis from a bar one night. Before we went inside, he said, 'I had better warn you, I can't put the light on.'

'Why ever not?' I asked.

He explained that he had a young boy living with him whose eyelids had been burnt away by napalm. He was in constant pain because he couldn't close his eyes, and the light made it worse.

'He might be a little afraid at first. He hides as soon as I leave, and I always have to look for him when I come back. He's got shellshock really badly and there is nothing I can do about it,' he said.

We found the boy, Chan, around twelve to fourteen years old, cowering under the kitchen table, swaying back and forth on his heels, moaning, his hands covering his scarred face. I looked at Dennis and could no longer see the self-assured war correspondent who had flirted with me a few minutes earlier. He was transformed into a caring, worried father, whose only concern was to make his son comfortable. He had to give the child morphine to dull the slow-burning pain of napalm. It must have been costing him a fortune.

⌒

Opium dens could be a real trap. More than one diplomat or diplomat's wife could be found any night at one of the many dens dotted around the city. They were mostly run and owned by Chinese. I only went once, out of curiosity.

The opium den was a normal Cambodian wooden house on stilts with steps up to the verandah. Once you were inside, the sickly sweet smoke of the poppy engulfed you. Straw mats divided the one large room, and each had a hard ceramic or wooden cushion for your head. A wooden or bamboo pipe, sometimes with an ornate porcelain bowl, was brought and lit for you by a Chinese youth, and you were basically left alone with only a pot of Chinese tea to sustain you. The night I was there I recognised several wives of French rubber plantation owners with their husbands, some high-ranking Cambodians in military uniform, a couple of high-class Cambodian bar girls, and a few up-market cyclo drivers, obviously out on the town for the night.

As I had never learned to smoke, I was able to get through the evening without worrying about getting hooked on opium. Although I took the pipe and put it to my lips, I only puffed away and never took the drug into my lungs. By only pretending to smoke, I was able get a good look around while all the others in the den were away with the fairies, including my Cambodian girlfriend who had agreed to show me the place. After a couple of hours I was bored stiff and took myself home. Life is too short to spend it lying drugged in an overpriced opium den.

A common diversion for expat men was to visit one of the city's many bars, which were filled with prostitutes. Some of the girls were shockingly young; thirteen year olds were popular. A lot of the prostitutes were Vietnamese, born in Cambodia but with no hope of being accepted there or in Vietnam. Some were hard-faced and bitter; others were sweet and innocent, fresh from the provinces, where they had probably been sold by their parents to feed the rest of the family. The girls' glittery, noisy, cheeriness was false, and I always felt depressed when I left the bars. However, they did at least give the appearance of being sociable places to go and drink; the brothels themselves were just bamboo shacks along the riverbank or on the roadside out of town.

As it was so commonplace for men to visit prostitutes, sexually transmitted diseases were rife. Among the war correspondents it was difficult to find someone who didn't have crabs or gonorrhoea, or even a disease without a name. It was all over town that a senior diplomat in a European embassy had caught a serious dose of syphilis. His posting was over, and he was preparing to go home to his wife and children. He was having penicillin injections several times a day, in the hope that he would recover in time for a loving reunion with his unsuspecting wife.

I remember being at a doctor's, getting a blood test after a case of dysentery. When he left the room to wash his hands, I noticed a wooden box on the desk, clearly marked 'The Diplomatic VD List'. I succumbed to the desire to flick quickly through the alphabetical cards for each embassy. I came away with more than I had wanted to know about my fellow diplomats in Phnom Penh! My new knowledge certainly made the many boring cocktail parties and National Day receptions that we had to attend far more entertaining.

Also, I had my suspicions about the background of our embassy male-only choir. I knew I could get the real story from Adrian, so I invited him over for a banquet of Chinese food, to tell me the story. He told me that it was an initiative of two communicators in the British embassy: an informal drinking and carousing group for bachelors in the British and Australian embassies and aid projects.

I plied him with a platter of fish baked with a ginger and chilli sauce, and he told me the choir had a dozen members. I handed him a bowl of finely minced beef in basil, peppers and mint to coax him to talk further. He told me that as the membership was confined to men who were unmarried or separated from their partners geographically, it was a statistical certainty that some of them would meet with medical misfortune while visiting bar girls. Contracting a disease was treated rather as a badge of courage, so he came up with the idea of using some old Cambodian medals and insignia he'd found in the registry to reward members for injuries sustained in the line of duty. (He was really enjoying the sweet and sour pork.) He then had the medals mounted on a display panel on the wall in the registry.

But when they started putting names under the medals, staff began asking what the connection was. He said they had to think of something believable, and decided to say that the choir was a bachelors' singing group and that medals were awarded for the best performers. (Adrian was smacking his lips before attacking the baby eggplant and lotus flower soup with bamboo shoots and noodles.)

He made me promise not to let on to anyone that I knew all about the choir. He said the blokes would have his balls on a plate if they knew he had told me the story. I seriously doubted that a plate that big existed in Phnom Penh, but assured him I would keep his secret. I served him his well-earned dessert of thinly sliced bananas and red beans in warm coconut milk. I imagined any guilt he may have felt was smothered by the satisfaction in his stomach.

Some changes were taking place at the embassy. A new person was replacing Ray, our stern security officer, and we wondered what we were in for. We were pleasantly surprised by the arrival of Sergeant Ian Hill from Sydney. He was about thirty-three years old and a real boy-next-door type – the kind of man who wasn't afraid to show how eager he was to receive his mother's weekly letter. If you closed your eyes you could see him as a little boy at school with his cap, shorts and socks falling down his legs. When he smiled his eyes lit up like those of a child blowing out the candles on a birthday cake. He was a real softie. How he ever ended up in the police force was beyond me.

Although he claimed to have worked in Sydney's notorious red-light district, Kings Cross, he had an endearing air of innocence. A group of us took him to his first Phnom Penh bar one night. All the girls flocked around what they saw as fresh meat with US dollars in his pocket.

They showered Ian with compliments and questions: 'You handsome boy!'; 'Me like big foreigner!'; 'You buy me drink?'

He was grinning from ear to ear.

'Gee, Geraldine,' he whispered, 'do you reckon one of these lovely ladies would go out for dinner with me one night if I asked her?' I didn't think it was possible for someone from the Sydney police force not to smell a working girl from fifty paces, but he looked genuinely surprised when I told him they were all prostitutes.

Ian became an embassy favourite and was such fun to play tricks on. He was always forgetting to lock his office, or locking himself out of it. I had a special trick of going into his office for a chat and closing the door softly when I left, locking him in. It was sometimes hours before he would bang on the door from the inside, saying: 'That bloody Geraldine. She's locked me in again. Someone get the key and let me out.'

One day this prank could have been disastrous.

Ian's office had only one door, that opened into the embassy reception area. One day Michael had the devil in him. He had noticed some Cambodians outside in the street with a fully grown black honey bear on a rope. They were trying to get money by prodding the poor animal with a stick to make it dance. Michael gave them some money and asked them to wait. For a joke he took the bear and led it on its rope straight into Ian's office, and pushed the bear inside, pressing the snib on the door to lock it before slamming it shut. He thought Ian had his key with him, but I had already slipped the key into my pocket as I was planning to lock him in as I usually did when I got bored.

News travelled quickly about the bear, and before long we were all waiting to see what would happen. I am sorry to say the staff was more interested in Ian's reactions than in the feelings the poor bear must have had about being shoved into a strange place away from his owners. He was less than impressed, and began to make his feelings known by throwing Ian's paperclips about the office and growling fiercely. Ian's shouts for help were heard up to the second floor, and probably also in the British embassy next door. Michael was no longer in a joking mood when he eventually found me in the registry upstairs, and he dragged me down to unlock Ian's door.

Ian's face was deathly pale by the time I opened the door, and Michael got the Cambodians to come in to coax the bear out. I don't like to think what might have happened if I had been out of the embassy at the time with the key. The bear had not been fed that day and Ian could very well have been lunch! From then on I was on notice: 'No more Mr Nice Guy, Geraldine. I've had enough.' I knew I was taking advantage of Ian's easygoing nature. I promised myself I would resist any further temptation to tease him.

⌒

Cambodia taught me something about myself: I loved danger. In Cambodia danger was really a matter of being in the wrong place at the wrong time. You could very easily get yourself blown up or shot. I adopted a fatalistic approach to life. I liked living on the edge, as long as I didn't fall over the cliff.

On nights when there were blackouts and the air conditioners no longer worked, I lay sweating in my bed, thinking of the cool water in the swimming pool at the Hotel Royal. (I had never seen anyone sweat like I did in Cambodia.) One night I couldn't bear the heat any longer and decided to test how dangerous the streets really were after the 6.00 p.m. curfew. After all, there were thousands of refugees sleeping out in the open. How dangerous could it be?

I woke the sleeping soldier provided as security for all diplomatic accommodation, and ignoring his plea not to go out, got him to unlock the gate. I ventured out into the dark night of Phnom Penh. I didn't have to walk far to find a driver asleep in his cyclo. I shook his shoulder softly so as not to scare him, and US$2 was all it took to wake him up properly. Soon we were racing through the night down the middle of a deserted Monivong. Deserted that is, except for the armed soldiers manning the main intersections.

As we approached the first barricade, my driver slowed down and shouted Khmer words I later learned meant: 'I have a round-eye with me. Don't shoot!' He was letting them know in advance that he had a foreigner with him. I was surrounded by tired, underpaid soldiers who were in no mood to bother with a crazy Western woman with a diplomatic ID card. They gave it and me a cursory glance by their weak torchlights and waved me on, signalling the soldiers with their walkie-talkies at the other checkpoints ahead to let me through. By the time I reached the Royal I was drenched in sweat, but it was the sweat of fear, not of heat.

I knew about a gate at the side of the Royal that was never locked. The journos who lived in the bungalows in the grounds of the hotel often used it to get in, as sometimes the night staff wouldn't let them through the front foyer if they had bar girls with them (which was almost always). I asked the cyclo driver to wait for me in the side street, and walked in the silence of the night across the unkempt lawn. I took off my clothes and swam naked in the dark. It was delicious, and even more enjoyable because I was completely aware of the risk I had taken. I had got away with it so far, but I still had to get home.

However, the journey back was easy, as the soldiers were expecting me. I smiled to myself as my cyclo glided through the streets and swung to a stop outside my gate, where the security guard was well and truly awake. As I snuggled down in my bed, refreshed from my swim, I imagined how Ian would tear his hair out when I told him what I had done.

After this, I often took myself out alone after curfew. Some cyclo drivers who knew of my eccentric behaviour parked their bikes outside my apartment after dark, hoping to get my late-night business. The checkpoint soldiers were usually the same men and I became quite well known among the guards. I sometimes brightened up the night for them by singing 'Waltzing Matilda' as I was swept past them, but that usually depended on how much I had had to drink earlier. But no night was as dangerous as the first one and no subsequent midnight swim in the pool at the Royal was ever as delightful.

When the rocket attacks became more frequent and began to start early in the evening, we had to change our working hours to a very early start at 7.00 a.m., and ate our lunches at our desks, so that we could get away at 2.00 p.m. This only gave us four hours of shopping and leisure time before the 6.00 p.m. to 6.00 a.m. curfew.

But it took more than a strict curfew to stop us Aussies! We started the practice of having all-night dinner parties. Guests would arrive just before 6.00 p.m. with sleeping bags, if they had them. When it was time to sleep, people's lounge room floors looked like the last scene of *Hamlet*, with bodies lying all over the place. At the weekends we often had formal champagne breakfasts. What a weird, callous bunch of foreigners we must have looked to the hungry, war-ravaged refugees as we rode down the main streets in the grimy cyclos early on Sunday mornings in ballgowns and dinner suits, clutching our icy bottles of Russian and French champagne.

As the rocket attacks got more regular and seemed to be coming from closer into the city, I thought I would have a look at our Evacuation Plan – Australian Eyes Only – Top Secret file, while I was relieving for the ambassador's secretary, who was on leave. The ambassador was at a luncheon from which he wouldn't return for a couple of hours at least. The file was held in his safe. I ordered a baguette with thick slices of juicy ham and cheese, sat back with the file and as I opened it, took a huge mouthful of my lunch. There was only one flimsy piece of paper in the folder. It said, 'The Americans will come back for us, if they can.'

I choked on my ham and cheese, and splattered the crisp white page with breadcrumbs. I read the few paragraphs beneath this incredible statement. The embassy's emergency evacuation plan was a farce, calling for us all to assemble at an open space near the Independence Monument in downtown Phnom Penh. Presumably we would protect ourselves from the fighting that would undoubtedly be raging around us by waving our diplomatic passports importantly in the air, while waiting for US military helicopters that *might* come back from Vietnam and evacuate us.

Later that day I told Michael and Adrian what I had seen, asking them not to let on. After a few days I learnt that they had cleverly put the evacuation plan on the agenda for the next weekly meeting. That way the plan could at least be brought out in the open and hopefully improved upon.

However, Adrian and Michael had little faith in the final arrangements, and devised their own escape route. They assembled ration packs, a couple of AK47s, Cambodian, Vietcong, South Vietnamese and Red Cross flags, and obtained an inflatable rubber dinghy they kept ready at a mooring on the Bassac. They planned that when the shit hit the fan they would head for the dinghy, and paddle and drift downstream to South Vietnam.

Everyone knew that the North Vietnamese were wolfing down great chunks of Cambodian territory and that it was just a matter of time before they reached the capital and took over the country. I didn't like the odds against the embassy's evacuation plan or Adrian and Michael's alternative method working. I had something much more colourful worked out. We were not allowed to have guns in our homes, although the embassy military personnel had weapons to defend themselves in case of an attack. I couldn't see the logic of being allowed to have weapons in the embassy but not in our homes, so I did a deal with the soldier assigned to guard the apartment block. Late one night, he handed over to me an M16 machine gun in good condition, which I promptly hid under my bed. The respectful looks I got from all the maids in the building increased significantly the next day.

I also had a North Vietnamese flag concealed in a locked box, and learnt how to say 'Long Live Ho Chi Minh' in Vietnamese. I figured the flag coupled with the spoken slogan, and with a sexy negligee and bottle of French champagne, might dissuade a band of Vietcong from slitting my throat.

⌒

Usually the rocket attacks started after midnight when most of the city was asleep. But one night I was home alone playing music in my lounge room, when the shooting and bombing started just after dark. The room was one flight up and faced the street, and I could hear the thud of bullets hitting the front of the concrete building. I dropped to the floor instinctively, knowing that with the lights on I would make an easy target for a soldier in the street. Somehow I had to turn them off without standing up, so that I could run to the back of the house.

I lay on my back and grabbed the broom that had been up against the wall, and turned the light switch off with it. Before I ran to my bedroom at the back of the apartment, I used the broomstick to poke my portable cassette recorder out onto the small verandah so that I could record the sounds of Phnom Penh under attack. My mother still has the tape that I sent to her.

But the night wasn't over. I heard the sound of a car horn blaring, and then the loud crash of metal against metal as a car broke through the locked iron gates downstairs. I heard footsteps running up the stairs to my front door and remembered too late that I had forgotten to lock it. My door burst open and I was prepared for the worst. Then my fear changed to laughter as I heard Michael swearing as he fell into my darkened lounge room. He said: 'Bloody hell, Geraldine! Are you all right?' He told me he was on his way to a dinner party when the attacks started and he had to decide whether to try to make it, or turn back. He wasn't going to get out of his car to find the guard so he could open the gates, so he drove his car right through them. Michael's eyes were sticking out of his head with fear, but he still wore his customary smile.

He and I tried to get information on the military radio but it was jammed with traffic. We had to wait till the morning to find out that there had been an eclipse of the moon, and that common practice was to make as loud a noise as possible to stop the dragon from eating it. In peacetime these noises had been made with saucepans and pots, but now people had guns and rockets, and they were much more effective in shooting the dragon.

⌒

By far the most dangerous time for me was one hot, sunny Saturday afternoon, when I was walking along the road near the Royal having just had a swim. There was no-one on the street except for a couple of Cambodian soldiers sitting in the shade of a lovely old *boab* tree. The next thing I heard was the shot from a single gun. I felt the bullet whiz by my head, its wind lifting my fringe with it as it narrowly missed my forehead. I froze in the middle of the footpath, and peed and peed and peed. I don't know how long I stood there, but I could hear the soldiers under the tree laughing at me and at how I had messed myself. They were just having some afternoon fun making the foreigner jump.

I was learning first hand what was really meant by 'shit-scared'. Soldiers throughout history have lost control of their bowels during battle and that day I wasn't far from doing the same. And this was due to the guys on our side!

I learned during my time in Cambodia never to waste time and energy worrying about things I couldn't change. But it was around about now that I was reaching saturation point in my lust for dangerous situations.

Paradise Found

Phnom Penh, October – December 1971

B y this time my disappointment over Theo was just a dim memory. What had not left me was the pain I felt every time I saw a beautiful, healthy baby. From the age of twenty-three when I first knew I couldn't have children, I had to leave the room during television commercials in which babies were used to promote products. If a movie went into the slightest detail of a baby being born, I would have to leave the cinema and go home. When married girlfriends joyfully told me they were pregnant, I made excuses not to see them. I couldn't force myself to be happy for them. Twice I had to stop myself from stealing babies their mothers had left in strollers outside supermarkets. Once I actually got my hand wrapped around the handle of a pram and was about to take off when I came to my senses.

I believed I would never be a mother but I was obsessed with children. I wanted to be with them, hold them, smell them, touch them and play with them. I had often thought about adoption since I was told I couldn't become pregnant. But in the 1970s it was impossible for a single woman to adopt a child. It simply had never been done and was not about to be encouraged.

In Cambodia I had pushed the hot tears away and no-one knew of the heartache that I carried with me always. But then I started asking around to see if I could visit one of the many Cambodian government orphanages in the city. I was given permission, and I arranged for a group of Australian women to come with me one Saturday morning. What happened when we arrived and walked through the orphanage gates for the first time was so unexpected and overwhelming that it still feels as though it happened yesterday.

At the sight of a gaggle of foreign women walking towards them, the children started running towards us laughing and shouting. Small ones clutched my legs as I tried to walk and they hung on to my arms. Older girls and boys fought to try to put their arms around my waist. They clung like little monkeys, fighting to occupy a part of my body. They were starved of love, of human touch. We all struggled not to cry, and walked along as best we could with our clumps of toddlers still hanging on as though they were physically attached to us.

The babies' dormitory was heartbreaking. There were many with cleft palates slowly starving to death because the untrained nurses didn't have the time to hold their bottles so that they could drink. When still full bottles fell away from their resting places on dirty pillows, the nurses came along and took them away. They probably never even realised that the children were starving. Babies were lying in their urine and runny stools, even though the staff knew we were visiting that day. At lunchtime, the children sat in little circles on low plastic stools, and a woman walked around giving them all a spoonful of rice porridge each one at a time off the same spoon. She walked around until the large bowl was finished. God knows what diseases were passed from one child to another on that spoon. After the children had their naps on the floor on mats, they were woken up for their baths, which consisted of standing them up against a wall and hosing them down, with their clothes on, without soap, with a garden hose like animals. The carers never touched them.

I was hyperventilating with rage I knew I could not show and a great wave of sadness consumed me. No-one could blame the staff. The government employed them and half of them received no salary, and worked there just to have a place to sleep and eat. None of the nurses was trained, and none that I saw had any obvious love or compassion for the orphans. They were so deadened by what they had suffered in their own lives during the war that it was impossible for them to understand that we were outraged at the way they were treating the children, who were identified by numbers. No files were kept.

As the novelty of our presence began to wear off, and the children started to lose interest in us, one blind boy of about six years old still held my hand tightly. I couldn't remember his identifying number. He was very animated and chattered away very seriously. His white, jelly-like eyes were rolling around in their sockets. I asked Kim from the embassy, who had come with us as our translator for the day, what he was saying. She told me: 'He says his mother felt fat like you, but he hasn't seen her for a long time and doesn't know where she is. He says the ring on your finger feels just like the ring his mother wore, and he is asking you if you are his mother coming back to take him home.' Kim was trying to conceal her feelings, and if maternal instincts were visible they would have oozed out of every pore of my body. I told Kim to tell him that I wasn't his mother, but that I would like to call him Sam. I carried Sam on my hip all day, and when it was time to go he had to be pried off me, screaming to be allowed to leave with me. I promised to return the next week and I left with his crying ringing in my ears.

I didn't blame the other women for not wanting to make regular trips back to the orphanage, but I spent most of my weekends there from then on. I befriended the directress, and slowly but surely the staff began to trust me. I asked if I could bring a group of the children to my home for an afternoon every weekend. I explained that I would give them fresh orange juice, a big bowl of fried rice and meat, and that they could swim in a plastic wading pool on the roof terrace.

When these afternoons started I think I looked forward to them more than the children did. I had a regular group of about a dozen of them. Some were blind, deaf or crippled, and some had cleft palates, club feet or tuberculosis. Some were normal children who suffered only from being unloved and unwanted. But Sam made it clear to me, and to the other children, that I was his special property, and he was always nearest to me throughout the whole day.

I don't know exactly when I first thought that maybe I could adopt a child in Cambodia. But the idea slowly nibbled away at me until I could think of nothing else. I saw that married couples from other Western embassies were going through adoption processes at other orphanages. These were mostly French people, but I thought, why not me?

Sam was becoming so much a part of my life that I knew I needed gently to distance myself from him, because even if I wanted desperately to adopt him, Australian immigration regulations would never allow me to adopt a blind child. Consular laws were extremely rigid as far as the health of overseas adoptive children was concerned. No deaf, dumb, blind or crippled children, or children with mental problems, or congenital diseases of any kind, were allowed entry. No, it would break my heart, but if I were seriously to attempt an adoption, I would have to choose a healthy child to have any chance of succeeding. The weekend visits continued and I tried to feel less attached to Sam, without success.

I told the directress that I would like to adopt a child. I explained to her how strict the laws were in Australia. I knew that almost all of the children at the orphanage had permanent deformities or serious illnesses, so I asked her, 'Please Madame, if you have a healthy child come to the orphanage, can you let me know?' I said that if she agreed I could take the child home while the paperwork was being processed so they would be less likely to catch the communicable diseases and skin rashes rife among the children. The directress had become a friend and she promised to help me.

⌒

The days went by and I tried not to think about where this child might come from or whether or not my plans to adopt would come to fruition. Then one day at work the phone rang, and it was the directress. She told me that the night before a soldier had brought in a baby girl, around six months old, and apparently normal but very malnourished. She asked if I would have time to go and see her.

You've never seen eighty kilos of flesh move as fast as I did that day. I got hold of a car and grabbed Moy to drive me to the orphanage. He was almost as excited as I was. We had become good friends, as he often ferried the orphans to and from my place at weekends and he knew I wanted to adopt a Cambodian child.

Moy stood behind me as I watched Baby Number 63 sleep on the dirty, torn plastic sheet on the crib. I could smell her urine and faeces from where I stood. They smelt like roses to me! It was hot and her hair was tangled, with greasy, feathery tendrils clinging to her tiny, sweet forehead. Her eyelashes were ridiculously long for an Asian baby, and she was, without a doubt, the most beautiful creature God had ever put breath into. She was going to be mine, and I actually heard bells ringing.

One of her upper arms was bandaged, and later the directress told me the story. 'There are some kind soldiers left in Cambodia, Geraldine,' she said with a dash of sarcasm. I had once told her that I thought the soldiers I saw in the street looked heartless and cruel. She informed me that the soldier had been going home after his curfew shift in Monivong, when he heard a baby cry in the alley where he had parked his jeep. He followed the screaming, and found the baby in a cardboard box surrounded by hungry dogs attacking her because she was too weak to defend herself. One of them had bitten a piece out of her arm. He shot the dogs, and took the baby straight to the orphanage, where they bandaged her arm and hoped she would not get tetanus or rabies. The directress said the baby was not yet strong enough to stand any inoculations, so she would allow me to take her home, as long as I signed something saying that I was responsible for her welfare until I decided if I wanted to adopt her or not.

Nothing was going to stop me from taking Baby Number 63 home that very day. Moy was grinning from ear to ear as I carried her out to the car. I was in heaven.

⌒

Al-aan was not so happy about the new addition to my household. I sent her off to the market to buy some clothes, baby oil, talcum powder, ear buds, tinned baby food, milk formula, and anything else she thought the baby would need. After milk and food the baby needed rest more than anything, and I thought she was too weak for a thorough bath. I wrapped her in a clean towel and lay down next to her, afraid to sleep in case she needed something during the night.

I had never been prone to praying, but that night I said: 'Thank you, Jesus, thank you, Buddha, thank you, Allah, thank you, God, whoever you are.' I lay wide awake gazing at Baby Number 63, trying to think of a name for her. I decided on Lisa Devi Cox. Devi means 'angel' in Khmer, and that is exactly what she was to me.

After the second day she seemed a little stronger, and was drinking milk and eating almost non-stop, so I decided to give her what was probably her first-ever bath, in the kitchen sink. The dirt on her head was so ingrained that it took several days of painstakingly rubbing her scalp with cotton wool balls soaked in baby oil to remove it.

One thing that tore at my heartstrings was that she wore badly crafted, but twenty-four carat, gold earrings. The places where the gold had pierced her ears were badly infected, so I had to remove the earrings as quickly as possible. As I placed them in a matchbox in some tissue paper, I made a promise to myself that when she was older I would tell her how she had had a natural mother who loved her enough to buy her solid gold earrings, and I would show them to her. I was convinced that her parents would never have abandoned her, and that they must have been killed in one of the rocket attacks in the city.

I couldn't bear to be separated from her for a minute. I still don't know how I got away with it, but I started taking her to work at the embassy in a bamboo basket that Michael and Monique had bought her. If anyone had any objections, one look at my face ensured that they kept them to themselves. She was no bother and never cried, and her presence never affected my work. I started the long process of completing all the Cambodian paperwork to adopt her under the local laws.

My happiness during those first precious days with Lisa was marred on Saturday when I went to the orphanage to collect the children for their usual outing. When I got there all the children were dressed and waiting for me. Except Sam.

I went looking for him, and found him in a darkened corner sitting on a battered plastic stool with his body turned towards the crumbling wall.

I called his name and he turned his head in the direction of my voice. Even though he was totally blind, he looked at me through his white, fleshy pupils with a mixture of hatred, disappointment, pain, rejection and hopelessness. I understood that he knew I had taken Lisa home and that I had chosen her over him. After that he was never around when I collected the children, and I tried over the years not even to imagine what might have become of him.

⌒

I immersed myself in my new role as a mother to the point that I even tried to breast-feed Lisa. I'd read that some women who have not given birth can produce milk. I was going to give it my best shot and held Lisa at my breast when she was hungry, hoping that her tugging at my nipples would stir some natural tendencies in my body. The agony was not worth it, and after a few nights I gave in and continued to bottle-feed her.

I loved carrying Lisa in a Cambodian cotton *kroma*, which is a woven cotton scarf used by Cambodians for everything from carrying babies and storing rice, to washing bikes and drying themselves. Her fragile body would be nestled on my belly with her face looking up at me while I walked around the food markets. Without meaning to, I caused quite a stir one day. I was used to being stared at because I was fat and foreign, and now I was a foreigner with a Cambodian baby.

'Madam, Madam, is that your baby?' one of the women I often bought goods from asked.

'Yes, she is,' I replied. 'Isn't she beautiful?'

'Very pretty, Madam, but who is the father? She looks a little Khmer, no?'

'Oh, I have no idea who the father is. I am not married. It could have been anybody,' I said, with a careless wave of my hand as I pocketed my change.

With that, the woman shrieked: 'Come and look at the foreign whore! She has had so many of our Cambodian men as lovers she does not even know which one is the father of her child. Come and see the foreign slut with her bastard baby!'

I was practically chased out of the market. I couldn't stop laughing, even though I knew the women would never understand why I would want a baby without a husband first. I had to find another market to do my shopping in, as I knew I would not be welcome back there again.

⌒

I got the legal adoption documents signed, approved and certified. Bob Devereaux attended the court hearing with me and spoke in French on my behalf, and I just nodded at the appropriate junctures. Cambodians love stamps and stickers, and to have as many official-looking seals and paraphernalia on the documents as possible. So along with about ten Australian postage stamps and a wax seal with a blue silk ribbon, I attached to the adoption papers the cardboard cutout of a popular football star that came in all the imported packets of an Australian breakfast cereal. It all looked perfectly normal to the judge, who stamped the papers and added a fancy signature. Before I knew it, I was Lisa's mother in the eyes of Cambodian law.

The first step was over. Now I had to get Australian approval to bring her back to Australia with me as my legally adopted daughter. To the best of my knowledge, no single woman had been able to adopt a child in Australia, and I knew I was trying to break new ground that the Australian government may not have wanted broken at all. I completed all the paperwork, sent the application back to Canberrra, and sat back trying to be patient. Time was beginning to be a factor, as the Vietcong were closing in on the capital day by day, and no-one knew how long the country could hold out against their superior fighting power. There were often rumours of pending embassy evacuations.

I slept with Lisa in my arms and was mystified at how soundly she slept through all the loud rocket attacks. I saw it as a blessing, as if she woke and cried I would never get any sleep. But I thought it was strange that noises didn't seem to affect her. She had been so dirty when I first got her that I had only lightly cleaned out her ears, which were full of hard wax. I thought that perhaps I had not probed them deeply enough and her ears were still clogged.

An American doctor from Vietnam was coming to see expats the next week, so I made an appointment for Lisa to have her ears looked at. I had already gone to the embassy-accredited paediatrician, who had pronounced her healthy, if a little underweight and malnourished.

The day for her doctor's appointment came.

'What seems to be the trouble, Miss Cox?' he asked. I told him my baby didn't stir from her sleep during deafening rocket attacks, and asked if he could drain her ears. The doctor laid her down on the examining table. He removed her pink booties while she smiled and gurgled at him. He then ran his thumb up and down the bottoms of her heels, looking for some kind of response that I didn't understand. He put her booties back on and placed her back in my lap.

'Why would you want to adopt a cerebral palsy baby?' he asked with a puzzled look on his craggy face.

'What do you mean? She's not from Cerebralpalsi. She's Cambodian.' I had never heard the term before and thought that Cerebralpalsi must be some country nearby.

For the next few minutes I listened in horror as he told me as much as he could about cerebral palsy. He did more tests on Lisa, and also gave me the news that her heart was on the wrong side, she appeared to be autistic, was probably epileptic and diabetic, would certainly be unlikely to walk unaided, and the chances of her being mentally normal were very slim. In addition, his tests indicated that she was profoundly deaf. All her problems were caused by brain damage and there was no cure.

'And she is far older than seven months old. She is closer to eighteen months and is far behind in her development. She can't hold her neck up at all and maybe never will. If I were you, Miss Cox, I would take her back where you got her and look for a more normal baby. I'm very sorry.'

I stumbled out of the surgery in shock. The nurse had to help me find Moy and the embassy car, as I was in tears. She explained the situation to Moy, who drove me back to my apartment in stunned silence. He came inside with me to talk to Al-aan, and they both helped me get into bed with Lisa. I lay for hours staring at the ceiling, refusing to believe any of the things I had just been told. I thought there must be a cure for her somewhere.

⟨⟩

News like this travels fast in a small place like Phnom Penh, and the next day Nicola Feakes took Lisa and me to the residence for lunch. She and Graham tried their best to counsel me. They told me that no-one would blame me if I returned Lisa to the orphanage; that to take on a multiple handicapped child like Lisa was madness and I must consider giving her up. 'Geraldine, don't you see that this new health report must be reported to Canberra and that the likelihood of her being accepted into Australia would be zero?' they tried to reason with me. They were very caring and only wanted me to make the right decision. I said that the embassy doctor had given her a clean bill of health and that I hadn't gone out on purpose to get a brain-damaged child. I told them I loved her and couldn't possibly abandon her.

I must have seemed demented. Everyone at the embassy was afraid to talk to me as I was in tears most of the time without even realising it. Graham told me to take a few days' sick leave, and I went home and tried to think what the future would hold for Lisa and me.

A little while later I got the news that the Australian government had rejected Lisa's entry into Australia on medical grounds. The story eventually reached the ears of Neil Davis and Dennis Cameron, who dropped in to see me. Between the two of them they had prepared a letter for the Australian Immigration Minister, Graham Forbes.

Without actually threatening anything tangible, the letter explained that as far as the Cambodian government was concerned, this baby was my legal and moral responsibility. Using the embassy medical resources I had done all that was expected of me to ensure that the child met all the consular health requirements before I had gone ahead with the Cambodian adoption procedures. Further, the world knew that the Khmer Rouge, who were touted as being more ruthless than the Vietnamese, were eventually going to take over Cambodia and that foreign nationals would all be evacuated.

The letter said that in this event, I had to make one of two decisions. One was to abandon Lisa in an orphanage, where she was unlikely to survive without special medical care which simply was not available. Alternatively, I would have to decide to stay behind after the embassy staff were evacuated, to take care of my legal daughter. It was expected that the Khmer Rouge would not give foreigners the red carpet treatment. Also the media community in Phnom Penh was very interested in the decision the Australian government was going to make in this case. Therefore, the Minister for Immigration should understand that this request to allow Australian citizenship for Lisa Devi Cox was one made on humanitarian grounds, not only from the point of view of the child, but from that of myself, as if approval was not given, my decision would be to remain behind in Cambodia.

Neil assured me that no minister would want the adverse media attention that a decision to refuse Lisa entry to Australia would attract, and that I should trust their opinion as seasoned journalists, and sign and send the letter they had prepared. I knew the letter was a loaded gun for me career-wise, but Lisa was more important to me than my career. I sent it.

Three weeks later I received Lisa's certificate of Australian citizenship in the diplomatic bag. It arrived with no covering letter of congratulations, nothing. I knew that the government was not pleased at being pushed into a corner, and that this was their way of letting me know this.

What did I care? I could take Lisa home with me. If I could achieve that, I could achieve anything. Maybe I could even find a cure for all her health problems. I felt I had passed a huge milestone in my life, but I also knew there were many more battles to fight for Lisa.

Om Kon,
My Angkorean Warrior

Phnom Penh, January – December 1972

A t this time, while I was acting as though there was nothing to worry about, planning my life with Lisa as though it was going to be completely normal and happy, Major Om Kon came into my life. Since I had adopted Lisa, all thoughts of a normal sex life had vanished from my mind, even though I still went to all the parties and receptions. I had reached the stage, God forbid, where I didn't even notice men any more. I was totally preoccupied with being a good mother to Lisa.

One night I was at a dancing party hosted by one of the American military advisors from the US embassy; he had invited a lot of Cambodian servicemen who were doing training courses with them. The party was in full swing and I had asked a waiter for a Coke with ice. I had to repeat my order three times because his English wasn't very good. In the end the poor guy returned with a bottle of Coke, carefully balancing a small block of fast-melting ice on the top of the opened bottle. I hadn't realised that there were no glasses, and everyone was drinking out of their bottles or through straws. A girlfriend and I were chuckling over his embarrassment when an immaculately dressed Cambodian man in full air force uniform, with a sleek black complexion, approached and asked if he could translate for us to the waiter. I watched him as he put the waiter out of his misery, and thought how kindly he had resolved the matter.

While he was talking, I felt the old Geraldine definitely stirring back to life as I noticed the rock-hard body under his tight air force shirt. He had powerful shoulders and large, strong hands. He had the usual short GI-type haircut, which set off his handsome Angkorean features. His face could have been used for the model of the Bayon temple. His mouth was wide and sensual, the kind designed for laughing and kissing. His teeth were perfect and almost ridiculously white. He was not delicately built like most Cambodian men, who had tiny waists and thin torsos. I could see just under his collar the beginning of a tattoo at the back of his neck. Many Khmer soldiers wore these Buddhist tattoos, which they were convinced would protect them from injury in battle. Some of the men were completely covered in tattoos, which were often whole texts in Pali from holy scriptures. I knew I wouldn't rest until I found out where his tattoo ended. My girlfriend was whisked off to the dance floor and I found myself alone standing close to him.

'I am Kon,' he said. 'I am a fighter pilot. May I ask your name?'

'My name is Geraldine and I work at the Australian embassy. Where did you learn such good English?' I asked.

'Oh, I have many foreign friends, but you are the first Australian woman I have met. Will you dance Cambodian style with me?' he said, as he took my elbow and led me to where the dancing was taking place on the rooftop.

Now, anyone not permanently crippled can dance Khmer style. The same steps and hand movements are repeated over and over by both men and women. But it is the hands that speak volumes. A woman's bent-back forefinger can either beckon with promises of unimaginable delights, or ban someone from her side forever. I have never seen a Westerner not look clumsy and awkward when joining in these dances, and I knew I stuck out like a country outhouse anyway, being twice the size of the slender young Khmer women gliding around in a graceful circle. But I did the best I could, and I sensed that Kon was enjoying the comments that were being tossed around in Khmer when it was obvious that he had chosen me for his dance partner. His friends called him Major Khmau, which means 'black', and his lovely wide grin almost cracked his face in half as he heard his nickname being called out every few minutes. He didn't leave my side all night and I didn't want him to.

We walked away from the crowds of people talking and laughing, and found a quiet spot at the edge of the balcony overlooking the empty street. I could see he had no idea how to treat a Western woman, and I knew I couldn't be my usual self and appear as available to him as I was. For once in my life I kept my mouth shut and let him do the talking.

'I have heard about an unmarried Australian woman who has adopted a Cambodian baby girl. Is this you?' he asked.

I needed no excuse to talk about Lisa and how much she meant to me. I didn't tell him about all her health problems because I was still refusing to believe they existed, and he listened to me with genuine interest. He finally asked if he could take me home so that he could see my baby. I thanked him, and mentioned that it was always a problem getting home from these parties when everyone had had so much to drink. I said I had noticed he didn't drink much.

'Oh, I like to drink, but it makes me sleepy and I don't want to be sleepy tonight,' he said, without understanding at all what he was implying. Or so I thought.

As we stood together our hands touched on the wall of the balcony, and it felt so good and natural as we moved closer together so that more of our bodies touched. He was not very tall, and we seemed to melt together at all the right places. His left hand was next to mine and it had no wedding ring. That was a huge relief, as I had almost forgotten that this was one of the things I always looked for on a man before entertaining the slightest possibility of a romance. But I wanted to be sure. I knew that in the military, men never wore wedding rings. Doing so would give the enemy a good weapon to use against them if they were captured and tortured: the threat of harm to their wives and children.

I was much too devious just to come out and ask if he was married or not. I usually tricked men into telling me the truth by asking them about their children. Most men who would lie about having a wife would never lie about having children.

'How many children do you have, Kon?' I asked. There, it was out.

'I have four daughters,' he replied proudly. 'Konnary is eight, Konnedy is five, Konnavy is four and Konnavine is just a few months old.'

I was so disappointed I could have wept. But I carried on as though his answer meant nothing to me.

On the way home, I knew I had to nip this in the bud as I was very attracted to him. The car came to a stop, and he turned the engine off in preparation for walking with me to my apartment. I told him I couldn't ask him in, as I never went out with married men. He told me his wife wouldn't mind at all if he had a mistress, because every time they made love she got pregnant and they didn't want any more babies. He said she loved him very much and he loved her, but that they didn't make love much any more.

I couldn't believe my ears! I said: 'No, Kon. I just can't. And I find your story hard to believe. But it was lovely to meet you and talk to you; perhaps I'll see you again at another party. Please, it's late, and you must get home before curfew. Goodnight.' I leant over and gave him a soft kiss on the side of his silky-smooth cheek, and got out of the car and inside my apartment as fast as I could. He sat there in his jeep for a long time before I heard the engine start up and he drove slowly away.

Bugger, bugger, bugger. Me and my stupid rules.

⌒

There were no secrets in Phnom Penh. So I wasn't surprised the next Saturday when I went to the orphanage to collect the children for the day to find Kon's jeep outside, with him waiting for me.

He asked if he could help with the children and said that he had something important to tell me. So he came home with me and finally met Lisa, and was a great help in bathing and playing with the children. They were happy to have someone there who could translate the many questions they had for me:

'How old is she?'

'Why isn't she married?'

'How much does she weigh?'

'Why is she so big?'

'Are you her boyfriend?'

'Why can't she take all of us back to Australia?'

We laughed and laughed at some of their questions. That day the embassy car took the children back without me. Kon was as exhausted as I was and we sat down to a cold beer.

Once settled in our chairs he asked me to listen to him. 'Before you say anything, please let me speak,' he said with a serious expression. He said he'd told Kruy, his wife, all about me and that she understood everything, and that he was free to do what made him happy. She had said she would not be jealous if he did not come home some nights, as long as he told her where he was so that she didn't worry. She said she was proud that her husband would have a Western mistress, as many of her friends' husbands went to prostitutes and she knew he would never do that. She knew I would not take him away from her, as she understood that I would leave Cambodia when my time with the embassy was up. His wife thought I must be a kind and good person because I was taking a Cambodian child out of the war and back to my safe country.

He went on to say: 'Kruy, my wife, makes only one condition. Every Sunday she would like to rest with the baby, Konnavine, and will give Konnavy, Konnedy, and Konnary to me to join you and your orphans at your house, so that she can sit in her hammock for the day and not have to worry about taking care of the children.

'So, now that you know my wife approves, can I please be your lover for as long as you are in Cambodia? I promise to be very kind and never do anything to hurt you, as I have promised Kruy I would never do anything to hurt her.'

I could picture Kruy telling him how she felt with dignity, simple honesty and a willingness to make her husband happy. Kon had told his wife that he didn't think I would believe him, and she had suggested he bring me home so that she could meet me and explain that I would not be hurting her. He offered to take me to his house that very day. But his eyes told me he was telling the truth and I believed every word he said. I was sure I was the only woman I knew in this situation!

⟜

Kon was a rare man. I have yet to meet another one so honest and uncomplicated. If he said he loved you, he loved you. If I did something to make him angry he told me immediately, and it was discussed and out of the way. If I did something not acceptable to Cambodian society, which was often, he explained how it would offend people.

One night I told Kon that I had played a trick on the guard downstairs, as he was always falling asleep when he was supposed to be awake in order to unlock the gates when we returned home at night. I had climbed the fence and, while he was peacefully snoring, took his machine gun upstairs to teach him a lesson. After that, there was a new guard the next evening. Kon was furious with me, explaining that what I had done probably resulted in the guard being sent to the most dangerous part of the front. He said that losing your weapon while on duty was unforgivable, and that when his superior officer inspected him the next morning, the guard would have been shipped off or put into military prison immediately. I had no idea my prank would have had such a serious consequence and wanted to crawl under a rock. Kon took the gun, and told me that he would try to find the guard and his commander to explain what I'd done.

He disapproved of me using the black market. He was adamant to the point where I had to cease this. He told me that people who used the black market were only increasing the misery in Cambodia and pandering to the warmongers. He said that many of his friends in the air force were getting rich by abusing their opportunities to use the black market and that I was helping to prolong the war and create more suffering.

Life was simple for him. He loved his wife, his children, his country, his religion and me. In that order. I was content simply to be on the list of such a man, even if I was last.

After Kon had graduated with an honours degree from a provincial college in Cambodia, he commenced his career with the Royal Cambodian Air Force in 1958, receiving training by the French. He climbed the ladder quickly, and by 1959 he was promoted to the rank of second lieutenant at Pochentong air force base. In 1961, he was sent to Okinawa, Japan, for advanced psychological training, and on his return in 1962 he was promoted to first lieutenant. Later, in 1962, the French sent him for further training with NATO. He then underwent training in Nancy, France, until 1964. In October of that year he became a flight commander, safety fly officer and pilot instructor, and was familiar with just about every aircraft used at that time, including MIG15s and MIG17s. In 1967, he was promoted to the rank of captain, and was a seasoned fighter pilot by the time of the military coup in March 1970.

When I met him in 1970 he was fully occupied fighting against the Vietcong invaders, as he liked to call them, along the eastern border of Cambodia. After the formation of the Khmer Republic in November 1970, Kon was promoted in January 1971 to major, and flew on fighter missions mainly in T28s, MIG17s and Fouga CM170 jets. He was now being trained further by the Americans. The US embassy military staff had great confidence in his abilities, and he was in charge of many secret missions where he flew in partnership with the American air force against the Vietcong and the Khmer Rouge.

In 1971 the American government selected him for training in advanced English, leadership and management courses at many establishments, including the Lackland air force base in San Antonio, Texas, and at the Kennedy Space Center, and other air force installations in Florida, Colorado, Washington D.C., and at the Air University at Maxwell air force base in Alabama. I really missed him while he was doing these courses in America but delighted in receiving his letters, which showed me another side of his many-faceted character.

When he returned to Phnom Penh, what we enjoyed most was the peace and quiet of evenings at home playing with Lisa before she slept. Often Kon would go into her bedroom after we had made love and carry her into our bed to lay her down to sleep between us. He taught me the Asian way of bringing up babies, which meant they sleep with their parents in the same bed. I honestly believe we in the West have got many basic things wrong.

I adored Kon's daughter Konnavy and told him that if we had been able to have a child together, I would have wanted her to be exactly like Konnavy. She had his beautiful face and calm personality. I even told him that if he and Kruy agreed, I would adopt her too and take her back to Australia with Lisa when my posting was over. He was touched, but never even responded to my suggestion. I could see from his face that he would never give a child of his away. I was ashamed that I had asked.

He would say: 'I love Lisa Devi like she is our child, Geraldine. As long as I know you are together, wherever you are in the world, you will have a part of me with you. She is of my race. She is a symbol of our love.' Kon said this as she slept calmly between us in the early hours of the morning before he had to leave to go up in a jet fighter plane.

He hated the North Vietnamese and the Vietcong, who were the enemies of Cambodia. He was happy to die protecting his country from the communists, and did not want to live in a Cambodia dominated by them.

He told me he didn't enjoy killing, but that when the Vietnamese, Thais, Burmese, Laotians, or any Cambodian neighbours, invaded his land it was his duty to defend his country, family and the Cambodian people. He said he would never invade another country, but would kill who he had to in order to 'keep Cambodia for Cambodians.'

Kon told me that at times he had to go against orders. One morning when he was given his combat mission for the day, he saw that the village in which his parents lived was one of those targeted for bombing. He marched off to his commander and said that he refused to accept this mission, and furthermore demanded the village be protected in the future. Or else. I never found out what 'or else' meant, but the village survived the war untouched.

Some nights he would come directly from the air base in his fly-suit, drenched with sweat, and with his survival-kit jacket, radio and Smith & Wesson 38 special revolver which he carried with him at all times. I never wanted him to bring his guns into my apartment; I made him take every weapon off and leave them outside the door (except the Smith & Wesson). As the apartment was guarded by a Cambodian soldier, he knew his weapons would be safe there.

Al-aan, being Vietnamese, was terrified each time he visited me, and her knees actually shook when she opened the door and let him in. Her behaviour when he was in my apartment made it very clear that she disapproved of my relationship with him. Fortunately, I was learning some sensitivity in this area, and if Kon was having dinner with me and staying the night, I asked her to prepare food in advance that I would heat up and serve myself so that she could leave before he arrived.

Some days he would make as many as five air strikes on battlefields all over Cambodia, attacking North Vietnamese troops and the Khmer Rouge.

'How many hits today, darling?' I asked one night.

'Many Charlie-Boys running like ants on my land. They were easy targets and many were killed or injured.'

I swallowed at this almost offhand remark about what were possibly dozens of human beings lying wounded and dying somewhere.

From that day on I made it a rule that we never talked about the war or politics.

⟝⟞

He loved to take me to Cambodian nightclubs where his friends would see us together. I spent many a night in a crowded disco dancing with Kon, being the only foreigner and the subject of much attention. There was clearly status in being seen with a European woman, and his rank of major meant that he was treated with respect. I never heard any unfavourable comments about us being together.

In some ways he reminded me a little of Theo. He made me laugh. Often he would leave the toilet door open. One day I noticed him sitting on the toilet the wrong way, facing the wall, reading a book placed on the top of the cistern.

'Darling! That's not the right way to use a Western toilet. You should sit around the other way,' I said, trying not to laugh.

'But you are wrong, Geraldine, this is much more comfortable. You can see for yourself next time you use the toilet. And then tell me if I am not right.'

I tried it and he was right! It was comfortable. I couldn't wait to tell all my friends that there was actually another way to sit on a toilet, especially if you were going to be there for a long time and wanted to read a book. I have to say, though, it only works for people with short legs.

Making love with Kon was in every way another expression of what he was as a person: honest, wholesome, clean, gentle, loving and natural. It was as important to him as eating and sleeping, and he thought it funny that Europeans made such a big deal out of what Cambodians took for granted as an everyday act between people who wanted to show their love and affection for each other.

He was my first Asian lover and the only thing I found disconcerting was to wake in the morning to find that the smoothest skin in the bed was not mine! The skin of Asian men is just as satiny as that of Asian women, but in Kon's case it never detracted from his complete masculinity. I never tired of tracing the tattoos around his neck and shoulders with my fingertips. He sincerely believed these tattoos of religious Pali script would protect him from enemy aircraft coming from behind while he was in the air.

Kon never lied, cheated or promised anything he couldn't give. We both knew there was a use-by date on our days together, and this made each minute precious. We promised to give pleasure every second we spent in each other's company, whether we were making love, sleeping, eating, dancing, playing with Lisa, talking together, entertaining his children on Sundays or just listening to his soft Cambodian music.

One night the distant bombing of a rocket attack woke us up. I felt him get up and start to dress. He said: 'Geraldine, I must go. The sound of the bombing is coming from near my home. I must go to check that my family is not afraid.'

I heard the clanking of the gate opening downstairs, and his jeep roared away into the dangerous streets of the city towards his house near the air base. He was taking an enormous risk driving after curfew during a heavy rocket attack, but I knew he could talk his way through any roadblocks, because he had many important friends and was well known.

I went back to sleep and an hour or so later I was woken again by another rocket attack, this time much closer to my apartment. I lay in the dark listening to the rockets hit targets not all that far from my street. But through the noise I could distinguish the unmistakable noise of Kon's jeep as it tooted for the guard to open the gates.

I threw a sarong around myself and ran to unlock my door. 'Are you completely mad?' I asked as he walked down the hall with me to our bedroom. 'What are you doing back here? You are out of your mind to drive around in the middle of an attack.'

Kon undressed and pulled me back into the bed. He said he had told Kruy that he had had to leave me because he wanted to be with his family to protect them. They had tried to sleep but once the attack had started near my house, he had told her he had to go to me now that the danger was over in their area. Kruy had understood, and was glad that he had gone to her and the children. But she also encouraged him to return to me if he thought I was afraid.

That night he had made love to me, driven through one rocket attack and comforted his wife and children, got back in his jeep and drove through a second rocket attack on the city, and made love to me again. When I woke up he had already left to take his plane up and fight another day over the skies of Cambodia. How he could even stay awake that day was beyond me.

With Kon I experienced for the first time how fear and danger can heighten sexual desire and the physical senses. With bombs dropping all around you it is in the back of your mind that if you are going to die, you might as well be doing something that brings you deep joy.

With him I shared one of the most intimate experiences I have ever had. He liked to fall asleep on his side facing me while I was on my side. He would position himself so that our nostrils were as close as possible to each other, and then he would ask me to time my breathing to his, so that as he breathed out, I inhaled his breath. It was a kind of loving meditation. 'This way, Geraldine, we are connected even in sleep.' I have never slept as peacefully as I did when I slept with Kon in this way.

⟵⟶

Although I was happy with Kon, there were others who were not so happy about our relationship. I think I can say for sure that I was the first woman in the history of the embassy to have had an affair with a local. It was considered normal for Western men of any nationality to go to the brothels and dally with young Cambodian bar girls, but for one of their own women to sleep with an Asian man was something else altogether. There were also women who made it known they were not impressed by my relationship with a Cambodian. But when was I ever concerned with what other people thought? I ignored the hints and comments, and did what I wanted, as always. I also knew there were others who were not in favour of me adopting a Cambodian child and taking her back to Australia. Racism was well and alive among many in the expat community in Cambodia.

Also, friends in the department have since told me that if I ever want to see my personnel file in Canberra, I should reserve a week to read all that has been recorded there. And I believe them.

⟵⟶

I had been in Cambodia for more than eighteen months and it was getting close to my departure date. There were the customary farewell parties planned. I was returning to Adelaide, where I was to work in the office of Foreign Affairs. I had to admit that the department was doing everything it could to help me. The people there knew I wanted to be close to my family to get the help I was going to need with all Lisa's medical problems. For this I will always be grateful.

One farewell party had a fancy-dress theme and Kon and I went, with me wearing his fly-suit. I had to travel standing up in the back of his jeep and leaning over the front seat, as his suit was so tight I couldn't sit down. 'My fly-suit looks far better on you than it does on me. Very tight, very sexy. I like to see you in my clothes,' Kon said, smiling as we drove to the party.

We entered into all the parties with gay abandon trying not to think of the day when we would have to say goodbye. The night before, we slept in an empty apartment surrounded by all my goods ready to be shipped.

We said goodbye the way lovers all over the world throughout time have said goodbye – with tears; sad, slow lovemaking; and promises to write and keep in touch. I told him how to address letters to me through the embassy, and said he should call every week or so to see if there were letters from me waiting for him to collect. I begged him to survive the war so that he could watch his lovely family grow up. He promised me he would.

I told Kon that on the morning I was to fly out of Phnom Penh I wanted him to leave while I was still asleep. He did as I asked, and I woke up alone in what I had come to think of as our bed.

My departure was a little different from all those before it. The local staff said that this was the first time a member of the embassy was leaving with a Cambodian child, and they all wanted to be in a photo with Lisa and me. We took the photo after Dusty and Moy argued over who was going to hold Lisa. Moy won and he held Lisa proudly. I was sure he felt closer to us than all the others did.

As I drove out of Phnom Penh along Pochentong Boulevard in a van full of my friends from the embassy, I saw through much more seasoned and sorrowful eyes the same scenes of what the war was doing to the Cambodian people as I had seen on my first trip along the same stretch of road. I ached for them and I wondered how it would all end.

After the always stressful check-in procedures, I hugged my colleagues goodbye and walked through immigration with my hand luggage and my priceless cargo, Lisa Devi. As I approached the plane, I saw with a mixture of joy and pain that Kon was running across the tarmac towards us. Of course, as a fighter pilot he was cleared to be anywhere in the airport he wanted to be.

He came to where I stood with Lisa, lifted her out of my arms, and without a word put his arm around me and guided me up the steps into my seat. Once I was seated, he kissed Lisa on her forehead and hugged her before placing her in my lap. Then Kon secured my seat belt before holding my face between his two strong, dark warrior's hands. He stared deeply into my eyes, stroked my hair tenderly and kissed me softly on my mouth, mixing his tears with mine. It was all over in a few seconds and then he was gone. Neither of us had said a word.

After take off I looked at the empty seat beside me. On it was a parcel wrapped in brown paper; he had left me a gift. I knew he had no money to spare on anything expensive and I couldn't imagine what it might be. I opened it, and there was one of Kon's air force fly-suits, complete with his name and rank in English, and Khmer sewn across the pocket. I lifted it to my face to drink in his scent one last time.

The Return of the Prodigal Daughter

Adelaide, January – June 1973

It's just as well I've always been able to change along with my environment, as the adjusting I had to do in taking care of Lisa without a full-time, devoted maid was quite a feat. From the very beginning of the journey Lisa was sickly, and my flight via Saigon and Singapore was delayed on both its legs, making the trip home to Adelaide very tiring for both of us.

At Saigon Airport I was the subject of very disapproving looks from all kinds of passengers who were also delayed. I must have been quite a sight trying to cope with a sick and crying baby. She had diarrhoea and needed constant diaper changing, and I had to do this on the airport seats as there were no facilities in the toilets.

Only one person seemed to take pity on me – an Englishman who asked if he could help by getting me a drink so that I didn't have to leave Lisa unattended. Then after a frenetic few hours we were finally boarding, and my rescuer again helped by carrying my hand luggage so that I could hold Lisa more comfortably. He started towards the steps at the back of the plane, and I had to tell him that I was in first class, and could he board with me at the front end of the plane. He seemed bemused by this. Before take off I asked the flight attendant if she would mind if the gentleman in economy, who had helped me board, could sit with me in first as it was empty except for me. She agreed, and this is how I met Ron Irons properly.

He helped me take care of a very sick Lisa all the way to Singapore but I was too worried about her to take much notice of him. However, upon disembarking in Singapore we discovered that both our flights were delayed, and he invited me to dinner in the transit lounge restaurant at Changi Airport.

I was still too preoccupied with Lisa and sad about saying goodbye to Kon to be in a flirtatious mood, but I couldn't help noticing he could have won a look-alike contest for James Coburn, the American actor. He was tall and lean, and his thick head of greying hair gave him an untidy craggy-lion look that was accentuated by his jet-black, bushy eyebrows. He was in his mid-forties, and had been in Vietnam trying to pull off a scrap-metal deal which didn't look as though it would succeed. He was separated and had three children who lived with their mother in London. He said that before he and his wife parted, they had lived high on the hog in Hong Kong until a business venture he was involved in had failed.

Ron said that he had heard some of the passengers discussing me at Saigon Airport. They assumed I had 'got myself into trouble' in Vietnam and was lumbered with an Asian baby. He admitted that this had been his initial opinion too and that when he had realised I was travelling first class, he thought I must have landed myself a rich South Vietnamese general.

He was interested in what I had been doing in Cambodia and was a good listener. As you do with fellow passengers you think you will never see again, I told him all about my fears; about how ill Lisa really was and that I was convinced I could find a way to make her well. I even told him how my mother had warned me that my father was not very pleased that I was bringing home a baby who he described as 'the Yellow Peril'. To Dad, all Asians were 'Japs', whom he hated with a passion. Trying to make him differentiate between a Chinese, Malaysian, Indonesian, Filipino,

Vietnamese or Cambodian person was pointless. Mum had tried to reason with him but he was immovable. She had told me in a letter that Dad had said I could only stay at home with Lisa until I found somewhere else to go. I had been stunned and deeply hurt by my father's callous decision.

I even went so far as to tell Ron that I hoped to find Theo again. Friends had written saying that his marriage had not worked out, his wife had returned to Greece and he was alone again. The child he had wanted never came. I was toying with the idea that, now I had a baby, perhaps we could make a life together.

My plane departed before Ron's, and he walked with me towards the departure gate, carrying my hand luggage. He put it down, proceeded to remove Lisa from my arms, and addressed the hostess on duty. 'Excuse me, Madam,' he said. 'Would you mind holding this baby for a minute so that I can kiss this lovely woman goodbye?' Before she could refuse, he handed Lisa over, took me in his arms and gave me a kiss he must have known few women could ever have forgotten. I was starting to go weak at the knees but pulled myself together in time to thank him for being so thoughtful. We hurriedly exchanged addresses at the departure gate, in front of the confused hostess still holding a sleeping Lisa.

During the flight to Sydney I thought about all I had been through in the last few hours. About my sorrow at leaving Cambodia and Kon, and my surprise at meeting a kind person such as Ron, who had really made a difference to what would otherwise have been a very difficult journey. I had been kissed by two gorgeous men in less than one day.

But I was not looking forward to what lay ahead with Dad.

As the plane approached Adelaide, I mused that all my serious decisions seemed to involve arriving at or leaving from an airport. On that day, although I had dressed Lisa in an exquisite pink dress, her frailty was painfully obvious. So, I thought, was her Asian-ness, and that was what Dad was going to see. Mum had told me that the whole family would meet me at the airport. I steeled myself, and walked through to the baggage area, where I could see them waiting for me.

Thinking back, it was like a B-grade movie. As everyone tried to hug everyone, Dad just seemed to loom over me. I had forgotten what a big man he was. He looked at the pathetic pink bundle in my arms, and I held my breath, not knowing what to expect from him. Spellbound, I watched as two huge tears rolled down each of his cheeks. It had been years since he had held a baby, but he just gathered her up in his arms, and walked out of the airport with his women trailing behind him, absolutely stumped for words. I had never seen my father cry before that day and never did after it; Lisa had won his heart without even trying.

A few weeks later Sandra's husband Evan, a real rock for the family, came home for dinner with Dad after a Saturday at the horse races. Evan took me aside and told me an amazing story. Apparently, some race club members at the bar were having a go at a couple of Asian waiters. The members were calling them 'Chinks' and 'slope-heads' and were just seconds away from being even more abusive when one of the waiters dropped a glass of beer and broke it. Evan said the poor devil was rattled by hearing what they were calling him.

Evan said he couldn't believe what happened next. Dad had just thumped the table really hard, and said: 'Jesus wept! Enough of that, you lot! That's my bloody granddaughter you're talking about. I don't want to hear that kind of talk around me ever again. Now, someone buy the next bloody round and let's get on with the bet on the next bloody race.'

Evan said you could have heard a pin drop; he thought Dad was marvellous. And the waiter! Evan thought he was going to kiss Dad, he was so grateful. I was so proud of my dear old Dad. What a corner he had turned, and Lisa had helped him to do it.

⟿

But it was tough taking care of Lisa. I needed to be alone, as she kept Mum and Dad awake at night and was generally very disruptive, so I moved to a small apartment. I arranged for Lisa to attend the Spastic Centre while I was at work and I had to pay for babysitters to be at home when she was dropped off before I got back from work. My girlfriends Cherie, Lyn and Gloria were all working too, but rallied around to help by doing what they could for me at the weekends. We had taken up our friendships where we had left them when I went to Cambodia, and without them things would have been far more difficult. But I was still exhausted every night, as Lisa demanded so much attention. I functioned like a robot most of the time.

I waited as long as I could before seeking Theo out. We had a tearful reunion and within a few days we were back to our old relationship, which was as strong as ever. But there was something very wrong. He didn't even try to hide that he did not want Lisa to be a part of our relationship. He tried to explain it to me, but I wasn't very receptive. I was torn between my old love for him and my new, overwhelming love for Lisa.

Theo begged me to try to understand that he had had a younger brother in Greece who was bedridden and deformed. No one knew the name of his disease, but he had died in his early teens. As a child, Theo had hated living in a house with someone that ill, although he had loved him and hadn't wanted him to die. He told me that he definitely didn't want to have another abnormal person so close to him in his life.

'I can't get rid of Lisa just because she doesn't fit into your plans. If I have to choose between you and her, then you lose,' I coldly told Theo one evening. Again we parted.

I regretted those words a few evenings later when a friend called me to say that Theo was in intensive care after suffering a heart attack. He had begged his friends not to tell me he was in hospital, as we had just broken up again, but thankfully this friend had been aware that I would have wanted to know. I rushed into the hospital to see him, and I knew I still loved him when I saw him so pale and still, lying against the pillow and hooked up to a machine recording his heart movements. I was so grateful to have the chance to say goodbye to him more lovingly than I had earlier. I felt guilty about leaving him that night, but I had already made my choice to take care of Lisa; Theo let me go with words of understanding. I will always remember him being so brave while he urged me to go on with my life with Lisa, and without him.

This time I was able to get a posting to Manila. At least there I would be able to have a maid to help with the care of Lisa. It was nothing short of a Herculean task to get the department to accept that Lisa should join me on future postings. It was equally difficult getting the adoption legalised in Adelaide, as the very concept of a single mother was beyond most of the social workers who worked on my case.

Anyone could see at a glance that Lisa's handicaps were multiple, her deafness and mental retardation pronounced. But the mother in me adamantly refused to concede the obvious, and I continued to cling to the flimsiest of hopes for a miracle cure.

What hurt me most, and what I pushed out of my mind, was Lisa's complete obliviousness to my love and devotion, to my very existence. I had a lot to learn about autism. Her cerebral palsy, mental retardation, crippled arm and leg, profound deafness, inability to speak, epilepsy and diabetes; all these I could live with. But for her not to know she was loved, and for me not to be loved in return, was unbearably cruel.

Before I left Adelaide for Manila, I went to the most expensive paediatrician in the city, confident that he could come up with something that would help Lisa. After he had examined her, he asked me to sit down.

'The Chinese have the answer to your problem,' he said.

'What is it? Where should I go?' I answered, leaning forward eagerly.

'They take babies like Lisa up to the top of a remote mountain, leave them there and get on with their lives,' the doctor said.

I was furious beyond words. I left his consulting rooms with considerably less respect for the medical profession than I had had when I arrived.

Paradise Lost

Manila, July 1973 – June 1978

It seems that often the momentous events in my life take place in July. Some are good, some are not so good, some are bloody calamitous.

Compared to Phnom Penh, Manila was a paradise. Admittedly, this was during the reign of Marcos and martial law had been declared. My first morning in Manila, I came down to the Intercontinental Hotel foyer to see the staff mopping and vacuuming a huge area of bloodied carpet where there had been a gun battle the night before between Marcos supporters and others.

Once again I was in a country where guns were the order of the day. I felt quite at home.

The work at the embassy was again enthralling, and I was even able to keep my eyes open for classified reports that came through to us about developments in the war in Cambodia. I found myself unable to forget completely about the country, the war and Kon.

I was in Manila during the worst of Imelda Marcos's excesses, those most of the world would have to wait years to hear about. I particularly remember the day she was expecting an important visit by a head of state. She was giving a garden party in the grounds of Malacanang Palace, and the grass was not the shade of green she wanted. She ordered in dozens of painters to paint the huge lawns until she was satisfied with their bright green colour. Of course, all the expensive grass died and thousands of dollars had to be spent replanting it. Then there was the time she was planning another outdoor event but the forecast was for rain. So as not to spoil the occasion, she ordered the entire Philippines air force into the skies to spray chemicals to send the clouds away from Manila.

Although the people in the city slums were miserably poor, and their lives were quite wretched, they seemed to love Imelda. They were actually, for some bizarre reason, quite proud of the way she threw her – or, more correctly, the government's – money around.

My life was as easy as falling off a log compared with the trials of living in Cambodia. But the Filipinos seemed to lack the soul I found in the Cambodians; they had it comparatively easy. Certainly there were injustices and hardship for many but as far as working for the embassy was concerned, there was very little to complain about.

I was in the middle of a pleasant, but not life-changing, affair with a man whose main attraction was that his name was Jesus. I could tell Jesus's time was up, but this was hastened by my receiving a postcard from Ron, the Englishman who had come to my aid in Saigon and Singapore after I had left Cambodia. He had written to my Adelaide address, saying he was going back to Asia to chase up some business opportunities while he waited for his divorce to go through. He wondered if I had taken another posting with the Australian government or whether I had settled down with my Greek boyfriend in Australia. He was planning a business trip to Manila but could be reached at the address on the postcard for a few more weeks. He asked how Lisa was. I couldn't believe my luck! He was actually coming to Manila without even knowing I was there.

I wrote back the same day and hoped that my letter would reach him so that we didn't miss each other in Manila. If he didn't get it there was no way he would know I was living there. Thankfully, I got a phone call from London to say he would arrive the next day. 'God, Geraldine, how amazing that you are actually in the Philippines!' he said. He asked if I could suggest a reasonably priced hotel and if I could get time off work to meet him at the airport.

I could still remember that kiss in Singapore. 'Yes, I'll be there, Ron,' I said to him demurely. With bells on, I told myself.

⟿

I had only spent a few hours with Ron before, but when I saw him at the airport I felt as though my whole life was walking towards me. I simply took him straight home, where he stayed for almost five years. 'Listen, God', I said to myself. 'If I've died and gone to heaven, I just want to say thank you.' It was the closest I have ever come in my life so far to being a wife and mother at the same time.

For the first time I was with a man who was stronger than me, a shoulder I could lean on during the rough times with Lisa. And there were plenty. Ron stayed up with me when Lisa had grand mal seizures in the middle of the night. He held me when I cried over the hopelessness of Lisa's condition. He was my complete support system, and my life was richer for having him in it.

I didn't believe that such compatibility was possible in a relationship. We never argued and always seemed to want to do the same things at the same time. We liked each other's friends and enjoyed socialising, although we were happiest when we were alone together.

Ron could be described at best as an entrepreneur; at worst as a con man. But the only person who ever lost money through his wild schemes was him, so perhaps 'con man' is rather harsh. He was the middleman in several grandiose deals he was trying to set up between the Filipino business sector and financial backers from Korea and Japan. As each deal disintegrated he always had another, equally meritorious, one up his sleeve. I never knew a man work so hard for such paltry financial reward. Each time he was defeated he bounced right back with a smile on his face, ready for the next deal.

A man can never fake wanting to be with a woman. Ron loved my company, and would always drive me to work, meet me for lunch and collect me at the end of the day, and even enjoyed boring trips to the supermarket. And, God, I even remember that he used to sit and wait patiently at the beauty salon while I had my hair and nails done on a Saturday morning. He would go everywhere I did, just to be with me. I took pleasure in being in our bedroom and hearing the car pull into the garage downstairs. Its door would slam shut, and I would hear him running up the stairs, taking them two by two in order to reach me more quickly. He would burst into the room and embrace me, even if it had only been a couple of hours since we had seen each other.

There were delicious weekends during the monsoon months when we retired to our bedroom on a Friday night. We would play with Lisa, watch television and have our meals brought to us on a tray by the maid, and never venture out until it was time to go to work on Monday morning. We were a constant source of entertainment to our maid, who giggled every time she came into our bedroom. I was so happy with Ron. He was an honest man and I always knew what he was thinking and feeling. We could never fool each other, nor did we want to try. Regretfully, I never really appreciated the way he treated me at the time. Love, sadly, often seems to be remembered, more than recognised at the time.

Ron accepted Lisa as part of his relationship with me. 'I don't love her like you do, Geraldine. That's the truth. But I love you for how you love her, and I will help you all I can,' Ron said to me many times. But he pointed out that, one day, I would have to put her in an institution. I would say: 'No, Ron. You are wrong. I am stronger than you think and I will never give her up.' Even though I knew I could never cope without the help of a maid and nanny while I worked, I hoped that Foreign Affairs would continue to send me to countries where I could provide these for her.

I spent a fortune on faith healers, Chinese herbal. medicine and acupuncturists. But I knew I was losing it when I wrote a cheque for $6000 to a Swiss clinic. This was to have an injectable substance made from the placenta of unborn lambs flown in because I had read that children like Lisa could be cured with this treatment.

I didn't have $6000. I called my bank manager in Australia to tell him

I had written the cheque and why. I begged him to honour it. I promised to pay it back out of my salary and said that he should look at it as an overdraft. 'Geraldine,' he said, somewhat annoyed, 'people go to jail for doing what you have done. I will honour the cheque this time, but if you do it again I can't help you.'

I knew I was not acting normally in refusing to accept Lisa's handicaps, and Ron just shook his head when I came home with the placenta injections packed in dry ice. Needless to say, they didn't make the slightest bit of difference to her condition. I kept on putting off the inevitable.

⌒

A girl can never have everything in a relationship, it seemed. What Ron didn't have was money.

He contributed financially to the household when he could. However, this was not often, as his 'big deal' was always just around the corner, but when he turned the corner, the deal would be halfway up another street.

I'm a firm believer that we pay for all our happiness in life one way or another, and Ron was one pleasure I didn't want to be without. I never thought an Englishman could make me so happy. But then he wasn't your everyday Anglo-Saxon. Although he was a Cockney with a heavy accent, his family could be traced back to when the British had African slaves; on his father's side an African man who had been bought as a slave and who was later freed, married an Englishwoman. Ron's dark skin and exotic features were a throwback, and he said he had an aunt who was almost completely black.

Ron was so nurturing as far as Lisa was concerned that he even put up with her sharing our bed (a habit I had never broken since my nights with Kon), until one night she nearly ruined his manhood by throwing her legs, still in her cruel little steel calipers, into his crotch. 'That's it, Geraldine! Lisa's almost four years old. It's time for her to be in her own bed. She doesn't have to be in another room, just in the cot she sleeps in during the day,' Ron reasoned. He was right, of course.

⌒

Since 1973 and up until early 1975 I was still receiving letters from Kon and was able to reply to him through the embassy in Phnom Penh where he collected my letters. He described his life and the progress of his children, and told me that he and Kruy had a fifth child, Konnwirak, a son, born in 1973. He had had even more training in the United States, in Fort Lauderdale, that was organised through the American embassy. America had made a great impression on him and his letters were full of his experiences there. He had been promoted to lieutenant colonel as vice-chief of the Air Force Intelligence Service and was immensely proud of this. His letters were noticeably free of any talk about the war and of the fact that Phnom Penh was coming closer and closer to being taken over completely.

I was following the reports that came through the embassy, and knew that even though the Paris Peace Agreement in January of 1973 officially ended the war in Vietnam, blood continued to be shed in Cambodia. The bombing by the Americans reached its height in August of that year. I remember reading that the American ambassador, Emory Coblentz 'Coby' Swank, during a farewell press conference, described Indochina's war in Cambodia as the 'most useless war' and I agreed with him totally. When Gerald Ford replaced Nixon in August 1974 I hoped a new president might be able to do something to stop the killing in Cambodia. But any hope of that was dashed when I learned that Ford had kept Kissinger on as Secretary of State.

I kept reading, with fear and anxiety for all Cambodians, the many political dispatches that were coming through about the military situation. I assumed that Kon would be sensible enough to stick with the Americans if he needed to. But then reports gave details of the American embassy evacuation on 12 April 1975, and I knew the future for the Cambodians was going to deteriorate even further, if that was at all possible. I knew in my heart that Kon would never leave his beloved homeland.

I received his last letter at the beginning of April 1975. When the international news broadcast the Khmer Rouge takeover of Cambodia on 17 April, I could only trust in Kon's promise to survive. I didn't even want to think of the fate of Moy, Dusty, Kim and the rest of our embassy staff; and what of Al-aan, Sophea and my other Cambodian friends?

⟵⟶

Despite my anxiety, I loved my life in Manila. I attended many receptions and national day affairs, and the social life was quite heady. The discos played the latest music, and Ron and I loved dancing. We went to and gave dinner parties. The restaurant scene was incredible, with any cuisine imaginable. The shopping was good and many designer labels were imported from Rome, Madrid and Paris.

We had wonderful weekends at the white-sand beaches dotted all over the Philippines. We took Lisa with us to deserted, pristine islands where we would spend the whole day completely naked, eating our prepared picnic lunches and drinking cold champagne under the clear Filipino skies.

But Lisa's condition was deteriorating at an alarming rate, and her grand mal seizures were becoming more frequent and beyond the control of the young nanny I had employed to care for her while I was at work. I was constantly getting frantic calls from her to come home because Lisa was having fits.

I applied through the Philippine network to be approved as a foster mother so that I could take in another child. I reasoned that having another one in the house might help Lisa to develop. The Filipinos accepted my request and within weeks I was given two little girls: one still a baby whose mother was in prison, and a toddler who was being adopted by an American family. I understood that these placements were temporary, and knowing this prevented me from bonding too closely with them. It was wonderful to have them around and watch them do normal things, but it did bring home to me how seriously retarded Lisa was. Instead of her copying their normal responses, they began mimicking her behaviour. Mealtimes were like being in a zoo, when the two girls would start throwing food around the kitchen after watching Lisa miss her mouth and constantly drop what she was eating. After a few months they left within days of each other and, although I missed them, it was bearable. I think I was pushing my luck with Ron too; although he had agreed to give the whole exercise a go for Lisa's sake, we were not getting enough quality time together with extra children to care for.

I then decided to apply to adopt a child. The Filipino agencies had been very pleased with how I had looked after the two girls and I thought my application had sufficient merit to succeed. I was devastated when their letter arrived declining my request because the attention my disabled daughter required would diminish the time and effort I could devote to bringing up a normal child. Ron comforted me as much as he could, but nothing really helped.

~

Soon after this Lisa's condition became critical. One night she was unconscious, and I drove like a maniac to the hospital with the terrified nanny holding Lisa in her arms. When we got to the emergency section of the Makati Medical Centre, I leapt out of the car and ran inside with Lisa. I didn't notice that the sarong I had been wearing had come undone and I was standing naked in the hospital with it around my ankles. Not only that, I had forgotten to put the handbrake on and my car had slowly rolled backwards into other cars in the parking lot, with the nanny sitting in it helplessly.

My work at the embassy was suffering and others had to do my share when I hurried home to take care of Lisa when she was sick. It was becoming clearer to me that if I didn't do something soon, I would be unable to handle my embassy duties efficiently.

Ron was on a six-week business trip to Japan and Korea, and I realised how much I depended on his strength to get through the days and nights. I didn't think things could get much worse, but they did.

Lisa started masturbating almost every waking moment. I tried putting her in overalls so that she could not get at herself, but nothing worked. If she was not amused constantly she would attack herself, sometimes with dangerous items such as dinner forks. Her little crotch was red raw and sometimes the skin around her vagina bled, but she didn't seem to feel the pain. I could see from her expression that she found a degree of satisfaction when she touched herself, but I knew that this was abnormal behaviour at the age of six.

I went to her doctor and the only remedy he had was anaesthetising spray to help deaden sensation in her genitals. I needed to apply it almost every thirty minutes and it was expensive; I knew it wasn't a permanent solution. Bedtime was the worst. Even with her sleeping medication Lisa always woke up and started to masturbate feverishly. As she began to drop off to sleep her hand would stop, and she would wake up and start again. The only way she could have a sound sleep was if I lay beside her, gently rocking and stroking her until she fell into a deep sleep.

I was hardly getting any sleep myself, and it was all I could do to drag myself to work in the mornings. Everyone commented on how tired I looked, and I could feel my depression worsening. I was becoming a recluse because I couldn't even take her with me to shop; I could no longer expose her to other children in the local playgrounds because of her unsociable, uncontrollable behaviour.

I looked into the future for Lisa and myself, and could only see our lives becoming more and more unbearable. I had reached the limits of my endurance, and contemplated ending my life and taking Lisa with me.

I had stocked up on sleeping pills and decided to do it the night before Ron was to return. I dressed us in identical lacy, white nightgowns, and even wrote a note to Ron and my family. I took great care with my makeup so that I would look my best when we were found the following morning. I made the bed with my best, carefully ironed, white satin sheets. I lit a candle and some incense, and sat Lisa up so that I could give her the pills before I took mine. Lisa smiled at me with such complete innocence, helplessness and trust that I realised that although I had the right to do what I wanted with my life, I didn't have the right to take hers. She wasn't really suffering; I was the one in pain.

This was my lowest point and from that night I knew there was only one way for me to go: up. I knew that there was nothing I couldn't bear in the future, nothing that I couldn't overcome, now that I had faced death lapping at the core of my being. I threw the pills into the toilet, and wept all night while hugging a blissfully sleeping Lisa to my breast.

⟷

I told Ron everything the next day when he returned. 'Geraldine, you know the time has come. You must do what you can to take her back to Australia and put her in a suitable institution,' he said gently as I wept uncontrollably on his shoulder. And so began the long search to get Lisa into a sheltered environment for 'special' children. I was able to find a place in Adelaide, meaning I could visit her whenever I was in Australia. But the mind-numbing guilt I felt the day I booked her in and signed the papers making her a ward of the state will be with me for as long as I live. She was only seven.

The last day we spent together as mother and daughter I sat in the bath with her and washed her tenderly, knowing that this would probably be the last time she would be bathed with a deep and personal love. I washed her beautiful long, wavy hair and brushed it slowly until it was dry. She loved having her hair brushed, and I knew there would not be this kind of special attention where she was going. I had been asked to cut her hair short, as long hair was not manageable by the staff at the institution. I sat Lisa in her highchair and plaited her hair, securing it at the base of her neck and at the end with satin ribbons. I reached for the scissors and, with hands shaking from grief, severed the plait. Lisa's hair lies in an antique Cambodian silver box and sometimes when I need strength, and other times when I just need to feel her, I lift her plait out and brush it against my cheek. The hair still has the sheen it had the day I cut it.

My mother and father were supportive of me, and tried to ease the guilt I felt when I was home making the arrangements for Lisa. They were quite shocked to see how despondent I had become, and wanted nothing more than for me to get back to normal and try to put my life with Lisa behind me. Dad didn't say goodbye to Lisa. He never visited her in the home after I had left and I knew it wasn't that he didn't love her. It was because he loved her so much he couldn't bear to see how she had regressed since the first day he had laid eyes on her. It was probably as difficult for my parents to give Lisa up as it was for me and to realise that she would never be a normal grandchild to them. My sisters had their own children and it was distressing for them to look at Lisa and realise how lucky they were that their own were normal. It was a dreadful time for the Cox family and I remember it only through a thick haze.

When Lisa was fourteen two angels found her. John and Ros Frazer were just an ordinary childless, middle-aged married couple, who wanted to foster a disabled child. Lisa was selected as being within their capabilities. Before agreeing to allow Lisa to be moved from the state home she was in, I met John and Ros in the Riverland of South Australia and became firmly convinced that angels do exist. Lisa brought the three of us together and we remain in constant touch so that I know how she is. I slept a lot easier knowing that she was out of an institution and living in a home in a loving relationship with a mother and a father figure. But the guilt that I couldn't take care of Lisa by myself will be with me forever.

⌒

I returned to Manila knowing that once again my life was going to change. But I had no idea how much until I received the news that I was to be posted to Bangkok. I was surprised to have got such a popular posting. I had caused Foreign Affairs more problems during my time in Manila. As I had finally got the department to accept Lisa as my legal daughter, the next step had been to be able to provide her with the kind of housing that people with families enjoyed. I won a long paper battle and had been able to move to a house that had a lovely little garden where Lisa could be during the day. I knew that any woman with a child deserved to be considered as having a family, but I also knew that breaking this new ground would not have endeared me to the powers that be in Canberra.

Any hopes of my love affair with Ron continuing were dashed. He had slowly built up a little business in Manila, and there was no way he could give that up to follow me to another Asian city, where he had no contacts and could not speak the language. We made all sorts of promises to each other, and he said he would try to follow me when he could, but we both knew these were empty words. I was aware that he no longer wanted to be a financial burden on me and that this was the end of our life together.

We had spent even more time together after I had returned from Australia alone. We were just as happy, but in a strange way we discovered that Lisa was a part of our love, and without her something integral had changed. I didn't need Ron so much, and we both felt this and talked about it. Neither of us was happy about it, but there was no doubt that a parting of the ways was inevitable with my assignment to Thailand looming.

Our farewell to each other at the airport was the stuff classic movies are made of, but I was getting more than a little tired of having to say goodbye to the men I loved. Goodbye Theo, goodbye Kon and now goodbye Ron.

I prepared for my new posting in Bangkok and, as an act of defiance, decided to dye my hair the most brilliant red I could find. I wanted a new image. Now I was single and available and Bangkok had better be ready for me.

Paying for Love

Bangkok and Adelaide, July 1978 – September 1981

I once heard the rock star Joe Cocker say in an interview that he couldn't remember any of the 1970s. I feel a bit like that about my three years in Bangkok. I had arrived there in a state of emotional shock – having institutionalised my daughter and parted from my lover of five years in a few short months, I was crazy with grief. But outwardly I functioned normally and did my job as well as ever.

But when my working day was over I didn't know what to do with myself. I had no Lisa to play with and care for. I had no Ron to laugh with and make love to through the long, hot nights. I had forgotten how to be single and if ever I had been going to turn to drink or drugs it would have been then.

But I had a much better diversion – sex. It was to be my solace for the next three years. Meaningless one-night stands were how I hid my sadness. That I never contracted HIV, or anything else for that matter, seems nothing short of divine intervention!

I didn't care what people thought, and threw myself into the Bangkok bar scene with an abandon I had never thought I was capable of. I was a regular at the five-star hotel bars, where I picked up whomever took my fancy. I relied on my intuition to steer me away from dangerous situations. I think the closest I ever got to one was at the Dusit Thani Hotel, where one night I was approached by a man in his thirties, who was a curious but very attractive mixture of what he said was Indian, Vietnamese and French parentage. He was seductive but respectful and knew just which buttons to push. But I heeded a very distant alarm bell that I had learned over the years never to ignore. I declined his invitation to visit a few more bars with him and after he had left, I felt a twinge of regret.

A few months later he made headlines worldwide for murdering I don't know how many Western women in Thailand. The face staring at me from the newspaper was that of Charles Sobhraj.

Even this narrow escape didn't slow me down.

My bar escapades aside, I had discovered Egypt Air, or rather, it had discovered me. I was able to juggle two affairs with captains over a four-month period. When one flew in he drove to Bangkok along the highway, while the one I had kissed goodbye drove past him in the other direction to pilot the plane back to Cairo. I would wait at the Dusit Thani Hotel bar to welcome the pilot who had flown in.

During this time I had the Egypt Air flight schedule up on the wall next to the diplomatic air bag timetable, to make sure I didn't get my pilots' arrival and departure times confused. The ambassador was quite perplexed as he couldn't imagine what Egypt Air flight details could have in common with our diplomatic freight details.

It was several months before the pilots actually got a chance to speak to each other and found out that they were both dating a plump redhead from the Australian embassy. They were far from pleased.

There was a bit of a lull after the pilots had sprung me. I shifted my interest to men of the sea, specifically Pryog, an Indian Sikh officer in the merchant navy, whose ship called into Bangkok regularly. One weekend when he was on shore leave he was at my house when another love interest, Omar, a Muslim Burmese/Pakistani and local journalist, dropped in unannounced. They both held their ground, making it clear they were each waiting for the other to leave. The Sikh had to return to his ship, so Omar won that night.

Omar and I had a very unusual relationship, without any strings or expectations. If Omar minded that I had other lovers he never showed it, and the relationship lasted on and off for years when later he worked in Dubai and I lived in Tehran and we visited each other often. We had a cerebral connection that was every bit as important as the sexual side, as he had a lively interest in politics.

⌇

But I had much more important things on my mind than my relationships with men. I actually thought that I might have a chance at adopting again. Australia's regulations were changing and it was now becoming possible for single women to adopt. As I had been turned down in the Philippines because I had a disabled child, I thought now that Lisa was not an issue, I might be considered suitable to take care of a normal child. I had submitted my application to the Australian authorities before I went to Thailand.

Just try to imagine how I felt when the official ruling was handed down that because I had admitted my adopted daughter into an institution, I was considered unfit to be a mother again through adoptive channels. I wanted to bash my head against a wall! Refused because I had a disabled child and then rejected because I gave her up.

Still, I was never good at accepting no for an answer and hadn't yet given up hope of having my own child. I had succeeded by unconventional means in adopting Lisa in Cambodia and now I had tried the accepted avenues in Australia and failed. It was time for something a little more drastic.

⌇

I enlisted the help of Douglas, a rich, gay English friend whom I had attempted to pick up on the beach at Pattaya one weekend before realising that his interests lay elsewhere. Douglas moved in the crème-de-la-crème of Thai business circles. He was tall, and ridiculously fit from working out in his own gym. He had the kind of English upper-class good looks that made it possible for him to look as immaculate in a Thai sarong as he did in his expensive hand-tailored suits from London.

Douglas was entertained by my outrageous lifestyle in Bangkok and loved the company of women, and when I wasn't sleeping around, I spent a lot of my spare time with him. We became very close friends, and he wined and dined me in Bangkok's finest restaurants.

He preferred to visit the gay bars that were everywhere in the city with me rather than going alone. We were only observers anyway. Douglas was much too careful to get caught with any of Bangkok's notorious bar-boys. Many people there thought we were married, and we enjoyed the game.

I lost interest in going to the bars when one night a ravishing transsexual approached me and was extremely friendly. She was madly curious about my cleavage and thrust her hand down the front of my low-cut dress. 'Darrrrling,' she purred, 'they are simply gorgeous! Where did you get them? Please tell me the name of your plastic surgeon.' Douglas was close to wetting himself with laughter and spent the rest of the night trying, unsuccessfully, to tell her that I was a real woman. Talk about demoralising!

For several months Douglas helped me with my plan. With his assistance I selected a series of handsome young male prostitutes to live with me one at a time for four weeks of my menstrual cycle. The deal was that I would pay and feed them, and all they had to do was take care of themselves, take no other lovers, male or female, and get me pregnant. If my period came, they had failed, and I employed the next one in line. I had a fleet of them lined up in alphabetical order!

To me this was my last-ditch effort at conceiving. It had been years since I was medically examined and I thought perhaps, if I tried sex with more partners for a condensed amount of time, I might find myself pregnant at last. I remembered the doctor in Adelaide telling me that Mother Nature sometimes corrects blocked tubes in her own time. I wasn't going to leave a stone unturned in my quest for children.

The first prostitute was a little nervous, but behaved in bed as though he thought he'd died and gone to heaven. One young man refused to take my money and another wanted to pay *me*! But after a few months of this, I tired of the mechanical sex and stopped the circus.

Of course I was aware that going to these lengths would have been shocking in most circles. But this was my last attempt to defy fate. If it didn't work I promised myself to forget about children altogether. Sperm banks didn't exist then. If they had, I would have saved myself a lot of trouble.

Douglas really cared about me in a way that many of my heterosexual friends could never understand. He understood my yearning for a child and offered his help. He had Thai citizenship and many friends in high places, and he was prepared to adopt a child for me in his name. I could choose the child and he would arrange the paperwork. When the child was officially his, he would marry me! The plan was that then he would prepare a paternity agreement for me to sign, indemnifying him from any financial claims from me. Then we would simply get divorced and part of the settlement would be that I got legal custody of the child. Douglas said that he had had legal advice and it could be done. I told him that the Australian government couldn't possibly deny me a child from a failed marriage. He was a genius and I didn't know how to thank him.

The night we talked about it Douglas just sat there with a satisfied smile. We celebrated our coming marriage with expensive French champagne and the only condition he made was that I had to wear white. Knowing what he did about how I had lived in the previous few months, he thought this was a glorious touch of theatre. We also planned to invite my brigade of would-be Thai fathers to be 'best men' at the wedding reception, which was to be held at Douglas's stylish apartment.

Douglas was true to his promise and within days helped me select a healthy three-year-old girl I named Jade. I wanted an older child this time so that I could see she was progressing normally. As Douglas was so well respected in the Thai community, he was able to get the authorities to allow me to take Jade home weeks before the papers were finalised. Jade was with me for six weeks and I was delirious with happiness. At last I had a normal child, and I had my friend Douglas to thank for this precious gift.

By this time the invitations for our wedding were out and my mother, who was in on the whole thing, was flying up for the ceremony and to see her new granddaughter. Douglas's papers were almost completed and he was to sign them the day before our Buddhist wedding ceremony. That day he called me.

'I wanted to make sure you were home. I'm coming over,' he said.

'Why, what's wrong?' I asked, sensing something serious was going on.

'Make us a strong drink. I'll be there soon,' Douglas said ominously and hung up.

After he arrived Douglas paced up and down my lounge room stroking his goatee beard distractedly.

He finally told me that when the authorities had examined his medical reports they discovered he had a serious heart condition. Because of this, and as he was over fifty years of age, they couldn't allow him to have Jade, as his health was a permanent impediment to him adopting any child in Thailand. They said they were sorry they had let the child leave the orphanage before checking these details and that she would have to go back as soon as possible.

'No, no, no!' I cried. 'Please tell me it's not true, Douglas. I can't bear it.'

I had thought I didn't have any tears left. Douglas put me to bed and he lay with me until the morning. We cried together, and the next day he insisted that I go to work while he and my maid packed all Jade's toys and clothes. I couldn't bring myself to look at her face and left without saying goodbye. What do you say to a three-year-old child who had been told she was leaving the orphanage to live with her new mother? It hurts almost as much to remember Jade as it does to talk about Lisa.

My mother was already on her way and it was too late to contact everyone to call off the wedding reception. Douglas met her at the airport and told her what had happened. He drugged me with Valium, and the party went ahead as planned with all the guests. The monks were sent away as there was no point in the actual marriage anymore. That night is just a dim memory. At least I had my mother there to comfort me in the coming days. I vowed I was never going to try to adopt again; I had had my fingers burnt too many times.

I hadn't spared a thought for Kon for ages. I knew he would have hated to hear that Lisa and I were not together, and that he would have deplored my promiscuous life in Thailand. Then in 1979 the story of how the Vietnamese had successfully marched into Cambodia and overthrown the Khmer Rouge was headline news. The Thais didn't do much to hide their dismay when thousands of Cambodian refugees starting pouring over the border.

International aid agencies were flying in from all over the world to offer assistance in caring for this wretched mass of humanity. The diplomatic community rallied, and sent teams of staff and wives of officers in convoys to the border refugee camps. My mother was still with me and wanted to come and help too. But I knew she would never be able to cope with the misery she would see, and I left her at home and went for the weekend with some friends to do whatever we could.

In Sakaen, the camp we visited, over 90,000 men, women and children had struggled out of the mountains into Thai territory in a forty-eight-hour period. The magnitude of the problem was staggering. I saw things that weekend I never want to see again in my life.

The road was clogged by diplomatic cars carrying volunteers and trucks loaded with food and medical supplies. Through the dust they created, I could see a sea of hastily erected open-sided canvas and plastic tents behind a wire fence. There weren't enough to house all the refugees and hundreds of them were lying in the boiling sun. Small family groups huddled together in a state of shock.

Together with other women from the embassy we were handed over to the aid agencies in charge.

'Are you a doctor or a nurse?' I was asked.

'I'm a secretary.' Just what they need, I thought to myself.

I was given a bucket of fresh water and a supply of paper cups, and told not to use the cups more than once to help prevent the spread of disease. I kept on tripping over the ropes attached to the peg holes in the ground holding the tents up. I felt desperately inadequate. All I could do was lift the heads of prostrate, exhausted people to help them drink water and then lay their heads down gently. Their skulls felt as fragile as eggshells and I was afraid that my mere touch would hurt them. Using makeshift taps I washed filthy, malnourished babies covered in their own excreta, and helped old men and women walk to the crudely built trench latrines and held on to them so that they didn't fall in. Some of them looked at me resentfully because I was robbing them of even the dignity of urinating and defecating privately. But others were grateful, and patted my hands as I helped them to lie back down on their donated straw mats. I lifted the head of a teenage girl and placed a cup of water against her lips. The water trickled down her chin because she had died a few seconds before.

Nurses worked around the clock to save the lives of those they could. The ones who didn't make it were carried on their woven mats to a place just outside the camp, and tipped like garbage onto a pile of continually burning corpses. They had no identification and had to be burnt as soon as possible to prevent more disease spreading. The mats were returned and given to the living, and often there was no time to wipe blood and body fluids off before other refugees were placed on them. The pungent smell of burning flesh filled my nostrils, impossible to ignore.

Margaret Boothby, a friend and the wife of one of our embassy officers, fell in love with a small baby girl who weighed less than a kilo even though she was several weeks old. She was so weak that the nurses feeding the babies could not hear her crying and Margaret took on the job of taking care of her, fashioning a shoebox for the child to sleep in. I could see Margaret's involvement every time her eyes filled with tears when she picked her up. The baby fitted neatly into the palm of her hand with just her spindly legs hanging over. Margaret knew the girl needed expert hospital care and she did her best to make arrangements with a hospital in Bangkok, but the baby died before she could be transferred. This was a personal tragedy for Margaret, but it didn't stop her from working in the camps for weeks on end. She did much more for these people than I could have managed.

⟜⟶

At one point I noticed great excitement coming from one of the medical tents. A volunteer had taken a dead Cambodian out to the cremation hill and while there he saw one of the bodies on the pile move. He looked closer, to find a woman who was still alive. He ran for help, and two men gently carried her into the doctors' tent for medical treatment. It was impossible to guess her age. She was totally naked and all the hair on her head and body had been burnt off. With shame I remember thinking that she resembled a large rare steak with a head and stick arms and legs. Three nurses worked for hours without a break trying to save her. They rigged up a kind of hammock so that very little of her body actually rested against anything, and they bent over her with long tweezers, painstakingly peeling off the charred scabs of dead flesh from her body in order to prevent infection. She was totally conscious and babbling incoherently in her own language. But whatever it was she said it was clear that she very much wanted to live. When it was time for her to eat, her burnt lips opened wide, and a nurse carefully dropped in a little morsel at a time.

But the human body can only take so much. She died quietly while the nurses were still working on her. These were seasoned, tough professionals but they were all hugging each other and crying uncontrollably. They had wanted her to live so much and couldn't bear it when she slipped away. 'Before she died, she looked at us with such gratitude. She knew she was dying and wanted us to know she understood how hard we were trying to help her. Her pain would have been beyond human endurance,' one of the nurses sobbed.

The scale of suffering was numbing. I turned away from one scene of tragedy to see another and another. A dead child had to be pried out of her living mother's arms. One woman was trying to force her dead baby to drink milk from her withered breast. Bangkok hotels had sent supplies of soap and some of the refugees had mistaken it for food and were violently sick from trying to eat it.

But by far the most tragic sight for me was the tent hospital full of children, most of them between four and twelve years old. The medical teams were trying to force-feed them with special nutritious rice porridge laced with vitamins. But these children, although literally starving, turned away and refused to accept the spoonfuls of hand-fed food. Some who had been forced to take a mouthful spat the food out.

'Why?' I asked a Thai nurse working in the tent.

'They have seen everyone in their family die. They know there is no-one left to take care of them and they have no will to live. There is nothing we can do for them. They won't even drink water. They could take days to die.'

I stumbled away, not bothering to hide my tears.

Just when I thought I'd seen every horror the camp had to offer, I was told about a group of children between the ages of twelve and fifteen who were segregated from the others. They looked stronger than the other children and I asked one of the nurses why they were kept apart from them. They had been trained to kill. Apparently all the children in one particular camp slept in a barracks and had been told by the Khmer Rouge cadre that there would be extra porridge for them in the morning if any dead children were found. The stronger children then strangled the weaker ones for more food. They were seriously emotionally disturbed and the doctors didn't think they would ever be able to assimilate into normal society. Efforts had been made to find counsellors to talk to them, but none could help, because nothing like this had ever been recorded in psychiatric history.

I felt guilty if I stopped working for a second. I could feel my body tiring and was afraid that I was actually going to faint. I wondered how long these people had gone on stumbling through the jungle without food and water, hoping not to step on a landmine. I compared my body and its rolls of fat to these creatures held together by skin and bones.

I only lasted two days. I knew it would break me physically and emotionally if I continued for longer. The other women and I drove back to Bangkok, all with distressing stories to tell. We had been told that these were the strongest Cambodians from the Pol Pot labour camps, the lucky ones who did not want to live under the foreign occupation of the Vietnamese. There had been many others who felt the same but were too weak to attempt the dangerous journey without food and water. We sat in the car silently wondering what these Cambodians could look like if the ones we had seen were the lucky ones.

I climbed the stairs to my apartment and rang the bell. My mother opened the door and looked at me. 'Stay right there, Geraldine. Don't come in,' she said.

She returned with a plastic bag and a fresh sarong. She made me strip naked on the landing, and she put my clothes, stained with urine, shit, vomit, blood, and every other possible bodily fluid in the bag, and covered me with the sarong before she allowed me into the hallway. She said nothing as she prepared a disinfected bubble bath for me, and brought me a stiff gin and tonic to drink while I lay there with my eyes closed, tears running down my cheeks. She sat on the toilet seat and just looked into my eyes. What she saw there stopped her from asking any questions. It was wonderful to have my mother with me then. I don't think I could have endured the night without her.

I had looked at the face of almost every man around Kon's age in the camp. Part of me wanted to find him there. But part of me hoped that I wouldn't have to see him reduced to the state that these Cambodian refugees were in.

~~~

After my visit to the camp, there was a bombshell waiting for me at the embassy.

I had tried to keep the whole charade of my intended wedding of convenience quiet, but the story eventually reached the ears of the ambassador. He was rather dour, not very popular in the embassy or back in Canberra.

Just a few days before, he had given me a bad assessment report. He waited for my response, which was later recorded in the special place on the assessment forms for officers to sign. 'Well, Ambassador,' I had said, smiling sweetly, 'I don't know how to thank you for these low grades. A bad assessment report from *you* can only *improve* my chances of promotion in the department.'

So I must admit I wasn't surprised that he took it upon himself to inform Canberra of how I had planned to hoodwink the government. Shortly after they heard this, I received an official letter from personnel telling me that they had heard of my plans, and that when my Thai posting was over I would not be sent overseas again. This was a disaster. The only pleasure left in my life was my work and travel with the Department of Foreign Affairs, and without the allowances paid to overseas officers there was no way I could provide for Lisa's future. I decided to fly back to Canberra at my own expense to try to talk them around.

I requested a meeting with a senior personnel officer. I grovelled, I begged. I hated myself. I said I would go *anywhere* in the world they wanted me to go, as long as I could still remain on the overseas list. I explained how I relied on my overseas allowances to put something aside for Lisa. My pleadings worked, because it was 1980, just after the Iranian hostage crisis, and they couldn't get anyone stupid or green enough to accept the posting coming up in Tehran.

'Send me! I'll go!' I offered. And they bloody well did. But not before I was asked to sign an undertaking saying 'that I would irrevocably, irreversibly, irrepealably, agree to never attempt any other undertaking to adopt a child at any future postings'. I think they must have run out of 'irre' words. Today such a request would be grounds for a court case I would probably win, but this was 1980.

I was told that children who 'were acts of God' were the only kind the department would accept as legal dependants of single officers. They went on to chastise me by saying that the department was not there for me to travel the world collecting children at their expense. The people in personnel don't know how close I came to strangling the lot of them then and there.

But my trip had been worth it. I returned to Bangkok, vowing that my behaviour would be different in my next posting.

⌒

My father was in the last stages of lung cancer in an Adelaide nursing home. I knew that I would never see him again, so I took three months' long-service leave to be with him and my mother before taking up my Iranian assignment. I have always been thankful that I was able to spend these last weeks with him.

I hate all nursing homes. The smell of disinfectant clings to everything, and in small rooms neglected old men and women gaze longingly at framed photos of children and grandchildren who never visit them. Dad was one of the lucky ones. Mum, Sandra and I visited him every day towards the end when we knew our precious days with him were numbered.

Dad had always been a giant in my eyes. He was a big man, and my fondest image is of him wearing his khaki Yakka overalls over his white singlet. He always left one brace hanging undone over his shoulder. I was shocked at how the cancer was eating him away. He was a shell of the man he once was, and his face on the white hospital pillow resembled a wounded bird's. Once I found him asleep, and he looked so peaceful that I didn't want to wake him. I sat by the bed and looked at his face and remembered happier, childhood days.

Before the advent of television Dad had really looked forward to listening to plays on the radio, and on Sunday nights the whole family would gather around to listen together. We would sit with cold lamb and salad sandwiches, the meat left over from the obligatory roast lunch, and I remember these times as ones of togetherness, until television put a stop to them.

I grew up with the smell of cigarettes in everything, my hair, clothes, the curtains and carpets. He hand-rolled Capstan tobacco and I can still recall his pleasure as he licked the white paper, fashioned his smoke to his own taste and lit up. I never smoked, but I think I got my love of food from Dad. When he arrived home early in the morning after delivering milk he would often cook his own breakfast. And what breakfasts! He would slice bread the size of a doorstep, and deep-fry it in oil together with onions, tomatoes, potatoes and eggs. He would place the loaded plate on the table and attack it with a knife and fork. Cups of tea with heaped teaspoons of sugar would follow. Regular breakfasts like this would have killed lesser men.

He loved his girls and we were denied nothing, but he never believed in what he called the never-never system of hire purchase. Dad would say that if he couldn't pay cash for what he wanted, he couldn't afford it. And true to his word he paid cash for our car and television.

Race day on Saturdays was his big treat for the week, and before he took Mum to the racetrack he delighted in annoying her by emerging from their bedroom in old-fashioned sports coats over mismatching trousers. Even though this happened every Saturday, Mum never caught on that he was teasing her. As she would rip his coat off and go to find something more suitable, he would wink at me as though it was our little secret.

Dad didn't have a mean bone in his body, but he did have difficulty displaying physical affection. I never felt unloved, he just wasn't the type of man to bounce his children on his knee. That only changed when Lisa came into his life and helped him discover how to express love. But he had always had a way of patting and stroking a horse that spoke volumes about what a gentle soul he was.

It became increasingly painful to visit Dad in the last couple of weeks before he died. His whole body was switching off, and his legs gave off a smell of decay that I recognised from my days in Cambodia. They had to change his dressings every day and he struggled for each breath. To me it seemed he was more likely to die of exhaustion from the great effort required to take air into what was left of his tar-caked lungs than from anything else. It was harder for Mum than anyone and she barely functioned towards the end. For the three months I was in Adelaide I spent my days sitting with Dad at the nursing home and trying to cheer Mum up. After the funeral I had to leave my distraught mother in the capable hands of warm, nurturing Sandra and supportive Evan, and headed out for my next adventure, in Iran. I had thought I was being punished for my promiscuous lifestyle in Thailand by having Jade taken away from me. I had often been desperately unhappy in Bangkok, and wondered what lay ahead of me in Iran, where revolution was taking place and war with Iraq was raging.

Veils, Vows and a Reunion

Tehran and Bangkok,
October 1981 – November 1984

I sat in my hotel room in Dubai, where I had a one-day stopover before continuing on to Tehran. I picked up the English-language newspaper as soon as it was pushed under the door. 'Bomb Wrecks Iran's Islamic Party Headquarters' was the headline. Dozens of leading mullahs and government religious leaders had been killed and wounded. Ayatollah Beheshti, the head of the party and one of the country's leading Islamic lights, had been among those murdered. The Islamic Republic of Iran's working Cabinet had been seriously decimated. I could imagine how busy the embassy would be investigating who the culprits were and how they had been able to get access to such a heavily guarded building.

The 444-day American hostage crisis was over and Iran was firmly in the hands of Khomeini, widely described as one of history's most fundamentalist and fanatical hardline Muslims. The American embassy no longer existed, and the State Department had to rely on political information passed on by the British, Canadians, Swiss and Australians. The war with Iraq was at its peak, with no sign of ending.

The Shah had been insensitive to the religious needs of the mostly peasant population in his desire to industrialise the country. The billions of dollars that came in from the oil industry was not used to help reduce the large gap between rich and poor. In some ways the revolution in Iran was like the Russian and French Revolutions; uneducated peasants overpowered the wealthy elites. The masses rebelled against him, the Shah was exiled, and Khomeini was flown in from France and installed as the head of state who would put Islam back into the lives of the masses. Death, poverty and unnecessary suffering would continue until the end of the war in 1988.

While sitting in my hotel room, I remembered with a start something that had happened years ago in the late 1970s when Sandra was visiting me in Bangkok. We were shopping in one of the many marketplaces when a small Indian man dressed in white stopped me in the street and held my arm. He gazed intently at the space between my eyes and told me in a clear voice that I would be going to live in the Middle East. Then he was gone. Sandra was not at all used to the ways of Asia and was quite unsettled. I'd long since learned not to dismiss things just because I didn't understand them. Maybe this was the part of the Middle East the Indian man had been talking about.

⌒

Strange things happened to me before I even set foot on Iranian soil. My flight was diverted to Dohar. The airport consisted of a shed; there were no baggage carousels or, from what I could see, immigration desks. I have yet to know why Dohar warrants an airport and I wasn't mad with curiosity to find out. What stands out most was that there were no toilets and I was seriously considering watering a nearby palm tree.

I was the only woman at the airport and the only woman on the plane when it did eventually take off for Tehran. I soon learned that in this part of the world any female under the age of eighty travelling without a male family member can only be a whore, and that's clearly how I was regarded by the regal Arab gentlemen. I had seen their lips curl in distaste at having to pass me in the terminal.

They must have been going to a hawk tournament, as each man who got on the plane held his bird proudly on his right arm, covered by a heavy leather glove the hawk sat on. A very tall man with an almost emaciated pockmarked face and the inevitable droopy moustache sat next to me, and pretended not to notice as his hawk, clearly agitated by the noise of the plane's engine, squawked as it emptied its bowels all over my left arm. When I was a child my mother had told me that if a bird shat on you it was a sign of good luck. I had my doubts.

I felt I did pretty well at ignoring this little dilemma, but wondered how the hawks were going to react to the noise of the engine when the plane actually took off. However, when it gathered momentum and the engines roared, all the men covered the heads of their hawks with beautifully embroidered silk hoods, and this seemed to quieten them down. The men stroked their birds and cooed soft words of affection to them. I wondered if they treated their women as gently as they treated their hawks.

⟵⟶

Without a doubt, my very first impression of Iran was how devastatingly handsome almost all the men were. I was going to stay with the ambassador until the woman I was replacing had trained me and had left her apartment. As the embassy car drove me to the residence I actually got a crick in my neck from turning to stare at all the good-looking men.

I was expecting living conditions to be modest considering the war was in full swing. I knew that there were many food restrictions, as most of the best food in the markets was snapped up by the army for the fighting soldiers.

Imagine my surprise at what was served for dinner at the ambassador's home. A distinguished, elderly Indian called Abdul served the finest Caspian Sea caviar, thinly spread on French toast, with a little crumbled hard-boiled egg, a delicate slice of onion and a dash of lemon juice. This was followed by a very impressive boneless salmon, also from the Caspian Sea, served with a tasty dill-flavoured white sauce and side dishes of crisp garden fresh vegetables. The food was washed down by appropriate red and white wines and a particularly good Russian champagne. Some war. I thought that I could get used to this.

⟜

It was in Tehran that I met Trish Labzin, and began a friendship that would span continents and endure all types of ordeals. She had been posted by Foreign Affairs to Jordan and from there to Tehran on a short-term mission, and I had been sent to meet her at the airport. I was miffed from the minute I noticed her naturally red hair partly hidden under the obligatory scarf. I didn't mind that she was beautiful, with a figure like Brigitte Bardot's and a face like Shirley MacLaine's. But how dare they send a *natural* redhead to my neck of the woods! I know I greeted her with much less enthusiasm than I would have had she been a blonde or a brunette. It was childish, but that's how I felt.

But I was fated not to dislike her, and after a couple of days I broke down and confessed why I had been so unfriendly. She laughed long and loudly at my explanation and the rest is history. We had so much in common, and by some strange coincidence, our lives would take parallel paths even though we often lived in different countries. I had no secrets from Trish and it was so good to have a female friend again. My close friends in Adelaide were far away, and in Manila I had been so involved with Lisa and Ron that I hadn't developed the close friendships with women that I had wanted to. In Bangkok, of course, my interests lay elsewhere. Trish and I giggled and gossiped like a couple of schoolgirls as we compared notes on our affairs with local Iranians and men from the diplomatic corps. Often we would sit around each other's houses listening to blues and jazz music, in which our tastes were so similar it was eerie. As in Phnom Penh, the restrictions placed upon us by war and, in Iran's case, a religious puritan government, meant friendships tended to be enduring. I really missed her when her short-term posting finished and she returned to Amman in Jordan.

But Iran then provided me with a further friend who would play a huge part in my life – Lynne Folster. She was another secretary at the embassy and she filled the space when Trish was no longer around. Lynne was a 'biggun' too, and I've always had a soft spot for other large women, especially ones with Lynne's sense of humour. We were inseparable, and among the partying crowd we were known as Tweedledum and Tweedledee. I knew, as I had with Trish, that Lynne and I would always stay in touch over the coming years.

My housing was embarrassingly opulent. Most embassies had leased the homes of those wealthy Iranians who had had the money and sense to flee the country before the Shah left. As in Cambodia, these homes could only be protected from seizure by the Iranian government by embassies using them to house their diplomats. The rents were ridiculously low.

I lived in the north of the city, in Farmanieh, in a beautifully appointed house with an almost Olympic-sized swimming pool, behind an eight-foot stone wall. It was all set on about an acre of manicured gardens, and boasted a solid silver chandelier over the hand-carved oak dining table. I vowed to brush up my musical skills on the white grand piano. The house was full of priceless antique silk carpets on Italian marble floors, and I could stand up in the hewn stone fireplace in the lounge room. The milkman's daughter had never had it so good.

The servants' quarters ran the whole length of the house, and were occupied by Edita, my Filipino maid, who thought I didn't know that she was having a raging affair with Reza, the gardener. I think the arrangement between them was driven more by practicality than by lust. A diplomatic home was the only place where a physical union could take place without the fear of being sprung by the Pasdars, male and female morality police who roamed the city streets. It would have been funny if it wasn't so tragic. Not even the rich could escape the fanaticism that soon overpowered all aspects of normal life for Iranians.

Iran was the most repressive of all my postings. I pitied my Iranian girlfriends, who if they didn't wear the full black *chador*, were forced to wear, summer and winter, the *ropoush*, a shapeless type of overcoat over all their clothing, and *hijab*, a headscarf completely covering their hair. They were prohibited from any self-expression in fashion, in their speech or lifestyle. I have many fascinating stories, but without the permission of those who told them to me, I must remain silent until they allow me to repeat these sad and shocking tales. Even all these years after I left in 1984, some people are still being harassed and questioned about their relationships with me and other foreigners. Many of my friends preferred to be described as Persian rather than Iranian. They felt that they belonged more to the old royal Shah Reza Pahlavi days when he was King of the Peacock Throne, than to the new Islamic Republic of Iran.

However, Khomeini was revered by the peasantry and hardline religious communities. True, he was apparently incorruptible, but that did not preclude those around him from being corrupt. Before the revolution the emerging middle class and the educated elite hadn't noticed that the religious masses were becoming tired of being ignored and that the royal government was bound to be replaced by a religious leader.

Something that angers me is the media's determination to portray all Iranians as an unruly crowd of bearded, unwashed, fanatical heretics, bent on killing off all but the Islamic races in dastardly terrorist acts. Of course these people exist, but the Iranian men and women I met were among the most cultured, poetic, educated, hospitable, passionate and tolerant people of any nationality amongst whom I have lived.

However, there was a curtain of fear hanging over the people. The Shah's dreaded secret police, the Organisation for National Security and Intelligence (SAVAK), had been replaced by the Islamic Republic National Security and Intelligence (SAVAMA), the same organisation, but working for the new Islamic Republic of Iran. Many of the officers were the old SAVAK ones and their interrogation tactics had not changed much. Midnight arrests, disappearances and imprisonments without trial were everyday occurrences. Life under the diplomatic umbrella was privileged indeed and I couldn't imagine behaving the way I had in Thailand. I would have ended up dead in a day!

I had two types of friends. There were those who were brave enough to be seen with a foreign woman who worked in a liberal Western embassy, and who had not yet been contacted by SAVAMA to try to get me to work with them, and there were those who had already been engaged to spy on me and did so under threat. I often didn't know who was who.

Iran's international spy network was admirable and is still one of the best. An Iranian man told me one evening, after more than his share of homemade vodka, that if I would just cooperate with him and tell him what he wanted to know about the Australian embassy and about how it was reporting on the political events concerning the war with Iraq, SAVAMA would give me what I wanted most.

'And pray tell, what is that?' I asked, intrigued. My friend hung his drunken head low, avoiding eye contact with me, and muttered the words into his chest. He was ashamed, but his fear was more real to him than his shame. He told me that SAVAMA knew I was not interested in money; they knew I wanted a child more than anything in the world. He said that if I worked with him, and with them, they would arrange a legal adoption of a child from an Iranian orphanage before I left Iran. I hid my shock and asked him to tell me more.

What he told me then sent a shiver down my spine. He said that SAVAMA had a file on me from when I had first joined the Foreign Service in 1970. They knew about every affair I had since then. They knew all about my family and my financial situation, and that I had got into debt trying to find a cure for my adopted daughter. They didn't like me, but thought that there was a chance I might work with them. If I refused to cooperate, he told me, he would be assigned to another person in another embassy. If he could not produce results, SAVAMA had told him they would not allow his sick father to leave the country for medical treatment. He begged me to work with him so that his father could leave Iran and check into a hospital in Europe.

I felt sorry for him, and told him so, but I said he should pass on to his SAVAMA dogs from me that I would rather eat dirt than be associated in any way with a bunch of warmongering, self-righteous, misguided, corrupt, moralising, fanatical thugs. I knew that there was a good chance they would hear firsthand how I felt about their offer. All our phones were tapped, and sometimes you could actually hear someone breathing or coughing on the other end. My friend visibly paled, sobered up and left. He never contacted me after that.

Files in Canberra are full of contact reports of this kind, recorded by officers serving in Iran during the Khomeini years. We in Australia are so lucky to live in a society free of this type of intimidation and intrusion.

⌐⟶

One day a letter arrived from Bangkok by way of the department in Canberra. On the envelope was a request for it to be forwarded to me. Inside was an almost illegible handwritten letter from someone whose name had no meaning for me, together with a black and white photo of an old man with bad teeth, smiling. A lot of people in Australia had been receiving letters from Cambodian and Vietnamese refugees begging to be sponsored to come to Australia. It was thought that lists of diplomats serving around the world were being sold to people in the camps with the promise that we might help. I tossed it in the bin and forgot all about it.

A few weeks later I got a similar letter in identical handwriting from the same man, whose name I still didn't know. But this time I could read it, and I couldn't believe my eyes when I read, 'And how is our darling Lisa Devi?' No one but Kon would write such a thing! I looked again at the second photo and this time I could see a slight resemblance. It was Kon! But why had he changed his name?

The letter was from Khao-I-Dang refugee camp, along the Thai border. There was no telephone number. The letter just asked for my help. My heart was pounding in my chest. Kon was alive! I applied for leave and two days later arrived in Bangkok.

⌐⟶

As soon as I arrived I called the aid agency in charge of Khao-I-Dang camp. I met the official in charge and showed him the letter. I told him that although the name was not known to me, I was sure it was that of Colonel Om Kon, who had fought with the Americans in the Cambodian air force. I said that he had even been sent on a training course to Eglen air force base in Florida, and gave him the approximate dates he had been in America before his letters stopped in 1975.

The officer looked up the file number given in the letter, and said that Kon was being used as a translator in the camp and his services were highly regarded. However, because he was so well educated it was considered possible that he might be one of the educated Khmer Rouge, some of whom had tried to escape being killed by the Vietnamese by masquerading as people who had suffered under the Pol Pot regime and slipping over the border, hoping to be accepted abroad as a refugee in a third country. Kon's file did mention that during his initial interviews he had said he was a colonel in the air force when the city fell. But the interviewing officer thought it was impossible that a well-known colonel could have survived without being recognised for all those years.

'Did he ever tell you his real name was Om Kon?' I asked.

The official replied that hardly any of the refugees gave their correct names. They were all still so afraid of the Khmer Rouge, members of whom they knew were living among them. In the camps there were still killings carried out by the Khmer Rouge, and the Cambodians were terrified to give their real names for fear that the information might fall into the wrong hands.

He arranged for Kon to come to Bangkok on an official pass, and told me that I would be held responsible if he didn't go back to the camp on Monday. After the weekend, when I verified who Kon was, he promised to arrange for him to meet the right people in the American embassy. If he had been one of their pilots, trained by them in America, they would do everything they could to get him to America as a legal refugee.

I left the official many photos I had of Kon and me together, having shown him the fly-suit with Kon's name on it as proof that we knew each other. I was to wait for Kon in the lobby of the Dusit Thani Hotel the next day.

After reaching the hotel I sat away from the entrance with my eyes glued to the door. I wanted to see him first and be prepared for how he might look. I recognised his walk first. He still walked like a warrior. He stood just inside the entrance looking very out of place. My hands flew to my mouth to stop me from calling his name. He was much thinner, but I had expected that. His hair was greying and his expression showed the expected traces of hardship. But he held his head high and his face was full of expectation.

I walked slowly towards him. I had to actually touch him before he recognised me.

'It's me, Kon!' I said, throwing my arms around him.

We just stood there in the middle of the crowded lobby, holding each other tightly. He broke the embrace first. He held me away from him, his arms holding my shoulders. His laugh was exactly the same.

'I wasn't looking for a lady with red hair!' he said.

Of course, I had been a brunette when we had last seen each other. We took the elevator to my room, where I longed to hold him and kiss him, but I dreaded hearing of all that must have happened to him. I was afraid to ask about Kruy and their children.

The moment was almost too sacred to make love. But not quite.

⌒⟶

After kisses and tears we slept; so much emotion had drained us both. I didn't want to ask him any questions.

In the morning we woke refreshed and ravenous. I was startled at the amount of food Kon ordered from room service. It seemed impossible for us to eat it all, but he proved me wrong and ate enough food to satisfy a whole football team.

After his meal he walked over to the window and closed the drapes, shutting out the bright sunlight. It could have been midnight. He got back into bed with me, tucked the sheets snugly around us and lay with his hands crossed behind his head. Kon told me that he wanted to tell me his story in the dark. There were many things that had happened he had never spoken about before and I would be the first one to hear his dreadful secrets. He thought I might not love him anymore when he had finished his tale. He believed he had done many bad things in order to survive. There were times he had almost been forced to kill to prevent others from informing the Khmer Rouge that he was a lieutenant colonel in the air force. He had committed acts that as a Buddhist he never thought he could commit and he believed that he would suffer in the next life because of what he had been forced to do. He reminded me that when we knew each other in Phnom Penh he had only killed Vietcong and Khmer Rouge. He had never foreseen a day when he would have to kill another Cambodian.

He had known bad things were going to happen when Lon Nol fled the country on 1 April 1975. It was announced that President Soeharto had invited Lon Nol to visit Indonesia on an official visit, but everyone knew that he was running away because he took his whole family with him. A few days later there were rumours that the Americans were pulling out, and that they could only take some high-ranking Cambodians with them. He said he hadn't believed the Americans would do that to them. But they did.

For the first time in Kon's life no Cambodian celebrated the New Year on 13 April. Soon after that Pochentong Airport was closed and he knew the end was very near. The Khmer Rouge were marching on the city by 15 April, a time when for years Cambodians have been happy and celebrating – but not in 1975. The Khmer Rouge broadcast by radio that Cabinet ministers, government leaders and military officers should surrender at the Ministry of Information, where they would be assigned new positions. Many of them went. Later he found out that people like Long Boret, Lon Non and Sirik Matak had all been assassinated and some beheaded. Kon lost many friends that day. He said he had told his friends not to surrender, that they couldn't trust the Khmer Rouge. But they had told him he was stupid to feel that way. They said the war was over; we will have peace now, they told him. Kon said that many military personnel and air force friends of his left in helicopters from the Olympic Stadium, but that he could never have left his family behind as many of them did.

Kon said that the Khmer Rouge broadcast that everyone should leave Phnom Penh as soon as possible, because the Americans were coming to bomb the city and they would only be safe in the provinces. People panicked. He and Kruy didn't know what to believe. They agreed to try to stay together and he knew that if he was to survive he should not wear his air force clothes. He dressed as a farmer, and the couple took all the children and joined the throngs of people walking out along the highway.

Kon had thought they would be back in a couple of days so they didn't take a lot of food with them, just some rice and dried fish. Relatives rushed to the hospitals to remove their sick and wounded families, afraid that if they left without them the Americans would bomb them. Some families were pushing hospital beds with the patients still attached to their drips. Kon said it had all been a trick to empty Phnom Penh. The Americans didn't bomb the city.

While walking, Kon saw many important people in government and the military, and they saw him. All were too afraid to acknowledge each other and just looked away. Kon's three older daughters were able to walk. Kruy was carrying their two-year-old son, and Kon was carrying their food supplies as well as nine-year-old Konnavy (the daughter I had felt so close to in Cambodia), who was very weak and dehydrated. They were all very tired, thirsty and hungry, but the Khmer Rouge were guarding everyone with guns and didn't let anyone stop. If they did, the soldiers beat them until they joined the line again. If they didn't obey, they shot them, and Kon passed many bodies on the side of the road.

He told me of one family who had stopped in the shade of a tree at the side of the road. They had a sick child who needed to rest, and were arguing with a Khmer Rouge soldier. The soldier said that if they didn't join the line of people immediately, he would shoot the entire family. The parents were carrying two children each and could not take the sick one. They were forced to leave her and continue their journey. Kon didn't look back when the family got back onto the road, but he heard a single rifle shot, and knew that the soldier must have shot the child.

There were many decomposing bodies along the road and he and Kruy tried to shield their children's eyes from the sight of them. Some had been shot and others had just lain down and died of thirst and exhaustion.

In the heat of the day, many people took a dip in the small creek at the side of the road. He warned his family not to drink the water, because of the contamination from all the dead bodies. But when Konnavy walked near the edge of the water she slipped. She screamed as she stepped into the stomach of a dead Chinese woman.

Kon gathered her in his arms and comforted her, and felt deep sorrow when she said that she had swallowed a lot of the water. She said she was sorry.

She developed violent diarrhoea and died that night. The family gathered around her, and Kon held her hand until it was cold, refusing to leave her side.

The Khmer Rouge would not allow him to cremate her as it would have taken too long to gather wood and for the body to burn. However, they did give permission for them to stay until Kon could dig a grave for Konnavy. His voice broke when he said that they could not imagine leaving her body at the side of the road, like all the others they had seen.

It was the hottest month of the year and the ground was as hard and dry as cement. It took Kon six hours to dig the small grave. Kon said he did not cry for Konnavy, but that as he dug the grave all he could think about was the time I had asked him if I could take Konnavy with me to Australia. He wished he had given her to me.

Kon tried to keep as close as possible to the area east of the bank of the Tonle Sap River, which made it easier for them eventually to flee to Vietnam in August 1975. There Kon supported them, working as a farmer. But he knew his family would not survive unless he could get them all to a refugee camp in Thailand and eventually to another country.

He was at risk every day. Kon saw the Khmer Rouge single men out of the forced labour camps for assassination because they were pointed out as members of Lon Nol's military force. The years of wearing air force boots that were laced tightly almost to his knees had left Kon with deep indentation marks on his calves. This alone was enough to identify him as a soldier of some kind. When he came out of the rice paddies he had to be sure to rub mud all over his legs until the telltale marks had faded.

Kon decided, with Kruy's agreement, to escape from Vietnam, and he walked for many days through the dense jungle, hiding and sleeping during the day and travelling at night, using the stars to guide him to the border. He saw what was left of those who had stepped on landmines. He said it was a miracle that he made it to the refugee camp in one piece. When he arrived at the camp he knew that he could never use his real name; he had hoped he could get a letter to me somehow and that I would understand the dangers of him using his own name. He wrote to many friends in France and America as well as to me, but no-one ever replied.

Being separated from his wife and children was almost more than he could bear. He had always loved and protected them, and he often regretted leaving them behind. But eventually word was passed to him that Kruy was alive and with their four remaining children. He told me how hard Kruy's life was in Vietnam, where she managed to eke out a living in the Dong Thap (Sadec) province as a street vendor to feed their children. He dared to hope they would be reunited one day. He told me he had stopped counting how many of his relatives had been killed by the Khmer Rouge. I said nothing and just put my head on his chest and held him.

Towards the end of the day Kon got up and opened the curtains. We stood at the window holding hands and watching the sunset. Neither of us ever mentioned any part of his story again. We only had one more day together before he had to return to the camp, but he was overjoyed that now there was proof of who he was and that he would eventually be able to go to America. He would do everything in his power to enable his family to join him there. Once again we promised to keep in touch, through letters sent to the Department of Foreign Affairs in Canberra. I didn't know how long I would be in Iran and Kon didn't know how long it would take for the authorities to process his papers for America.

The last night when we said goodbye, I presented him with his fly-suit. Now that he was out of danger and had survived, I knew it meant a lot to him. He had not been able to save one personal belonging to remind him of his previous life before Pol Pot, so I gave him back his past. He had proof of who he had been. I told him that I'd carried his fly-suit to Australia, the Philippines, Thailand and Iran and that I had felt that as long as I could see it, he was alive. I said: 'Now I don't need it anymore. Please have it back, darling.' Kon left me exactly the way I had asked him to in Cambodia so many years before – while I was sleeping.

When I returned to Tehran I felt as though I had lived a complete lifetime. For once a chapter of my life had ended happily for someone I loved.

⌒

Now if there were a Lotto prize offered to the woman who could find the most unsuitable and doomed-to-failure candidate for a love affair, I would be a millionairess. Enter Sion.

I met him just a few weeks after my return from Bangkok. He was a couple of years younger than I was, in his early thirties, and he owned a Persian carpet shop not far from my house. The sparks flew when I went there to buy a rug. He was tall, with slightly stooped shoulders, and his hair was dark and wavy. His complexion was unusually fair, which set off his black, sad yet smouldering, eyes. Our affair got under way the same day, when Sion delivered the rug I selected to my home.

The relationship was stormy, and he was passionate and madly jealous. But I never doubted his feelings for me and for the first time since I was with Ron in Manila, I could feel myself falling in love.

Sion was the only son of a conservative Jewish family. For him, continuing the family name was paramount in any marriage he might have. I told him that I could never give him a child. Sion introduced me to his parents, having already explained that we were in love and wanted to marry. The only way he or his family would accept me as his wife was for me to get pregnant before marriage. They were good Jews, but it was more important to them that their son be assured of having a childbearing wife. I was surprised at this modern approach, but could see its sense.

Sion correctly pointed out that it had been years since I had last had fertility tests and that if I underwent the new process of microscopic fallopian tube surgery, maybe we could have our own child. After knowing Sion for less than six months, I flew home to Adelaide and had the operation. It was not a success. I broke the news when I returned to Tehran, and Sion behaved as badly as it was possible to behave. I was dumped even before the normal swelling from my operation had disappeared.

I was beginning to be an expert on rejection by this stage. But my reaction, as always, was to bury my sorrow with sex. In a twisted way I felt that being sexy and promiscuous was how I could prove I was as much a woman as the ones I envied who had their own children. I was in my late thirties and getting really tired of hauling my barren arse around the world proving to spineless men like Sion that I was as worthy to be a wife as the next woman, whether I could produce a child or not.

⌒

I embarked on indiscriminate affairs with members of the diplomatic corps, including senior diplomats from Somalia and Oman. I also managed to squeeze in a dalliance with a talented underground Iranian painter who later made a name for himself in the Paris art scene. It was far safer to stick to the diplomatic corps. SAVAMA didn't care much what infidel diplomats did with other infidel diplomats, but for one to get involved with a local Muslim could lead to a disastrous backlash against the Iranian. And I use the word 'backlash' literally.

More than one of my friends had been publicly whipped. One night SAVAMA stormed the house of an Iranian couple to which diplomats had brought alcohol. The diplomats were allowed to go free, but the Iranian man was dragged from his home and whipped within an inch of his life. It was months before he could sleep on his back. To be true to Shariah Law, these whippings were carried out with a book of the blessed Koran held firmly under one arm while the other is used to administer the whipping.

⟜

I hadn't heard from Sion in months when he called one Friday morning to see if I was home alone. I thought he wanted a reconciliation and waited nervously for him to arrive. A reconciliation was the last thing on his mind. He had got wind of my many affairs and was in a mad, jealous rage. The minute he was inside the door he ripped the telephone off the wall so I couldn't call for help and systematically set about giving me the thrashing of my life. He smashed everything in the kitchen and hit me over the head with a broken wine bottle. I still have glass in my head. In the bathroom I tried to get away from him by crouching down between the toilet and the handbasin. He just tore the basin completely away from the wall and dragged me out by my hair. Water was gushing everywhere.

I was paralysed with fear and never thought to fight back. I just cringed like a dog and let him tire himself out. When he came to his senses I was on the floor with my dress half ripped off and blood running down my face, and I was sure I had several broken ribs. I made out I was unconscious, and when he gave me a final kick I didn't move or make a sound. Before he left he locked the front door from the outside with the key so I couldn't get help. I could have bled to death for all he knew or cared.

As luck would have it, I was expecting a new Iranian admirer who was to take me out for lunch. I had to wait a couple of hours for Massoud to arrive. When the doorbell rang I crawled to the front door, and asked him to look on the ground for the key and let himself in. He stood there staring at me. I had been able to stand up but was bent double holding my side, my clothes were half off and blood was still running down my face. And this was our first date!

The apartment was trashed and I didn't want the landlord to find out, and I especially didn't want to report to the embassy what had happened. I didn't want to lay any charges against Sion either, so that meant I couldn't go to the hospital. Massoud called a friend who was a doctor, who came to dress my head wound and said that possibly I had broken ribs but that there was nothing he could do about them. He also called in painters and plumbers, and arranged for all the repairs to be done immediately. We became good friends, but I think he thought I was definitely too dangerous for him to want to get to know me any better.

I was in emotional as well as physical pain after this and there were no other women in the embassy I was friendly with. I called Trish, who was now with the Australian embassy in Paris, and told her what had happened. She took leave and was in Tehran the next day; that's the kind of friend she was. I cried on her shoulder and she stayed for about a week until she was sure I was beginning to recover.

⌒

Iran more than sated my appetite for danger. I took my life in my hands if I ventured out on the streets wearing lipstick.

The sight of the mustard-gas-affected soldiers from the front was more than I could handle. They just lingered on in badly understaffed hospitals, and hoped that somehow supplies of pain-killing medicine would arrive.

The Khomeini government had a quaint method of clearing the country of landmines in preparation for soldiers to attack the Iraqis. A particular favourite was to empty the mental hospitals, and homes for the elderly, and handicapped children. A bus would arrive to take them on an 'outing', complete with a picnic lunch. When they reached the picnic spot they were herded out and forced to walk over the land to set off the landmines, making it safer for the military assault. Those who understood were told that their sacrifice would confirm them as martyrs. As a bonus, there was then room in the empty hospitals for the wounded soldiers.

⟜⟶

Despite these horrors and the Sion episode, I was enjoying Iran. The politics were intriguing and mercurial, and the ambassador I worked for, John Dauth, treated me as an equal and gave me scope to develop and verbalise my opinion of local politics. This gave me more self-confidence, and made my job far more interesting.

I got on well with all the embassy staff and had a lot of Persian friends. I was always either giving a dinner party or going to one. If despite this, the local restrictions did start to close in on me, there was the diplomatic bag run for a weekend to a European capital city. Every week someone was scheduled to carry highly classified diplomatic reports to London, Athens or Vienna. There we would link up with couriers who would take the top secret despatches to the Minister of Foreign Affairs in Canberra. I was actually travelling far more than I would have from any other posting available to me at that time and I had more men asking me out than I could poke a stick at. Why would I want to leave Tehran? I decided to request an extension.

Personnel in Canberra were beside themselves with frustration. Tehran was meant to be a punishment for me, but here I was extending a one-year posting to a second and then a third year. They were forced to accept my requests because no-one else in their right mind wanted to go to a country suffering the turmoil of war and run by a radical religious-backed government.

⟜⟶

In my third year in Tehran, towards the end of 1983, I met Mahmoud at a party in my apartment. I had asked my married friends to bring an extra swag of unmarried men, as I had a surplus of female guests, mostly gorgeous Scandinavians from other embassies.

I was busy being the hostess with the mostest when a guest brought a tall, dark and handsome specimen of Persian manhood to me. 'This is Mahmoud, he would like to meet the woman who lives here and reads the poetry and political books in the bookcase, and who plays the classical and jazz music piled up next to it,' he said, before slipping away in quick pursuit of one of the girls from the Finnish embassy.

Mahmoud stood there looking slightly shy. I was distracted and didn't take too much notice of him, as I was busy pouring drinks and putting out food. I did notice that he had beautiful hands, dark and smooth, with long fingers wrapped around his glass.

'Do you really like Hafez, Rumi and the other old Persian poets?' Mahmoud asked. He said he hadn't heard jazz since studying in England and America, and asked me to invite him back some other time so he could hear jazz again.

'Yes, why not? Come by next Wednesday night after dinner. I'll be home,' I said, almost carelessly, as I moved away to take care of some new guests. When Mahmoud arrived the next week bearing flowers and chocolates, I had almost forgotten that he was coming.

Our relationship was not based on sex or physical attraction, but on poetry, politics and music. Of course, all the rest followed, but by then we really knew and cared about each other. Mahmoud was only two years older than I was, but had been married and had a seven-year-old boy, who lived with his remarried ex-wife. He often said that he hoped to have his son live with him in the future if he remarried.

Mahmoud was something of a computer genius. He worked for Computer Sciences Corporation, a well-known American company that acted as a sole distributor of Honeywell hardware to the Iran government. He had set up a large-scale management information system for the Imperial Iranian Air Force and later for the supreme commander's staff. He had travelled outside Iran for his employers, and had a good network of Western friends inside and outside the country.

He proposed and we decided to get married in Tehran before a Western wedding ceremony in Adelaide with my family, planned for August 1984. But before I agreed to marry Mahmoud I wanted to make sure he knew what he was getting. After dinner one night, I closed all the dining room curtains and put the lights on. I took my clothes off in front of a startled Mahmoud and stood up on the table.

'What on earth are you doing, Geraldine?' Mahmoud said.

'I'm already thirty-nine, darling. I want you to understand that my body is never going to be better than it is tonight. I just don't want you to ever think you made a mistake, so have a good long look,' I said, as I turned slowly under the harsh lights.

That ended up as one of our most romantic nights together, even though I had shocked Mahmoud. He wasn't used to such a lack of inhibition in a woman.

One Saturday morning Mahmoud called me to say he had found a mullah who would sign a marriage certificate.

'You mean I'm getting married today and I won't even be there?' I exclaimed.

'Don't argue with me. Just have your passport ready and by the time I get back in the afternoon, we will legally be man and wife,' Mahmoud said.

While I arranged a romantic dinner, I wondered what name the mullah would choose for me. I had to sign a paper saying I had converted to Islam, and when this happened the mullah always chose a new Muslim name for the convert. (I felt a few qualms about signing the conversion paper, but as my religious faith was confused at the best of times I didn't feel it was an unforgivable betrayal.) I was thinking of all the lovely feminine names I knew, such as Soraya, Parvonne, Farangis and Scheher-ezade. I would have been happy with any of those.

Mahmoud finally returned, waving an undecipherable document that was written in Farsi in a rather shaky hand. Nonetheless it was the real thing. 'It's done, darling! Take this certificate to the embassy tomorrow and have it legally translated into English, and make dozens of copies in both languages. It's worth more than gold. I can actually stay here with you tonight. We are married!'

'I can't believe it. We are actually married and the mullah didn't even ask you if I wanted to marry you or not? This is a very strange country. What if I didn't want to marry you?' I asked. I couldn't get my head around the fact that it was that simple.

'Don't you want to know what your new married name is?' Mahmoud asked mischievously.

'Yes, yes! What is it? Don't keep me in suspense. Tell me!'

'Fatima!'

'What!' I screamed, screwing up my face. 'Fatima?'

'Yes, Fatima was the favourite daughter of Mohamed the Prophet. It's a very honourable Persian name. Don't you like it?' Mahmoud asked.

'Oh, I hate it! Can't we change it?' I pleaded.

'No, it's in the certificate. You are now Fatima, so start getting used to it,' Mahmoud reasoned with me.

'But darling, you Persians shorten all names. How do you shorten Fatima?' I asked, half-knowing the answer.

'The nickname for Fatima is Fatty,' Mahmoud said unconcernedly.

'Oh, shit, Mahmoud. How could you let him call me Fatima? I already weigh close to eighty kilos and now I'm going to be called Fatty by all our friends.' I didn't know whether to laugh or cry.

From then on, we were known as Mahmoud and Fatty. I ask you, what chance did the marriage have with a start like that?

We spent our honeymoon in Paris, where we stayed with Trish. After a more conventional wedding in Adelaide with my family and friends, we proceeded on to Washington D.C., where I was to work in the political section of the embassy.

As I was to have access to top secret material, Mahmoud had to be cleared by ASIO so that he could be granted Australian citizenship. It was not possible for security reasons for me to go to Washington with a husband who had an Iranian passport. Once again I was causing work for the department.

The ASIO agents were thorough, and spent hours grilling us together and separately to make sure he wasn't planted by SAVAMA. After the clearance, Mahmoud was the proud owner of an Australian passport.

The Great Satan and Another Reunion

Washington D.C. and Sydney,
December 1984 – June 1990

Just a few months into my marriage to Mahmoud, I had to face the fact that he and I had problems. Mahmoud was exhausted by the demands of living in a new country, and at night would often fall into a deep sleep on the lounge. For me, being married was far lonelier than being single.

I was also having more than my share of problems coping with housework. I had had maids for fourteen years and Mahmoud had grown up with servants. One of the most embarrassing situations we found ourselves in arose when I commented to Mahmoud that our expensive vacuum cleaner was not sucking as well as it should have been, considering we had only had it for six months. We went to Bloomingdales department store with our guarantee clutched in our hands, and explained our problem to a very glamorous-looking woman behind the counter of the complaints department.

'When did Madam last empty the bag?' she asked, with a supercilious look on her face.

'The bag? What bag?' I asked in all innocence.

As the woman took the vacuum cleaner from us, she flicked open the back. We could see the bag bulging fit to burst with six months' worth of dust, dirt and cat and dog hair collected from our apartment floors.

'*This* bag, Madam. May I inquire where you thought all the dirt was going when you cleaned your carpets?' the woman asked disdainfully.

We got out of the store as quickly as possible, and argued all the way home over who should have known about the bag.

⌐⌐⌐

I was also feeling sad because it looked as though Mahmoud's young son would not be joining us as originally promised in Tehran. Mahmoud was even more upset than I was at this.

My behaviour, too, was far from exemplary. I deeply resented Mahmoud's withdrawal from me and was also a little scared when I saw him sleep so deeply. Often on my way to bed I would stop at the lounge where he was lying, light a match and hold it under his bare feet. If he flinched I knew he was not unconscious and I would trot off to bed quite happily. After a while he started to complain that his feet hurt him, and I felt quite ashamed of myself. I changed to pricking his feet with a pin. It had the same effect without causing the lasting pain of the matches. It was years before I owned up to these antics. It's a wonder he still talks to me!

Mahmoud's unhappiness was also exacerbated by the fact that his older sister, Farangis, a dermatologist who lived near us in Virginia, was not expected to live for more than a few months. She had breast cancer and was recovering from unsuccessful chemotherapy. She knew she was going to die and leave her two children behind. I could see how disturbed Mahmoud was by bearing this sorrow every day. He and his sister were very close, and I also grew to love her in the six months we knew each other. We spent all our spare time either in the hospital or taking care of her son, who was only ten when his mother died.

We promised Farangis that we would take her son into our home and bring him up as our own after she died, and for a few months I was able to lavish my affection on him. Mahmoud and I were in the middle of adoption proceedings when his father arrived from Iran to take him away. He was a lecturer in psychiatry at the University of London Medical School and his behaviour when he found out his wife had cancer had left much to be desired. He had deserted her and the children, and left them to fend for themselves financially and emotionally. But he still didn't want me or Mahmoud to have his son. The boy was physically dragged out of our house by his estranged Iranian father one year after his mother died, and Mahmoud and I cried for days.

Mahmoud's misery was also added to by the fact that many Washingtonians were racist, especially as far as Iranians were concerned. It was the time of the TWA hijacking and when Mahmoud finally succeeded, after many months' searching, in finding employment, he came home very dejected. After only a few days in the job, he had found graffiti in the men's toilets. He was working as the head of technical administration at Hughes Satellite Communication, an international organisation in Maryland.

'On the first day the toilets were all clean. But after three days every one I went into had "Nuke Iran", "Iranians Go Home" plastered all over the toilet doors. And no-one is friendly, Geraldine. Some of them never even answer me when I say hello or look up when I pass by,' Mahmoud complained. I had no words of comfort for him.

Mahmoud was wrestling with the loss of his country, the death of his sister, the loss of his nephew and the realisation he might never see his son again, not to mention working in a new cultural environment with hostile staff. On top of all this, he was married to a woman who amused herself by setting fire to his bare feet at night!

Although we lived in the same house we were becoming more distant with each passing day. I didn't know how to begin to improve things. And like so many other married couples who are no longer happy, but afraid to do something about it, we just limped along.

Then Mahmoud left Washington on a business trip. I was miserable and had few female friends at the embassy. As always I called Trish, who was working at the Australian embassy in Tokyo. She had also married a Persian, whom she had met when we were together in Iran, and we often talked about how similar our lives were. She took unpaid leave as she had no holidays left and spent some time with me in Washington. She always answered my pleas for help. It was good to have her with me to listen to my bitching about Mahmoud, but there was little Trish could really do to change things.

⟿

Then out of the blue I received a letter addressed to me from Canberra, which had been sent on to my Springfield Virginia address. It was from Kon, and he was living just a couple of hours away from me in Warrenton, Virginia.

I always felt I could tell Mahmoud the truth about anything that had happened in my life before we were married. He was most unusual in this respect. He knew all about my affairs, my life in Bangkok, the lot. He was only concerned about my fidelity to him. He trusted me.

I told Mahmoud that I would really love to surprise Kon with a visit. I explained that Kon had no idea I was married and certainly no inkling that I was living in America. I read him Kon's letter in which he told me that he had finally been able to get approval to bring his wife and remaining children to America. I told Mahmoud I was thrilled for Kon, and would give anything to see his face. I asked him to come with me to see Kon.

'No, Geraldine,' Mahmoud said. 'You go and see your old friend. You've told me what a good man he is, and you should see that he is all right and doesn't need any help. I'll be here when you get back.'

I got maps out and charted my way to Kon's house in Warrenton.

⟿

It was winter and snow was falling gently. While driving I recalled everything about Kon. I savoured our first meeting and our strange love affair that had had his wife's blessing. I remembered with a sweet sadness the day Lisa and I left Phnom Penh, and how much I had worried about him when his letters stopped in 1975. I relived the moment in Tehran when I had received his letter telling me that he had kept his promise to survive and remembered how I couldn't wait to get to Bangkok to see him again. It was as if our lives were forever linked in some way.

It was no longer a sexual longing, but something much stronger and more pure. I felt I could see his soul. My need to reassure myself that he was well and wanted for nothing was strong. I tried to push away the nightmarish images I had of his life during the Pol Pot years. I wanted him to know that I still cared about him, not just as an old lover, but as a fellow human being who deserved some peace in his life. I hugged myself with pleasure at the thought of how he would react when he saw me.

His letter had told me that he was working in a huge nursery where flowers and plants were grown commercially, and that he was happy to be working with the soil. His employers had provided him with a small house in the nursery grounds, and he was busy getting it ready for the family he hadn't seen since 1975, nearly twelve years before. The nursery grounds were huge and I had to ask at the office where I could find him. A pretty young woman was at the reception desk.

'Excuse me, I'm looking for Om Kon. Can you tell me how to get to his house, please?'

Her expression was very inquisitive. 'I can page him for you if you like. Who shall I say wants to see him?' she asked.

'I'm an old friend and he doesn't know I'm in America. So would you mind helping me surprise him? I really would appreciate it', I explained.

'You do know his wife and family are coming in a few weeks, don't you?' She was about as tactful as a sledgehammer.

'Yes, I am very happy that Kruy and the children are coming. I will be visiting the whole family when they have settled in. Now, can you ask Kon to come to the office without saying there is anyone here to see him?'

'Sure. Sorry. It's just that Kon's never had any visitors before. We all love him here. I'm glad that he has a friend.' She was being so protective.

While I waited I remembered how shocked I had been at his appearance when I was reunited with him in Bangkok. The crushing work in the paddy fields and the lack of food had really taken their toll. But I knew that he would have put on weight in America.

The door squeaked as Kon's foot, encased in a heavy workman's boot, pushed it open. He walked right past me up to the desk. 'What do you want? I'm busy shovelling snow from the paths,' Kon said, removing his thick gloves and shaking the snow from them.

'You have a visitor, Kon,' the receptionist said, pointing to where I stood behind him.

He turned and faced me.

'It's you! Is it really you? Where did you come from? I wrote to Australia a few weeks ago after I arrived here. This is wonderful.'

Kon's face was wreathed in smiles. His once beautiful white teeth were discoloured from the bad diet he had had for the four years he toiled under the Khmer Rouge and as a farmer in Vietnam. But the warmth in his smile was still there.

In the car I told him I had married after I had seen him in Bangkok and that I was working at the embassy in Washington. Kon directed me through some picturesque country lanes to a cosy wooden house.

'It is good you have someone to take care of you now,' he said as he started to boil water for tea in the kitchen.

Later, we sat together on the couch, drinking each other in. 'Is your husband good to you? Is he a kind man? You must tell me this,' he said.

Our eyes spoke the words we didn't say. We both felt the change in our feelings for each other and knew we could never go back to our previous relationship. I was now married and he was looking forward to being with his family, who had suffered incredibly. But this in no way lessened our love; it just changed it to something that would never die the way physical love so often does.

We talked about anything and everything. I told him about Mahmoud's problems and the distance between us they were creating. But he offered no advice, he just shook his handsome greying head in sympathy.

When I drove home I felt as though I had been sprinkled with some kind of exquisite fairy dust that protected me from harm and showered me with love. Just being with Kon gave me the strength I knew I was going to need to do what had to be done with Mahmoud.

When Kruy and the children arrived, and had got over the initial culture shock and cold weather, I was invited to their house for the day.

I had been very nervous about meeting his wife for the first time and was almost moved to tears by the way she greeted me. Her pleasure could not have been feigned. Kon translated, as she had not started to learn English yet.

She said it was an honour to have me in their house. She had always considered me a sister, and a godmother to her children. She said she was very sorry to hear about Lisa Devi. Kon had told her all about how sick she was and she understood the loss of a child, that although Lisa Devi was not dead, I was mourning.

Kon told me that Kruy wanted me to know that he had told her everything about me, back from when we first met in Phnom Penh. While she was waiting for the immigration papers to come through, she had reminded all the children not to forget the Australian lady they had met in Cambodia. She told them that they had a godmother in Australia and that maybe one day they would see her again.

For no apparent reason, Kruy started to laugh so much that tears ran down her wrinkled face.

'What's so funny, Kon?' I asked.

He said Kruy was asking if I remembered when he drove backwards and forwards between her and me the night of the rocket attacks. She said she had often thought about that over the years and still thought it was funny!

What a remarkable woman Kruy was. There was no embarrassment, no awkwardness. I knew no-one could ever comprehend the bond between the three of us.

Kon's eldest girl, Konnary, was eleven years old when she used to come to my house in Phnom Penh. She was now a young lady, and told me in halting English that she remembered visiting me with her father and brothers and sisters. She said she remembered it clearly because I had many chairs and she had thought I was very rich.

I became a regular visitor to Kon and Kruy's happy home, where I was always welcomed like family. It was wonderful to see a Cambodian family survive and be able to start again.

I was also focused on my work and there was plenty of it to do. I had arrived during the hoopla surrounding President Reagan's second inauguration and, without a doubt, Washington was the busiest post I had ever been assigned to. During my three years there I worked on reports on the end of the Marcos regime and the progress of the new Aquino government, the decline of the ANZUS agreement, the UN's General Assembly and National Security Council meetings in New York, international anti-terrorist contingency plans, the Chernobyl nuclear disaster, Star Wars and the Geneva Peace Talks. I also assisted the Australian Prime Minister, Bob Hawke, the Foreign Minister, Bill Hayden, and the Defence Minister, Kim Beazley, during their official visits to Washington D.C. and San Francisco.

But by far the most riveting political comedy of errors was the Irangate scandal. After watching months of public trials and interviews on television, I was pretty much convinced that the Iranians were not far off in their assessment of America as being the Great Satan. Irangate disgusted me, and I saw for the first time what a corrupt game politics can be. I wanted out.

In November 1987 I decided to resign. I packed up to return to live in Australia for the first time in seventeen years.

So much in Australia had changed since I had left in 1970. Especially prices. I once complained in a restaurant that its public telephone didn't work; I was inserting twenty cents, having had no idea the cost of calls had increased to forty cents. When buying a ticket to travel from Sydney to Adelaide for a family celebration I was staggered to learn what it cost. Before, the government had taken care of all my travel needs and I had never even inquired what airfares cost. Also, my rent, gas and electricity bills were paid for as part of my package when I lived and worked overseas as a public servant.

I started pounding the pavements to find a job. No job ads ever asked for a woman over forty. It was hard going. But I eventually succeeded in landing one with the Chase Manhattan Bank after explaining to them that

'I was a forty-three-year-old thirty-six year old'. I settled into corporate life, which was crushingly boring compared with being able to monitor political events.

Mahmoud was having problems finding work as well. Employment agencies were suggesting to him that he change his name to Mike. He stuck to his guns and refused. 'Even if I call myself Mike, I will never look like a Mike,' he said wryly. Nothing I did could shake him out of his unhappiness.

⌒

The only bright spot in my life was the time I had with Trish, who was back in Sydney. We spent most of our spare time together, as Mahmoud wasn't interested in going out and Trish was separated from her Persian husband, and also at a loose end. She was my solace; I always left her feeling stronger and less sorry for myself. But I soon learned I was going to have to be her solace for a change.

I felt a cold hand squeeze my heart when she told me that a lump in her breast was malignant, and that it was so serious they would have to operate immediately, on Christmas Eve 1989. Trish was going to die; I knew it. How could I live without her? She refused to tell her family in Queensland because she didn't want them to worry. But I was around every day and she couldn't lie to me. I remembered all the times I had needed her and how she was always there for me and how she was still there for me. At last I could be there for her.

She was as close to death as anyone gets without actually crossing over. I was with her when she was grappling with the knowledge that, instead of just the lump being removed, they had removed her breast and scraped her flesh down to her rib cage to catch the virulent cancer. It seemed a miracle when she bounced back.

However, the cancer returned with a vengeance. Trish submitted herself to months of radiation and chemotherapy so they could make sure all the venomous cells were dead. Ultimately, the radiation treatment was bungled and almost killed her. By the time she recovered from the poison pumped into her now mutilated body, her thyroid gland had been permanently damaged, which meant she would be on medication for life. For Trish, the hardest thing to come to terms with was the knowledge that her dysfunctional thyroid would never allow her to sing again. She had always sung for the sheer love of it and this was a truly cruel side effect of all her suffering.

She was the most important person in my life at that time. When her disease was at its zenith, she went to live in Queensland with her parents, who could give her more constant care than I could. I phoned her every day, obsessed with the fear of losing someone I loved as a sister. I could not bear even to think about a world without her in it.

But I also have to admit that when I watched her suffer I was grateful I wasn't going through the same torment. Once I recognised this feeling I was consumed with self-loathing, and guilt that I was so healthy. Trish never cried in my presence once in all this time. It was often she who dried my tears, when I broke down at the sight of her agony.

Trish had done so much to help me cross barriers. In the same way that Theo had awakened in me a deep interest in world politics, she gave me insight into myself so that I could accept and understand my flaws. Trish came through this period of her life with a definite gift for being able to heal other people's pain, both physical and emotional. Strangers came from miles around to meet her and be counselled by her. It was almost as if she was rewarded for her endurance by this wondrous gift.

It was so hard for her in the beginning to look at herself naked in the mirror. She had always had such a beautiful body. But when she finally came to terms with her prosthesis, she would have me in fits of laughter when she visited and took it off, laying it down on my coffee table. Once she forgot to take it with her and called me when she got home. 'Hang on to my tit for me will you, love? I'll pick it up tomorrow. It doesn't need food and water. Just make sure no-one fools around with it until I get there. I don't want to miss out on any fun!'

What a woman she was. I thanked the universe for giving her to me.

Happily, Mahmoud eventually secured a job with IBM, the company he had worked for in Iran before the revolution. Luckily IBM still had his personnel records and was pleased to have him back. He was over the moon about it and worked harder than he really needed to, so what was left of our marriage took more of a back seat than ever. I was working long hours too and in the end there seemed no point in our being together. It was a relief for both of us when we finally divorced in June 1990. Still, the failure of my marriage was a deep disappointment to me. There is something infinitely sad about the words 'irreconcilable differences' in divorce papers.

Full Moon over Angkor

Phnom Penh and Siem Reap, November 1992

Before I tried to find a place in which to live alone once again, I took six weeks' leave. I planned a long trip, taking in Cambodia, where I particularly wanted to see Angkor Wat from the ground. The image I had seen from the helicopter twenty-one years before of temples reaching through the jungle, had made me want to see the world's largest religious edifice in more detail.

I had already spent a fortune on myself in London, San Francisco, Ottawa, New Delhi and Bangkok before I found myself once again flying over Cambodia. The ambassador was an old friend and I was to be his guest. He told me he would send his driver to collect me from the airport.

As I went through arrivals I saw an old Cambodian man with grey hair waving frantically at me and calling out my name.

'Miss Gelladine, Miss Gelladine! Over here. It's Moy!'

My God, it really was Moy.

I don't usually make a practice of kissing and hugging embassy drivers, but this was an exception. I engulfed the poor embarrassed man with my bulk, and we attracted quite a crowd of amused bystanders who wondered why the big foreign lady with the red hair was kissing the old man so passionately. I knew that in Cambodia public displays of affection were considered very impolite, but I just couldn't help myself.

Moy had weathered all the tribulations of the Pol Pot years and I listened with sadness and even amusement to his tale. When the embassy staff evacuated Phnom Penh, the then ambassador gave Moy the keys to the embassy Mercedes and residence, and asked him to take care of them. Moy moved into the residence, but the political climate deteriorated so rapidly that he deserted the car and moved as far away from the residence as possible. The Khmer Rouge were killing on sight any people identified as having worked with any diplomatic personnel. No one had ever accused Moy of being stupid, and he was farsighted enough to wrap his Australian embassy ID card with his photo on it, together with the keys to the residence and the Mercedes, in waterproof plastic and bury the package under a tree several miles out of the city.

After carefully committing the hiding place to memory, he joined the thousands of refugees flowing out of the city, and he and his family were put to work in the labour camps around Battambang. He didn't go into detail, but few of his immediate family survived the years of hard work, deprivation and physical abuse. He said his life had been no different from that of oxen, except that oxen often got more to eat than he did.

The Vietnamese liberated him and his people from the Khmer Rouge in 1979, but as he had no means of returning to Phnom Penh, he stayed in Battambang and became a rice farmer. He had heard that thousands of people had swarmed back into the capital, and that they squatted in whatever empty house they could find. He was sure there would already be people living in his home and that he should stay where he was. He moved to Phnom Penh and worked for a while for the Hun Sen government until he discovered in late 1981 that the Australian embassy had reopened its doors and that there was a new ambassador and other diplomatic staff.

He presented himself at the reception desk of the new embassy, demanding to speak to the ambassador. If he had spoken one word of English or French during the year under the Khmer Rouge it would have meant instant death, so he had forgotten a lot of the language. The receptionist thought she had a madman on her hands, especially when he said he was an Australian embassy staff member and would not budge until he had spoken to the ambassador. The ambassador agreed to listen

With my sisters Sandra (left) and
Marlene (right), Adelaide 1945

First and last beauty contest,
Adelaide 1950

At home with my parents, Norman
and Dorothy Cox, Adelaide 1963

In London, 1965

With nieces Karyn and Amanda Powell, Adelaide 1964

Theo (right) and a colleague in the doorway of the pharmacy, Adelaide 1968

Michael and Monique's Lao marriage ceremony, Phnom Penh 1971

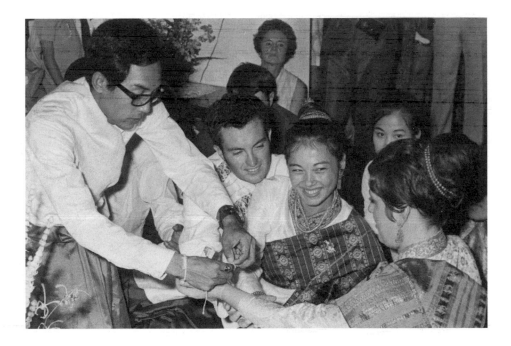

Weekends with the orphans.
On the roof terrace of the
'Birdcage' apartment building,
Phnom Penh 1971

Feeding time in Lisa's orphanage,
Phnom Penh 1971

Lisa and me in Phnom Penh shortly after I brought her home, 1971

Major Om Kon, Phnom
Penh 1971

Wearing Kon's air force fly-suit,
Phnom Penh 1971

Ron, Manila 1978

Douglas, Bangkok 1978

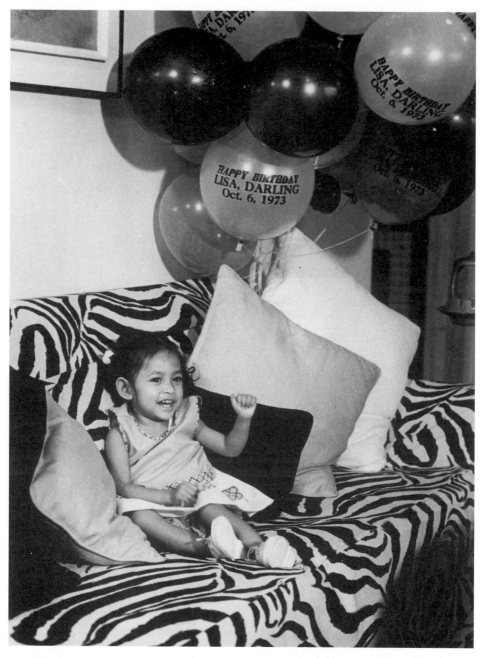

Lisa in Manila, 1973

Jade, Bangkok 1979

Lisa and me, Adelaide 1982

Honeymoon with Mahmoud,
Paris 1984

Trish, Sydney 1991

With the ambassador's driver, Moy,
outside the Australian embassy,
Phnom Penh 1992

From left, my sisters Marlene
and Sandra, my mother and me,
at my mother's eightieth birthday,
Adelaide 1994

Riddth, Wotjek and me with Cambodian friends in Royal North Shore
Hospital, September 1995

HRH Princess Marie Norodom Ranariddh visiting the children at the
orphanage, 1995

Presenting donation cheque from
Chase Manhattan Bank to Princess
Marie, Phnom Penh 1995

Riddth and me, Sydney April 1996

Last farewell. Riddth's funeral in the local village near the
orphanage outside Phnom Penh, July 1996

Orphans' dormitory after the coup, Phnom Penh August 1997

With members of the Phon family at the orphanage, September 1997

Audience with King Norodom Sihanouk, Siem Reap September 1997

Me receiving my Member of the Order of Australia Award from the Governor of South Australia, Sir Eric Neal, AC CVO, Adelaide 6 April 2000

to his story, and they drove together to the place where Moy had buried his ID card. He dug up his parcel and handed it over to the ambassador, who heartily congratulated him on surviving.

Moy thanked him but wanted to know when he would get his job back. He said he had been told in 1975 that he was still official staff until further notice. As he was never asked to leave his job he thought he was entitled to be re-employed! The ambassador supported his request and Moy was reinstated as the ambassador's driver, and became quite a celebrity among the Australian expat community.

If Canberra had not honoured his request I think there would have been a lot of unhappy Australians who felt very guilty at the way the Australian government deserted not just the Cambodian people generally, but the local staff at the embassy. Moy is the only one who survived.

I feel that Australia should have done something for the Cambodian staff at that time. However, with what has been done since by the Australian government, for example, by Senator Gareth Evans in helping establish the UN framework that set the scene for the 1993 elections, perhaps we have taken a few steps in the direction of earning the forgiveness of the Cambodian people.

Moy was overjoyed to see me back in Cambodia and was full of questions about Lisa. His face was sympathetic when I told him how handicapped she still was.

'Don't feel bad, Gelladine,' he said. 'She is alive and in good hands. If you did not take her away I know what would have happened to her.'

'Do you know what happened to the children at the orphanage we used to visit, Moy?' I asked.

I had tried to find the place while I was in Phnom Penh, but it had been replaced with another government building.

'Yes, I know what happened. It was very, very bad, Gelladine.'

'Go on, Moy,' I told him gently. I was prepared for just about anything, but what he told me reduced me to tears of rage.

He spoke of when the Khmer Rouge soldiers entered all buildings, forcing the people occupying them into the streets and out to the provinces. Lisa's orphanage was one of the places they went. In the labour camp he was sent to he recognised one of the women who worked there and she recognised him as the embassy driver. Moy said she promised not to divulge that he used to work for the embassy, as she knew it would have condemned him to death. The woman told Moy that the Khmer Rouge soldiers forced all the children who could walk out into the streets to join the streams of people. The babies and children who were blind, crippled or too sick to move were lined up, and a soldier held as many of their heads together as possible, so that one bullet could kill several of them at a time. The soldiers systematically went through the wards and killed the children until there was no-one left, shooting small babies as they slept in their cots. Moy said that the Khmer Rouge believed there was no room for babies and handicapped children, who could not contribute to the rural workforce they were planning.

He told me that Lisa would have met this fate if I had not taken her to Australia.

I could only think about Sam.

⟿

I was very nostalgic in Cambodia. I drove past my old apartment late one afternoon; it was still standing, but very much in need of maintenance. I was able to go inside and felt like a ghost walking through the empty rooms, my footsteps echoing on the green and white floor tiles. I even climbed the back stairs to the roof terrace, but the memories of the nights I had spent up there with Kon were too intense, and I hurried away.

I was only in Phnom Penh for a day or two before I flew to Siem Reap to achieve my dream of seeing Angkor Wat. I remember carefully choosing my clothes for my first day in the temples – a most impractical white outfit with long sleeves. I felt that I was making a pilgrimage.

There were few tourists, and I chose to go in the middle of the day when I knew that most people would be out of the noonday sun, enjoying their lunches or taking naps. It was strangely important to me to be alone when I first walked through the temples. And I was.

Even the monks and beggars were nowhere to be seen. I didn't take a guide as I had been reading about Angkor Wat for years and felt I knew so much about the place. I ran my hand tenderly along the walls of exquisitely crafted bas-relief carvings. The smooth stone was cool and felt oddly familiar beneath my touch. The stories of heaven and hell seemed to speak to me as I walked very slowly down the shaded corridors. I climbed the steps of the highest temple and sat there alone, feeling like an ancient queen.

Nothing I had seen had prepared me for the perfection of the stone carvings. But now war and genocide had killed off the artisans and others with creative skills. You were hard pressed to find a carpenter who could make a door that shut properly, and the people were afraid to show their artistic talents. They remembered how the artists and musicians were among the first to have been murdered by the Khmer Rouge.

I spent the whole day at Angkor Wat and after watching the sunset I stayed behind after the tourists had left. It was going to be a full moon, and no-one else seemed to realise how magnificent it would be to see it rise up behind the stone towers. I arranged for a car to come back for me later, and sat at the edge of the lotus pond in front of Angkor Wat, waiting for the moon.

I wondered what the temples would tell me if they could speak. I thought they would tell of the Cambodians' love and respect for their Buddha and the many Hindu gods introduced by India. They would speak of the countless wars with the Siamese. They would talk of good kings and bad kings, reveal palace treacheries and intrigues but also speak of the devotion Cambodians felt to their Angkorean royal families. They would tell of the many slaves who worked to build them.

When I left I felt that if I died in my sleep that night, I would die a happy woman. I had been completely at peace among the centuries-old stone ruins. I had felt a serenity in Angkor Wat that I knew I would return to in my thoughts and dreams for the rest of my life.

⟵⟶

I completed my long holiday, and went back to Sydney, found a new place to live and went back to work at Chase. I had spent all my savings and knew it would be a long time before I could contemplate a holiday like that again. I would find that it was extremely difficult to get back into the swing of the boring old routine of corporate life.

The Beginning

Sydney, June 1993

I was definitely restless. I was reading voraciously all the news I could find on Cambodia in *Newsweek*, *Time* and *The Economist*. That Prince Norodom Ranariddh had been voted in as the First Prime Minister, sharing power in a coalition government with Hun Sen as the Second Prime Minister, seemed weird, but as almost everything I had ever experienced in Cambodia was weird, I accepted it.

Shortly after this a friend called me one night while I was enjoying one of my favourite television shows, the British comedy *Absolutely Fabulous*, with a bottle of icy cold Hunter Valley white wine close by. She had just seen a documentary produced by Jack Thompson, the Australian actor, about his involvement in moving orphaned Cambodian refugee children from one of the camps in Thailand back to Cambodia, where he had helped set up an orphanage called Krousar Thmei (New Family). She had been very moved by the program, as she had lived in Cambodia and had a soft spot for the country. She had been friendlier with Princess Marie Norodom Ranariddh than I had been. She told me that she had contact details for Princess Marie and she felt we could 'do something' for Cambodia.

'If Jack Thompson can do it, I don't see why we can't,' I agreed with her.

Within a day or so we were able to telephone Princess Marie in Bangkok, and asked her if we could do anything to help. The relief in her voice was tangible as she told us how worried she was about a group of twenty-four orphans from Site B Refugee Camp, or Prince Sihanouk's Camp, as it was generally known, as it housed the families of soldiers who had fought for the royal family. They had become lost in the repatriation program, as they were in an orphanage inside the camp and no-one wanted to take responsibility for them back home.

She had moved them to a poor village called Ampil, in the province of Oddar Meancheay, not far from the Thai border. But they were living in a deserted schoolhouse and the princess had no way to contact them, or get food or other supplies to them. Princess Marie had known all these children in the camps in Thailand; they loved and trusted her, and she wanted to continue to assist them. But her hands were tied and she could do nothing from Phnom Penh. If we could go to them she would be eternally grateful.

Her brother, Roland Eng, was in Bangkok and if we contacted him he would give us all the assistance we needed to get across the border to reach them. If we were able to get to the children, she asked us to tell them that she had sent us, and that she loved them and had not forgotten them.

The next three weeks were spent networking on the telephone with colleagues, friends and family and collecting a ton of clothes, toys, medical supplies, English language books and audiocassettes, and anything else that could be shoved into cardboard boxes. I thought that it was not a coincidence that my boss at Chase was away on a long business trip so I could spend many of my working hours putting all this together. Also, my taking leave at that time suited the bank.

In 1993 my friend and her husband would work long and hard setting up our little charity, The Australia Cambodia Foundation, and getting it legally registered and established. The whole idea to set up some kind of an orphanage was hers, and although neither she nor her husband have had anything to do with the children or the foundation for some years, and sadly we have drifted apart, their original idea, vision and commitment were invaluable. Without their foresight, I would never have had the courage to continue. I would like to speak more of my friend's involvement, but she prefers not to be a part of my story.

But without her suggestion, I would still be bent over the profit sheets of Chase Manhattan Bank. Thank you, my friend.

Sihanouk's Babies

Ampil and Sydney, July 1993 – January 1994

I met Roland on my first day in Bangkok. I'm sure he will one day be in Cambodia's history books. His love for his people is legendary, and he has been the Minister for Tourism, Cambodian ambassador to Thailand and in 1999 was appointed as Cambodia's ambassador to the United States. But when I met him in 1993 he was just a Cambodian eager to take someone to a little group of orphans he had helped his sister care for in the refugee camps in Thailand during the 1970s.

'They call me Papa Roland,' he said. 'I wish I could do more to help them, but at least I can take you over the border and to the village where they are sheltering until Marie can find a better place for them.' We loaded dozens of cartons into a minivan he had organised, and set off to drive through elephant country to Surin before reaching the Cambodian border. During the seven-hour drive, Roland talked with passion and pity for the orphans he hadn't seen for two months.

He explained why the refugee camp the children came from was also known as Prince Sihanouk's Camp. Many of the children I would meet were the offspring of those who died serving the king and his son, Prince Ranariddh, but many children from other backgrounds were also accepted.

Roland said that the children had relied on money from him and his sister for their very existence, and that there was a limit to how long they could financially support the orphans. He hoped I would not be just a one-day wonder.

Roland's own story emerged bit by bit as we drove through the Thai countryside, lush and green from the rainy season. He had left Cambodia in 1969 to be educated in an exclusive French boarding school. He became Prince Sihanouk's chief adviser in the south of France, before returning to Cambodia in 1983 to fight in the jungles as part of the royalist resistance to the Vietnamese occupation. As the days passed I learned that Roland's only surviving relatives from a large extended family were his two elder sisters. Everyone else had been slaughtered.

Roland's bodyguard started to talk in Khmer and pointed at some oxen pulling a plough in a nearby rice paddy. Roland translated for him while he spoke softly with a faraway look in his eyes. The bodyguard said that when he was a boy in the Khmer Rouge labour camps he had hated the oxen because they could eat grass but it made him throw up. He would pray to Buddha to make him an ox so that he could eat the grass and not feel hungry. I smiled at the soldier and then gazed at the passing scenery. How could I tell this man that I had never felt real hunger in my life?

We reached Surin before the supermarkets closed. Roland said there were many things he knew the children would need, such as washing powder, salt, cooking oil and tinned food. After much debate he allowed me to pay for the items he had selected. However, when he took me to dinner he refused to let me pay. He said there would be plenty of things for me to spend my money on after I had seen the children. And before that, in the morning, we would need to get up very early to go to the market to buy fresh pork, beef, chicken, noodles, fruit and vegetables so that we could have a big party for them when we arrived.

⌒

The next morning, very early, we hit the main highway out of town. The van was chock-a-block with fresh food, much of it tied to the roof.

I had asked Ron where I could get a Cambodian visa several times since leaving Bangkok, but I never got an answer. Now we were very close to the border.

The van rolled to a stop near the side of the road. A small open truck was parked and in it were six Cambodian government soldiers armed with a mixture of AK47s and M16s. The roof of the truck even had an automatic machine gun affixed to it.

'Compliments of Prince Ranariddh and Princess Marie,' Roland said to me with a gracious wave to them. 'They sent these bodyguards to meet us here because there is a lot of banditry and kidnapping in this area.'

The truck travelled ahead of us with our van close behind. I could see how we would be an attractive target for any hungry band of Cambodians living in the area, and was grateful for the extra protection.

We stopped in front of a boom gate made of very tired-looking bamboo, and Roland got out to wake a soldier who was fast asleep with his gun resting up against a tree. The soldier looked uninterestedly at us, accepted a US$20 note Roland handed him and sleepily raised the boom gate to allow the van to pass.

'Welcome to Cambodia!' Roland said with a grin.

Bloody perfect, I thought. An illegal entry into Cambodia was a great start. If anything happened to me, immigration records would show that I was still in Thailand. From most people's point of view this completely illegal entry into any country was most irresponsible, but it was the only way to get to the children. The roads in Cambodia from Phnom Penh were impassable during the rainy season, and had not had any maintenance for over thirty years.

As we sped along, I noticed every few hundred metres the black, red and white posters showing a skull and crossbones that indicated that the whole area was still heavily mined. Conservative estimates were that for each of the ten million people in Cambodia there was a landmine. The mines would never be cleared in my lifetime.

Years of travelling have taught me always to carry a toilet roll. This was just as well as the Thai dinner we had had the night before was sending me urgent messages. Roland was asleep so I asked the driver to pull over to the side of the road, waving my toilet roll wildly to make sure he understood why. I got out of the car as fast as I could, and started to walk towards a well-worn track I could see in between the landmine warning signs. I thought this would surely be safe, as it had obviously recently been used by the local villagers. I had barely got to the edge of the paved road when the head bodyguard, Som Kiat, jumped off the lead car and lunged in front of me, barring my way with his automatic weapon. I put out my arm to brush him aside but he wasn't budging. I gesticulated urgently to the nearby bushes and again to my toilet roll, leaving him in no doubt that the matter was becoming extremely urgent. He stepped towards me, forcing me back onto the paved road. I could see he was trying very hard to speak in English.

'Commander say me, if Madam die, I die. So, Madam, please shit here!'

I got the message.

The safest place was at the side of the road itself, as most landmines were just off the shoulders of roads, where they were more likely to be stepped on. The soldier directed me to the back of the van and then left me to it.

Cambodia this time around was certainly giving me more new experiences.

⟜

As we neared the orphanage Roland woke up and wanted to talk. He said: 'We are not far away now, Geraldine. This road is particularly dear to me. You have noticed how good it is?'

He said that a year ago it hadn't existed. He and 150 others had cleared the jungle of mines with dynamite, and built the road with only picks, shovels and their bare hands. Most of the volunteers were demobilised soldiers who had become farmers. They had wanted to open up a food and market line from the border to very poor villages, and it only took them ninety days. A lot of the men who worked alongside him had said they were happy to do the work for food only. This was the kind of forced labour they had to do at the point of a gun during the Pol Pot years; now they could see that they were working to improve life for their families.

Out of nowhere appeared a checkpoint manned by the handsome English UN colonel David Viccars. I didn't know it then, but I was going to see a lot of him over the coming days. He was visibly annoyed, as it was rare to get motor traffic along this stretch of road. As he was in charge of the

UN communications network in the province, I think he felt that someone should have let him know we were coming. He gave us the standard lecture about bandits and kidnappings, and waved us on after we explained we had supplies for a group of orphans.

By lunchtime we had reached Roland's little wooden shack on stilts, which he said was within walking distance from the children. The women and children living in it were overjoyed to see him, and with their smiles of welcome wore expressions of relief that they hadn't been forgotten.

We unpacked the food. Roland sent it over to the staff taking care of the children, with a message that they should cook up a storm for dinner, and that he was bringing a friend and gifts later in the afternoon. Now that I was actually minutes away from seeing the children I couldn't believe it had only been three weeks and three days since Princess Marie had first asked for help.

After a simple lunch of French bread, cheese and pâté we drove for all of one minute to the wooden schoolhouse. The children came running from everywhere to greet their 'Papa Roland'. They were poorly clothed and not very clean, but they generally looked physically healthy. I had been prepared for much worse.

They hung back from me and were very shy. Without being told, they formed a line and started to unload the cartons until they were all stacked up in the middle of the main room. They stood there looking at the unopened boxes, and Roland explained to them in Khmer that I had been sent by Princess Marie to help them, and that there were many things for all of them in the boxes. He asked them to wait until his video battery charged before they opened them, as he wanted to film them unpacking their gifts.

The mountain of clothes, toys and books were finally all unpacked. I will never forget their faces as they looked uncomprehendingly at the pile. No-one made a move towards it. But I didn't have to understand Khmer to understand the sorts of things they were excitedly saying to each other.

'Is this a dream?'

'That doll is mine!'

'That dress will fit me!'

'I want that red T-shirt!'

'What *is* that toy over there?'

I waited for them to throw themselves into the mountain of gifts and grab what they wanted, but they were strangely still. Then a teenage boy pushed another boy called Cham Chern forward. He was in a dilapidated wheelchair fashioned out of a wooden chair and bicycle wheels, because his legs were badly deformed by polio. They wheeled him around, and as he pointed to clothes and toys, a smaller child crawled in, got what he wanted and put it in his lap. Only when they were all sure that Chern had all he wanted did they go for it.

I was so touched by their thoughtfulness. They knew he couldn't get things for himself and without a word being spoken, it had been arranged that he have first choice. Chern sat there, the proud owner of a 'World Expo Brisbane' T-shirt with gold lettering, jeans, a white sailing cap, (complete with gold braid), and a pair of blue knitted slippers with satin bows, which he put on to cover his tiny withered feet. He turned his rickety wheelchair towards Roland and me, and posed for the video with his treasures.

After that though, I had to stand up on a chair so as not to get knocked over in the rush. I had been prepared to fight back tears, but with all the laughter and chattering going on, and the obvious pleasure everything we had brought was giving them, it never occurred to me to cry. In fact, I was laughing with them.

Teenage girls who had never seen themselves in a mirror before were holding up new Western-style clothes and asking others what they thought. The older and more aggressive boys were using their new T-shirts to bundle up whatever they could get their hands on. Young children were trying desperately to get their feet into Reebok shoes two sizes too small for them. Other small girls and boys were choosing dolls and soft, cuddly toys, poking them to see if they were alive or not. Never had they seen such wonders! Within ten minutes, the youngest boy, Pros, about four years old, had found all the bits of a train set and had worked out how to link the carriages together.

Some, however, held back. They had to be coaxed over to the pile, and asked others to choose things for them. Many of the little ones just held on tight to as much as they could and stood perfectly still. It was as if they were testing us to see if they could actually keep their treasures or if it was all a trick.

On a more sombre note, later Roland and I were taken to the bed of a little girl who was very sick with malaria. Upon seeing him she just burst into tears and said in Khmer, 'Hot, pain, hot pain, help me.' Her urine was completely red, a symptom of one of the more serious strains of the disease.

Roland noticed that she also had infected gums and an abscessed tooth. She was very weak and Roland gave her medication to help her pain. However, she clearly needed proper medical attention, and soon. There was no doctor or hospital close to the village. I was saddened but not surprised to hear a month later that malaria had finally claimed her.

⟷

Roland and I sat together at dinner and ate with the children, who were eating like there was no tomorrow. I might as well have come from Mars, but I had expected it to take a while for the children to accept me. I went home with Roland in the twilight with an intense pressure in my chest that it took me a while to name. It had been so long since I'd felt it. It was happiness.

Roland showed me where I was to sleep and told me that a French deminer, who was training local soldiers in detecting and deactivating landmines, usually slept there. Roland explained the sensible 'punishment' the French have for those convicted of misdemeanors. They are given the option of doing community service work in a third world country for a year, and this was what this man was doing.

The bed was a fold-up canvas army stretcher, but with a pair of pink pure satin, lace-edged sheets! This was hardly what I was expecting in the middle of a dirt-poor village in the wilds of Cambodia. I think I was asleep before my head touched the pillow. My dreams were full of children clutching toys and laughing.

⟷

The next day I arranged to be driven to the nearest UN station, where Colonel Viccars was in charge. From there I could place a call to Thailand to follow up some cartons we had not been able to bring with us. I made this trip every day as the UN lines were out of order; I had to keep going back on the off-chance they were open.

Roland had arranged a pick-up truck for me to make the trip in. It had no brakes, but hey, this was Cambodia. He had informed me that village etiquette was to offer rides to whomever was on the road. As we slowed down, people ran alongside and jumped in when they could.

One day I looked behind me to see how many people we had in the back. I counted two monks in saffron robes, smoking their heads off; eight soldiers in various kinds of Cambodian army uniforms, all comparing the condition of their boots and guns; four old ladies with shaved heads chewing betel nut, their mouths gaping holes showing red-stained gums; and half-a-dozen ragged children.

'Don't look now,' I said to the driver Roland had given me, 'but isn't that a Khmer Rouge soldier in the back with the plain black uniform, and red and white check *kroma*? I know the uniform well from when I was in Thailand working in the refugee camps.'

The driver looked back unconcernedly.

'Oh, that's Saren from my village. He is Khmer Rouge, but he's OK. Many of the farmers here fight for them, because they give rice to their villages. He wouldn't hurt anyone.'

Small comfort. The black uniform could still strike terror into the heart of anyone who remembered what its wearers were capable of.

One day while I was at the UN station waiting for my call to be put through, Colonel Viccars said he would like to talk to me about the orphans and Roland.

'I don't think you are aware that this group of children is not considered by the UN to be orphans in the true sense of the word,' he said firmly. 'Roland is very well known in the area, and we know that many of these children have parents who abandoned them because they knew Roland would find ways, through people like you, to give them a better life.'

I tried to stop him there, but he continued.

'This is not necessarily my point of view,' he said, 'but it is the UN's stand on the issue.' He said that Roland had approached them for financial assistance but that the UN saw his efforts as destroying the fragile structure of the Cambodian extended family system. They had tried to tell him that when families saw he could take better care of their children than they could, he would find hundreds on his doorstep looking for a better life.

I was quite depressed by what Roland was up against. I couldn't help thinking there should be more Rolands in the world and fewer United Nations High Commissioner for Refugees employees with their 'official opinions' formed in a building in New York.

I had been a long-time supporter of the concept of the UN but then I went to Cambodia and saw its operations on the ground. There is no doubt that the UN helped make the elections successful, but there were many destructive aspects of its presence while I was there.

General Sanderson, the Australian who headed the United Nations Transitional Authority in Cambodia, was capable, respected and liked, but his task was colossal. No matter how professional he was, he would have been heavily criticised for every mistake made by individual UN soldiers.

It had been suggested that short orientation courses be held for the troops to ensure they understood local customs and traditions before they arrived. However, this never moved beyond the agreement that it was a good idea.

To be fair, pouring 20,000 troops from 100 different countries into a country not much bigger than Tasmania, already set the stage for serious problems. HIV/AIDS and other sexual diseases were rampant while the troops were there, and the prostitutes who serviced them were left in a pathetic situation after they had gone.

Traffic accidents escalated. UN soldiers involved in them didn't seem to understand that financial settlement had to be swift so that any bodies could be cremated within twenty-four hours. This was necessary due to the Cambodian heat, which led to rapid decomposition.

Many UN troops smuggled out priceless stone and bronze artefacts they came across in the fields while performing de-mining exercises. A friend in Bangkok with an antique shop told me that one of her regular clients came in every month with statues taken from the Cambodian countryside.

To make matters worse, the UN paid unrealistic prices for everything from house rentals to vehicles, food and clothing. These things then soared beyond the reach of the average Cambodian. A UN employee received something in the vicinity of US$145 per day allowance aside from their salaries. Young Cambodian men found it very hard to watch as their lovely young women chased after the UN soldiers, who could offer them so much more than they ever could.

For some reason unfathomable to a mere civilian like myself, the UN arranged to release many prisoners from jail. Street crime in the cities escalated to the point that Cambodians were far more afraid to venture out at night than they had been before the UN peacekeeping force came.

Also, there were mixed feelings about the repatriation program to send Cambodians home from Thai refugee camps. Many of them didn't want to go. Not much thought had been given to how a family who had lived in a refugee camp for thirteen years was going to manage working on a farm when some of them had never seen a buffalo, or grown rice, which in the camps had been delivered in bags to their doorstep. Much of the land that was earmarked for them on their return had not been cleared of mines and new plans had to be made at the last minute.

But from people I spoke to in Ampil, the overriding fear was that returnees would be despised for having fled the country when other Cambodians were trapped and had to stay throughout the killing fields and Vietnamese foreign occupation. They thought they would be branded as cowardly and that others would find ways to punish them. They also said that the money and housing materials donated to them by the UN would cause immense resentment towards them by the other farmers and villagers with whom they were supposed to integrate, and who were not going to get anything for all they had suffered from remaining in Cambodia.

Of course, I heard of good UN commanders, and high-up ones too, who felt fury and real grief about all the problems that were brought to their attention. But by the time most of the serious problems were recognised, it was too late for them to be fixed.

Cambodia loses again.

⌒

I started taking Polaroid photos of the children in the orphanage and preparing short biographies describing what they remembered of their lives.

'I don't have any memory of family life.'

'My parents starved to death in the jungle before they reached the refugee camp.'

'My family packed up and left me when I was eleven, because I was crippled with polio and too difficult to take care of. Someone took me to the orphanage.'

'My father was killed by a landmine and my mother ran away.'

'My mother was killed by a landmine and my father ran away.'

'I escaped from a village where I was being used as a slave in the rice paddies after my parents died of TB.'

'I was stolen from my family's farm by soldiers when I was twelve and trained to kill by the army, before I escaped and was taken to the refugee camp.'

'I only remember being alone, until an old soldier found me in the jungle and carried me to the refugee camp. But he had to go back and fight so he put me in the orphanage.'

'I got lost during a battle in the jungle when my mother and father were trying to escape from the Vietnamese and I couldn't find them. I ate leaves from trees until I ran into some other Cambodians who took me with them. But when we reached the camps, they couldn't keep me with their family and put me in the orphanage there. I want to try to find my family but don't know where they are.'

'Only my grandmother was alive when the Vietnamese came and she is too old to take care of me, so she put me in the orphanage.'

'I hid when the Vietnamese came to our village, and they beheaded my father and cut my mother's throat. I ran away with my sisters but we got lost, and when I was found and taken to the refugee camp, I couldn't find them.'

The tragic litanies continued all day as one child after another sat in a chair next to the interpreter. What astounded me was the matter-of-fact way these relatively small children told their stories, hopped off the chair and went to join their friends to play. These tragedies were all they had ever known and all that anyone they knew had ever known. I was deeply affected listening to these children tell of how they had suffered, with a type of courage and acceptance that no child on this earth should have to display.

Some did cry when asked questions and others just refused to answer, no matter how gently I asked them. I later learned that many of the children were petrified by 'interview' situations, as often in the past giving a wrong answer had meant cruel punishment. Just giving their ages was agonising for them. Even the older ones were not sure of their correct ages. Some felt if they were thought to be too young they would be sent somewhere else and if they were thought to be too old they would be turned away and have to take care of themselves.

It was heartrending when a lot of them told me they had no memory of any family life at all, and could only remember being alone, until they came to the refugee camp. Many of them had never known a mother's or father's kisses or caresses, strength and protection.

I couldn't begin to imagine the mental scars of children who carry with them every day scenes of death, torture, starvation, disease, and running for their lives, with what was left of their families, through countryside filled with mines, never knowing where they would sleep or where they would find food. But this was normal for refugee children from any country, who have been confronted with armed conflict.

These innocent children had lost the essence of who they were, and of what they might aspire to be. I asked them what they wanted to be when they grew up, and they couldn't see further than the world they knew, the inhabitants of which were soldiers, military police or drivers if they were men, or seamstresses and cooks if they were women. I knew enough to realise that the real futures for these children would probably be as beggars, thieves, prostitutes or servants.

⟳

I tried to cheer myself up by making a game of taking their photos, and slowly they began to accept me. To them I was a magic lady: I just pressed a button, there was a lightning flash and in a few seconds something spat out the bottom of my small black box, something in which their faces slowly appeared.

I told them I could teach them to be magicians too. Through the translator, I said that they musn't look away from their photos or they wouldn't come out, because it was their eyes that were developing the photos.

Then they were three deep around me waiting for their turn and you could have heard a pin drop. After I had shared my magic with them I was definitely in. I couldn't move from then on without half a dozen of them tagging along holding my hand or grabbing hold of my skirt.

Some of the little ones squeezed the flaps of fat under my armpits, enjoying the experience far more than I did. The older girls, in particular, became very adventurous. They fought to brush my hair, intrigued by its redness and finer texture compared with their thick, glossy black tresses. They were giggling and whispering behind their hands, trying to see how far they could go.

Then they made me lie down so that they could massage me. What they really wanted was to make sure that I had all the same bits and pieces they did. I let them explore my vast territory as I lay flat on a mat on one of the girl's beds, with one girl on each arm and leg, and two more on my back and buttocks. (In Cambodia a body massage is an everyday thing. Husbands and wives, brothers and sisters give them to each other, as do friends in the workplace. Once I saw it was a public thing and culturally very acceptable, I relaxed, and enjoyed a massage whenever the children offered one.)

'I see you've won their trust; I knew you would. Welcome to the club,' Roland said as he popped his head into the dormitory. We both knew without further conversation that there was now a bond between us through the children. When he had to leave, the children and staff were visibly upset. It was as though he took with him their light of hope, and courage to go on.

⟿

I was secretly happy to have the orphans to myself for the next week. I had more than twenty beautiful children all fighting to call me 'mother'.

To be exact, they had decided to call me 'Madai Thom Thom', which in Khmer means 'Big Big Mother'. I would have settled for just one 'Big'.

I never had to rely on an alarm clock. Just after dawn a group of children would come in to wake me up, wait for me while I dressed and walk with me to breakfast. The children would eat *bor bor*, a rice gruel made with salt and scraps of dried fish. I attempted to eat it, but usually ended up having a banana and a muesli bar I would try to eat without the children seeing as I didn't have enough to share.

Every day I saw Lisa in the faces of the children in the orphanage and the village. I only went to the market to help buy food once, because so many people there thrust their babies at me. None of them asked for money; they just wanted their babies to have a better life. I found it all too much.

With the stories the children were telling me every day and all the poverty around me, I started to have bad dreams. I hadn't suffered from them in the 1970s when people were actually worse off. But here in Ampil, I was living among them, not in a nice embassy apartment with air conditioning and a maid.

But for every down there was an up. I remember the time little Pros jumped up on my lap, coyly pulled the top of my blouse open and peered with wonder inside. Whatever he saw must have mightily impressed him as he scurried off shouting something in Khmer that made all the other small children line up in front of me for their turn.

Each day I could feel the children coming to adore me. Slowly but surely, I could feel the old wounds inside me healing.

⌒

The following days were full of many other new images and experiences, some of them hilarious. I was fast learning that Cambodia could make you laugh and cry within the same hour.

One unnerving, definitely unfunny, thing was the 5.00 p.m. explosion of all landmines detected on a particular day. The UN policy was not to explode each mine as it was detected, as that would have scared too many people too often. So they scared just about everybody half to death with one almighty deafening blast.

One morning I heard music and saw a happy crowd marching towards the Indian UN headquarters. A few of the children and I joined the little procession.

I couldn't believe my ears when I was told what was going on. A few days before, a Cambodian soldier the Indian UN was training made a mistake during a de-mining exercise and lost his eye. The UN took him to the clinic and paid him compensation, and he and his family were thanking them with the music and parade, paid for out of the money he was awarded. He was thankful to them, saying he could still see out of his other eye, and would never have been able to earn that much money in his life. He even asked them how much the UN would pay for the loss of a hand or leg! The UN had a sliding-fee scale for compensation to de-miners for loss of body parts. But I couldn't help thinking about the thousands of villagers who were maimed and killed, and who were not beneficiaries of the UN trainee scheme.

I knew, too, I could never tell my animal-loving friends at home how long it took an elephant to die when it stepped on a landmine. I was told by soldiers that usually the mine itself would not actually kill it, but would bring it to the ground. Once down the elephant could not get up with an injury such as a blown-off hoof, so it was the prey of other wild animals, that would slowly eat it while it was still alive.

A soldier told me that the landmines exploding all over the country, either by accident or through de-mining services, also affected the country's birdlife. Many species of birds unique to Cambodia had stopped breeding altogether. The blasts had frightened them so much the males were no longer capable of playing their part in reproduction.

But landmines don't just kill people and animals: they also kill art and culture. The glorious Cambodian silk sarongs traditionally worn by both men and women were for centuries woven by hand. Their designs were handed down from mother to daughter. The silk was dyed with natural juices from leaves and berries once plentiful in the jungles, and the fabric's vibrant hues of red, blue, green and yellow were what made it typically Cambodian. But now the villagers were too scared to venture into the jungles to gather the leaves and berries. Too many of them had been killed and maimed by landmines.

One night there was a party in the village, and Som Kiat, my trusty bodyguard, assigned by Roland, asked if I would like to go. He and I danced together in a clearing where the villagers played their motley collection of musical instruments. The crowd whooped with glee and shouted encouragement as we did the traditional butterfly dance together.

My life was completely in Som Kiat's hands as I followed him home in the dark along a pathway from the village. He walked ahead of me and lit each step I took with his torch. I never felt afraid when he was around.

There were many contingents of UN soldiers around Ampil and some of them became my friends. They had dozens of stories of danger. One told me that a UN soldier was held up at gunpoint on a provincial road by bandits who wanted to steal his brand-new Land Rover. They made him get out and lie face down on the side of the road. He could hear a lot of banging and noise, and after a few minutes the bandits came back. Through sign language they made it clear they didn't know how to drive and asked him to give them a lesson! When they got the hang of it, they let him out of the car, waved him a friendly goodbye and lurched off having a grand time!

Another time a UN car was stolen. Its owner, with a machine gun pointing at him, told the bandits that they could have the car, but asked if they could drop him off near headquarters, because he was late for a meeting. And they did!

One day we had to take a little girl with malaria, whose name I never discovered, to a clinic some miles away from the orphanage. It was clean but desperately needed more drugs and staff. The sick were lying listlessly on mats on wooden beds and were being treated by a Cambodian doctor who had been trained in China. His English was quite impressive and he gave me a tour of the clinic.

I will always remember the sight of a young man sleeping with his young son in the crook of his arm. They were both only semiconscious and the man was deliriously mumbling gibberish. Next to them on the bed lay a simple black headband. I asked who had shared the bed with them.

The doctor said: 'That was the man's wife and boy's mother. They were admitted together with malaria. The woman died last night. We will have to tell them when they recover, if they do, that she is dead.'

I have been haunted for years by the image of them waking to see that all they had left of her was that one black headband.

One particular day as I drove along the dusty potholed road to the UN headquarters, I was at a loss to understand the affinity I felt with the country. I slowed down to pick up all kinds of passengers along the way; charred stumps of trees upturned by landmines were dotted starkly against late afternoon skies. Then a bird of a brilliant blue flew across my path, close to the windscreen, almost in greeting. I had never seen such a bright blue, even in a painting. It was like I was seeing everything in life more clearly.

My mind was in overdrive during these days in Ampil. Each night in bed I would review all that had happened that day. So many stories and images crowded my mind, like mosquitoes buzzing around an electric light bulb. They hovered around my brain all night, waiting to be filed away as part of my memories of the poor, unforgettable village of Ampil.

⌒

On my last morning there was great excitement and activity in the kitchen. The older children had gone to the market at dawn to be sure to get the finest pig's head they had, to be served in my honour at my farewell lunch. I could hardly wait.

I watched as the pig's head was given a perfunctory wash in some dubious dark-brown water in a bucket. It was dunked a couple of times, and then placed in boiling water in the huge tin cooking pot on the wood-fired stove. The head went in complete with long, thick bristles, eyes, tongue, the works. I remember wishing that someone would clean the crunchy balls of wax out of the pig's ears while it was being washed, but alas, no.

Vegetables of every kind, shape and colour were added to the pot, and someone was always on duty to keep the fire going and the pot stirred. Children kept going into the kitchen to smell the pig soup, which they were looking forward to with great relish. I was glad *they* were hungry.

I was served first, at the wooden table with a cheap plastic tablecloth they used only for guests. I smiled wanly as I accepted a full plate of soup and a big bowl of steamed rice. I pretended to be ravenous but stirred the soup carefully before taking my first mouthful. I was checking to make sure that my first bite was not an eyeball. But then I remembered my hateful meal of monkey brains years before, and comforted myself with the knowledge that at least the pig was dead before I started eating it.

It was actually quite delicious, although I did have to fish out a few prickly bristles and yellow teeth. The pot was scraped clean.

Some of the children came with me to my room to watch me pack. They lined up in a guard of honour in order of height to kiss me goodbye. Everyone was sad.

I told them in English, through the translator, that this was the first of many trips I would make, and that I loved them and would be back soon. I could see from their expressions that they didn't believe a word of it.

I was still crying when I reached the border of Thailand some hours later.

⌒

Once at the border, though, I had other things to occupy my mind. Som Kiat and my translator had to explain to the Thai border guard why I didn't have a visa to get into Cambodia or a visa to re-enter Thailand. I did my best to look inconspicuous every time the border guard looked over at me.

There was a lot of gesticulating and head shaking. The main problem was that they wouldn't let the Cambodian translator over the border into Thailand. We had to drive to a nearby village to get permission from the owner of the car for me to drive into Thailand alone; there someone would collect the car and drive it back to the village.

I said goodbye to Som Kiat and the translator, and continued into Surin, where I caught the night train to Bangkok. I had just got comfortable in a sleeper when I heard what the Thai woman in the bunk next to mine was asking the conductor. 'Could you find me another bunk away from the very smelly foreigner?' she was asking in a disgusted tone.

I hadn't bathed properly for days. The water in Roland's shack was downright scary. It was stored in a huge plastic rubbish tin, was dark brown and had 'thingies' swimming around in it. To bathe, you just scooped it up in a plastic dipper and tossed it over your head until you thought you were clean. I had brought lots of expensive perfume with me and just hoped that it might mask my body odour. However, my fellow passengers were obviously unimpressed with my personal hygiene. I chuckled to myself before I fell asleep, vowing that the bubble bath I would have the next day would be long and hot enough to be recorded in the *Guinness Book of Records*.

⌒

As I slept on the flight from Bangkok to Sydney, I dreamt of black eyes, brown skin, brilliant-blue birds, green jungles, carved grey temple stones, landmine signs, a pig's head, potholed roads and the childrens' sad stories. I also dreamt of how it felt to hold their cool, small hands in mine as they walked me back to my thatched shack after dinner.

Had it only been fourteen days I had spent with the children? It felt like a lifetime. I knew that it would take a real effort to fit back into a modern Western community.

⌒

So I expected to be depressed when I returned. This was largely due to missing the children. But there were other things too. I had diarrhoea in the middle of the night and strange rashes were appearing on my body. I couldn't sleep, and was irritable and unsociable. I was tired and refused invitations from friends. I was off sex altogether and this was a real worry. This is it, I thought, the dreaded menopause. After at least three months of putting up with all these weird symptoms I went to the doctor to have my blood tested.

'While you are taking blood, perhaps you should do other tests as I was living in a remote jungle area in Cambodia a few months ago,' I suggested.

A couple of days later the doctor asked me to come in for the results. He told me I was far from being menopausal, but that there was an enormous number of parasites in my blood. He said I would have to take in some stool samples to the Tropical Diseases Centre at Royal North Shore Hospital as soon as possible. He said he had never seen a blood count like mine in his entire career.

I wasted no time in getting my little gifts ready, and took myself to the Tropical Diseases Centre. As I stood there with the jar in my hand, a doctor came towards me rubbing his hands in anticipation. 'We are very interested in what your problem might be, Ms Cox,' he said, taking my stool samples. 'We will call you as soon as we know what you've got and how to treat it.'

The parasites were diagnosed as *strongeloides*, which can be fatal if not treated in time. The doctor told me the most common way of contracting this was through the feet and warned me against going barefoot in Cambodia again. They hadn't had a case of this particular parasite since 1950!

I was given a prescription, and directions to place an old dinner plate in the toilet so that I could collect the worm with a fork that looked like a small backscratcher, as they wanted me to take it to them for further testing. I took the medicine and spent two days following these instructions, but to no avail. I called the centre to say that I hadn't been able to find anything, so they gave me another, stronger prescription.

I took it into the chemist's shop close to Chase Manhattan, where many of my colleagues also went. I stood there in my navy-blue suit complete with padded shoulders and gold braid, very high-heeled shoes and matching blue stockings. As I chatted with some friends from the bank, the chemist, also a friend, called out loudly: 'Geraldine love, can you come back for this tomorrow? I have to get the prescription filled from a vet. It's what they give sheep and cows on farms.'

Well, you've never seen a shop empty so fast. Everyone took a step back from me and rushed out.

'Thanks a lot,' I said to the chemist. 'Could you have said that any louder? Now it will be all over the bank that I've got the pox or something.'

'Sorry, I didn't realise there were so many people you knew in here. Come back tomorrow and I'll have the pills ready for you,' the chemist said.

The next morning I collected the pills, which were about as big as the palm of my hand and had to be chopped up with a knife and fork. (I could just imagine a farmer opening a cow's mouth, pulling its tongue out and shoving the pill to the back of its throat.) I took them just before going to sleep and was woken early in the morning with violent stomach pain. If childbirth's anything like this you can have it, I thought, as I scrambled for the toilet. What resulted was the passing of a worm about a foot long and as thick as a large knitting needle. The thing was almost human; I felt like putting a bonnet on it and giving it a name!

Exhausted, I went back to bed and fell immediately into the best sleep I had had for months. I proudly deposited what I had called 'Bruce' with the doctors at the Tropical Diseases Centre, who were so delighted I was afraid they were going to burst into song.

What a relief! I could feel my energy levels rise almost overnight. I promised myself never to walk without shoes in Cambodia again.

⌒

Once my health problems were solved I was so fired up with enthusiasm I had to be restrained from going ahead with scatterbrained ideas. One was to accept the offer of some local farmers to donate their rusting farm tractors and other machinery to the orphanage. I even contacted friends in the Australian army to see if I could get this equipment shipped on military transport that I knew went to Cambodia from time to time. I never gave a thought to how it would be serviced and maintained if by some miracle it did arrive there.

However, another idea I had was to approach the Rockefeller Foundation for funds to build an airstrip near Ampil so that supplies could be sent in to the children. I had, quite by accident, read a file about the foundation. It had been set up to fund worldwide projects for agriculture, health, the arts and humanitarian causes, as well as working towards the abolition of weapons of mass destruction. The file explained how to apply for funding from the foundation by making proposals through the Chase International grant system. I had no idea how crazy my airstrip plan was; building an airport in such a remote area was not a practical project!

Nonetheless, a grant that I applied for through the Chase Foundation, the philanthropic arm of the Rockefeller Foundation, for a kick-off donation of US$15,000 was approved. As far as the children were concerned it might as well have been US$1 million; it turned their lives around.

Before they received the money, though, Chase Manhattan's accountant asked me to explain how the money would reach the children. 'Your money's quite safe,' I started out carefully. I told him that it would go into the foundation's bank account in Sydney. Then a cheque for US dollars would be sent via the diplomatic bag in Canberra to the Australian embassy in Phnom Penh, where it would be deposited into Princess Marie's account with the Indo-Suez Bank. He looked quite satisfied with my explanation, thus far, but he didn't know what was coming. I informed him that an eighteen-year-old translator would withdraw the cash, and stick it in his shoes and socks before he hitched a ride to Battambang, from where he would hire a taxi to Sisophon. There it would be given to the orphanage cook. When it was dark she would bury it in the ground in three or four different places, and before she went to bed each night she'd dig up what she needed to go to the market the next day. I can still see the look on the accountant's face.

'There are no telegraphic transfer facilities in Cambodia yet, and there are no banks at all in Sisophon,' I explained. 'But so far we haven't lost a cent.'

The fact is that without this initial injection of funds the orphanage never would have got off the ground. And for the next five years Chase Manhattan continued to approve grants for special projects to help the children.

Promised Return

Sisophon, February 1994

I visited Cambodia again six months later. This time the children had been moved from Ampil, where the unrest between the government soldiers and the Khmer Rouge was increasing alarmingly. They were now in the small city of Sisophon, also in the province of Oddar Meancheay. Just weeks before, Roland had written to tell me the details of the inhuman death of one of the orphanage boys, thirteen-year-old Ong Samrith.

The Cambodian woman Princess Marie had put in charge of the orphanage decided to move all the children to the relative safety of the pagoda where the local monks lived. She left Samrith and Vichet, Samrith's seventeen-year-old brother, behind to take care of the fruit and vegetables they were growing and guard their other meagre belongings.

Two Khmer Rouge soldiers strolled up the path to the orphanage one day, eating some of the fruit. They didn't seem threatening, so Samrith walked out and asked them not to take their food. Still eating, one soldier lifted his machine gun and casually sprayed Samrith with bullets.

Vichet peeped through a window and saw the two soldiers sit down, and calmly hack off his younger brother's limbs and head. They also ripped him open to remove his liver, which they ate with great gusto, squatting at the side of the body. (Ancient Khmer tradition has it that if you eat the liver of your enemy you will be rewarded with his strength and courage.)

Vichet ran to the children and monks, asking them to help carry his brother to be cremated. These small children, as young as four years old, had to carry what was left of Samrith, in many plastic bags, back to the pagoda.

Roland's letter said that Vichet was not recovering. He blamed himself for not going to his younger brother's aid, and was suffering from intense guilt. He had withdrawn from the rest of the orphans, most of whom he had known all his life. He didn't join in games, and often took his meals away from the dining area and sat alone to eat. He felt so unworthy.

Roland was ready to kill someone. He told me he had posted a reward for anyone who could bring him the head of either of the soldiers who had committed this heinous crime. Apparently they were known in the area. I knew Roland well enough to believe that he would do the deed himself if he got the chance.

When I heard this devastating news I applied for more leave from the bank and took off again for the wilds of Cambodia. I flew into Phnom Penh, then took a domestic flight to Battambang, and had a gut-wrenching three-hour drive on bad roads to Sisophon.

Before planning the road trip from Battambang to Sisophon I had asked for a security briefing at the Australian embassy, and they advised me against making the trip. It was suggested that if I was determined to go, I take with me two or three truckloads of soldiers, especially as I was travelling with cartons of supplies for the children and would therefore be a target. (They also advised that I should not depart before 6.00 a.m.; often fresh mines were laid along the sides of the road overnight, but by that time the road would have been well travelled, and any mines detected 'one way or another'!)

Prince Ranariddh provided armed bodyguards in two pick-up trucks, one in front of and one behind the car I was to travel in, complete with rocket launchers fitted into their roofs. After loading all the cartons there wasn't enough room for me in the car, so I ended up riding in the front seat of the first 'shotgun' car. In theory I was sitting in the death seat all the way. Apart from this I felt like I was in a kitchen blender for the two hours of the trip. To protect my breasts from flying all over the place I had to sit with my arms folded tight under them.

⟼

Sisophon had even less to offer the children than Ampil. They were living in an abandoned garage left behind by the departing UN troops, open on three sides with just blue plastic tent flaps nailed up to protect them from the elements. Worse than this it didn't appear that they would be much safer from the Khmer Rouge.

I was part of the group in this open garage for nine days, and at night I was as afraid as they were when heavy fighting could be heard just a couple of hundred metres from us. Toddlers would whimper, and the older ones lay rigid with terror in their beds. We were afraid that if we made a noise the soldiers would come and kill us.

They didn't need a reason to kill; they just wanted to assert themselves. One day when I went into a nearby village, I found that its small marketplace had been completely burned down in the night, just as a reminder that the Khmer Rouge was close by and had power over the area.

Landmines were just as serious a problem in Sisophon as they had been in Ampil. Every day there were reports of landmine accidents and many cases were never reported. This was because there was nothing left of some of the bodies. They were shredded, like human confetti, by a mine designed specifically to shoot out nails at over 300 kilometres per hour from the ground to a height of one metre.

One day I was in the countryside around Sisophon picking up recently orphaned children to join our group. On the way into the village I saw a little girl of about four years old, tied up to a tree on a chain, crying. I was enraged at this cruelty and got out of the car to see if I could speak to her parents. The neighbours told me with extremely clear sign language that the mother had gone to the market for food and couldn't take her daughter with her, as she needed her hands free to carry the shopping. This was the only way she could protect her from wandering off the road into the minefields.

I got back into the car wiser but sadder.

Amid all this insecurity and madness, every evening at sunset Ong Vichet lit a stick of incense for his brother, Samrith.

⌒

On a lighter note, somehow the girls had been able to prepare a bed for me in the garage with a hard mattress they had acquired from somewhere. Each night the mosquito net was tied up for me and my sheets turned back lovingly. The Hilton could not have taken more care.

On more than one morning I awoke to find myself staring eyeball to eyeball with a duck that had adopted me and chose to sleep next to my pillow. I know I've had many strange bedfellows in my life, but the duck was a hard act to follow. Still, the duck was by no means the *worst* bedfellow. There are few things worse than being in complete darkness and knowing there is a cockroach in your bed trying to get out.

Since those days in Sisophon I never get into a clean bed without part of me registering how comfortable I feel, compared to how I felt on those dark, scary nights in Sisophon with a duck on top of the bed, cockroaches in it, and the Khmer Rouge firing just metres away.

I went every day with the children to the river where they bathed. It was the fun part of their day. They all immersed themselves and jumped from the top of the bridge into the murky waters, and tried to coax me in. But I could see the water buffalo shit, with swarms of flies happily hovering over it, as it made its way downstream towards where the children were washing themselves. The closest I got to swimming was to stand up to my ankles with my thongs on while I dried off the small ones with a kroma when they came out. I could still remember 'Bruce' vividly.

⌒

I was there when more children were brought to us. Some were allowed to join us and some were sent away. I watched one day as the woman put in charge of the children by Princess Marie talked to a wizened old lady who held the hand of a boy of around eleven years old. He was very thin and sick, constantly coughing up blood and spitting it on the ground.

Even someone like me with no medical training could see he was in the advanced stage of tuberculosis.

The two women talked together for a while and then the old lady just turned and walked away, taking the child with her. None of the children had been inoculated against any disease and if just one child with TB began eating and sleeping with us we would soon have a raging epidemic on our hands.

I wondered where the old woman would turn for help. If the dangerous living conditions we were in looked good to her, I hated to think where and how she lived.

There were eighteen more children we did accept during my nine days in Sisophon. I hid my pity as I wrote down their heartbreaking stories for their files.

All these children were born in a country at war, and so were many of their dead parents who were born after 1970. They had no experience of what life could be like without foreign invasion; bombs, soldiers, guns, tanks, landmines, and having to flee their homes in only the clothes on their backs, and with what they could carry.

They suffered deep anxiety about their lives, constantly. They distrusted just about everybody, and had pitifully low expectations for their future. They didn't have any desires, beyond wanting to know where their next meal was coming from.

Every one suffered some kind of post-traumatic stress syndrome. Symptoms were easy to identify, ranging from bed-wetting to difficulty in concentrating. It's a wicked thing to see distrust in the eyes of a three-year-old child. It distressed me when walking through the dorms at night to see some of them crying in their sleep. I knew their files intimately, and what grief they were reliving in their dreams.

Boys as young as eight and nine told me stories of being used as slaves in their villages after their parents had died, working for only a bowl of rice. Other boys were forced to climb mountains to carry down hidden guns for soldiers who didn't want to risk the minefields. These boys made it but many of their young friends didn't.

Also, in Cambodia, and many other developing countries, soldiers don't wear dogtags and telegrams are never sent to inform families of their losses. The dead are simply burnt at the end of each fighting day. Most often mothers, wives and children wait for years, hoping their men will return, never really knowing if they are dead, disabled or have abandoned them.

To any child, the sight of a soldier with a gun is a sight to fear, and a landmine can kill you or reduce you to being a beggar, regardless of who laid it. Children don't understand which side is fighting for or against them, or even why there is fighting in the first place. They only understand that they could die, be orphaned or maimed.

In developed countries, children who have seen acts of brutality and killings, receive, as is their right, months of professional counselling to help them put the memories behind them, and become well-adjusted adults, who fall in love, have babies and otherwise go on to be functioning members of society. This is not so in countries at war like Cambodia, Rwanda, Bosnia, Angola, Somalia and Afghanistan. The children's horrific memories seem to rob them of their souls, preventing them from reacting normally to real-life situations as they mature. How could they *not* be filled with fear, hatred, suspicion and despair, and sometimes place little value on human life?

I noticed also that often the children had scant respect for the few belongings they did have. When I chided them for this I got the impression they felt nothing was going to be theirs forever. Everything had been taken away from their parents and grandparents, or destroyed at some time or another, during the Vietnam War, the carpet bombing by America or the desecration and slaughter carried out by Pol Pot and the Vietnamese-led government that occupied Cambodia from 1979 to 1989.

I believe much of the present sad situation in Cambodia, and other war-torn countries, is due to the fact that many of the country's adults, from all walks of life, have grown up in this very same environment of fear and uncertainty. Thousands of children were abandoned in orphanages or inside refugee camps in Thailand, to which their families had fled either from Pol Pot and his ruthless genocide program or from Vietnamese-led 'liberation'. Even living in 'freedom' in Thailand, they were not safe from bomb attacks, and unfriendly Thai villagers who thought they threatened their own fragile livelihoods. Children living under such conditions usually don't grow up to be very sensitive adults.

In an attempt to try to understand more of what my kids had been through, I asked them to draw pictures of their saddest and happiest memories. One ten-year-old girl, Phon Thay, was very worried by this request, saying she didn't have a happy memory. I fought back tears at the sight of her face.

As was the case in Ampil, the children did not attend school. There was no money to pay teachers or make uniforms, and we knew they were not staying there permanently. Without school many of the children spent the days just staring into space or playing games. The favourite game was 'thong', where a child placed a beer bottle cap on the ground and then groups of them would try to throw their rubber thongs as closely as possible to hit it.

Many children from troubled countries are not motivated to study hard; they truly believe their lives will be short and can't see the use of learning anything. They have often watched their families die in the camps, from untreated TB, malaria, cancer, or unknown causes.

On the bright side, Roland called from Thailand, where he was then the Cambodian ambassador, to say that two scholarships were available in the sculpture department of a university there. He asked me to send him two boys from the orphanage. I gave the older boys a simple drawing test, and sent the two most likely students to Thailand. Their names were Tek Lak and Eng Sophea and they were both around eighteen years old at the time. They had never before had paints or papers to try their hand at art.

Within weeks Roland called to tell me that the sculpture teacher had said that these two orphaned peasant boys were born sculptors. He believed their ancestors must have been among the grand artisans who carved Angkor Wat, they were so good. I was so proud of them I could have burst! Who knows? All over Cambodia there could be disadvantaged children who are, with the right opportunities, potential Mozarts, Rembrandts, and even Einsteins! Einstein was himself a poor refugee as a child.

There were other little rays of sunshine – like when six-year-old Phon

Chaab was asked what he wanted to do when he grew up. After much pondering, he slapped his knee and, with great certainty, declared that he wanted to be the person in charge of feeding all the elephants of Cambodia. (I didn't have the heart to tell him that landmines had killed most of his country's proud elephants.) And there was Roi Sophal, fifteen, who, although her first desire was for a husband, decided that, on second thoughts, she would prefer to have a sewing machine. This was because if she married, her husband would probably be a soldier and she would never know if he was coming back to her. But with her sewing machine she could earn an honest living, and, what's more, she would always know where it was!

⟞⟶

I knew it was time for me to think about going back to Sydney when I was taking an old issue of *Time* or *Newsweek* with me to read in the latrine! The putrid odour that had almost knocked me over on the first day was barely noticeable after a week. I really knew I should be heading back when I started to spit on the ground along with the children! Also, I was aware that if I wanted to help the children I could do it best by raising money for them in Australia.

I left some money for supplies to last them until their next move, to the city of Battambang, where it was expected they would be better housed and much safer. Again, I made my promise to return, facing disbelieving expressions, as they knew that conditions in Sisophon were bad enough to scare anyone off. I began my bumpy journey back to Battambang to catch a flight to Phnom Penh.

On the way the driver stopped for lunch at his favourite noodle restaurant. I ordered some grilled fish that they promised me was fresh, and made my way to the toilet at the back of the shop. Most rural toilets in Cambodia have no flushing system, and if there is an Asian-style toilet to squat over, 'flushing' is done by filling a small plastic dipper with water from a concrete tank, which has been filled by hand with buckets of water from the local river.

As I stood up to fill the dipper with water, a hand reached into the tank, which I saw extended through into the kitchen. Then a large fish was caught in a net and yanked out. My 'fish of the day' had been swimming contentedly in the water people used for washing their hands and flushing the toilet.

I knew that no-one was going to believe me at home when I told them this story. I must say, the fish was delicious, even though I knew where it had been before it was served to me on a plate. (I admit that I did try to kill any germs by adding lots of chilies.)

In Battambang I boarded a 1956 Russian-built plane with no little trepidation. This only increased when I noticed that the Russian pilot stumbling down the aisle to the cockpit was clearly drunk. Many of the seat belts didn't work and neither did the air conditioning. Everyone was fanning themselves so vigorously with fans or their boarding passes that it would almost have been possible for the plane to take off without the services of the drunk captain.

I was beginning to think my chances might be better with the Khmer Rouge back in Sisophon!

⌒

Back in Phnom Penh there was only time for a quick lunch with Prince Ranariddh and Princess Marie, who were going to arrange the children's move first to Battambang, and then on to Phnom Penh when a more secure piece of land could be found for them. A bank account in the name of 'Princess Marie's Orphanage' had been opened into which the Chase Manhattan donation and other money that had been raised by my friends in Sydney would be deposited. I headed back once again to my boring job in Sydney, but I had a grateful heart. If I hadn't been working for the bank it would never have occurred to me to ask for money from their headquarters in New York.

But once I was in Australia it was even harder than before to keep from searching the newspapers for news of Cambodia and to keep my mind on my job. I had already been planning my next trip back before I had even unpacked.

⌒

I was able to return in April 1995. This time I could see huge improvements had taken place in Cambodia. For one, Phnom Penh's Pochentong Airport was unrecognisable; I thought I had landed in the wrong country. Although still small it was comparable with modern Asian airports. In a few years it would be classed as being of international standard. Also, the city had a commercial bustle I hadn't seen before. Shops were selling new cars and motorbikes. Some enterprising women had caught on to the Western concept of selling clothes in boutiques, instead of at the open-air market stalls. Many hotels were being built, obviously in preparation for an upsurge in tourism.

Princess Marie had found a safe place for the children thirteen kilometres from Phnom Penh, where they were housed in concrete military barracks on six hectares of land. She had also organised for a group of war widows to stay there and they earned a living weaving silk for export.

The princess had done all within her power as wife of the First Prime Minister to make life better for the children. The land itself had so much potential. All that was needed to develop it and repair the existing buildings was money. I knew I had a challenge ahead of me. But at least I could see for myself that the children were settled, and for the first time in their short lives, they were safe. They were taking great pleasure in attending a regular school for the first time, and were even planting flowers and fern trees in pots to make their new home beautiful.

The children adored Princess Marie. They knew she had stood by them during the days of Site B refugee camp, and had arranged the housing in Ampil and Sisophon, and temporary accommodation in Battambang in 1994. I once again stressed to the children that my commitment was real, by reminding them that this was the second time I had kept my promise to come back. I explained that in Australia we had organised a small charity to which people donated money towards the cost of their day-to-day expenses, and they thought this was remarkable.

I was enjoying adult company as well. There was a new orphanage 'mother', a woman in her late forties named Douch Touch who had a young daughter, Socheata, with her. Although she didn't speak English I knew that we would become great friends and we did. I called her Ming, meaning 'auntie', a term of endearment, even though I was a few years older than she was.

There was even a bit of the glamour of my old embassy days during this trip. Bill Hayden, the Governor-General of Australia, was paying an official visit to Cambodia, and the embassy had invited me to the reception at the Cambodiana Hotel. I am not a big drinker, but that night it was so hot I drank gin and tonics purely out of thirst. I ended up a little the worse for wear and gave my views on all and sundry to any Westerners unfortunate enough to be in the group I had cornered. No one is a pretty sight drunk, and although I was not *that* drunk, I was very self-opinionated. I made a few enemies that night, I believe!

When I flew back to Sydney after nearly three weeks in Cambodia, I felt much more at ease. This was because I was more confident about how the children were going to survive and because I knew that our foundation was slowly but steadily raising money through the efforts of friends in Sydney.

Fired and Fifty

Sydney, March 1994 – August 1995

My life consisted of one frantic week after another, as the executive assistant to the Chase Manhattan CEO in Australia. The pay was very good but they certainly got their pound of flesh. I pushed paper and people around from early on Monday mornings to late on Friday nights and rarely had the inclination or energy to socialise during the week. Weekends were taken up with shopping, housework, and what time I could spare for a frenzied workout in bed with my Polish boyfriend, Wojtek. He deserved a medal for putting up with my cantankerous moods during what was the closest I had come in years to a normal relationship with a man.

I had met Wojtek at what I'd like to think of as an upmarket singles club in Sydney. As usual my antennae were rearing to go, and I managed to sniff out the one and only not-born-in-Australia man in the room. I wasn't looking for anything more than a one-night stand, but I finally succumbed to Wojtek's persistent courting. He made many of my fantasies come true – from doing the vacuuming before I woke up on Sunday mornings, to turning up with the entire weekend's meals precooked to be served at indecent intervals with chilled champagne.

Any woman in her right mind would have accepted one of his many offers of marriage. He was a hard worker, sincere, generous, as faithful as a bloodhound, and devoted to doing whatever he could to make my life easier. And his prowess in bed for a man in his late fifties put men in their thirties to shame. He worked out regularly and his body was as hard as a rock. Everywhere.

But I felt smothered. He was so jealous and possessive he truly thought that any man left alone with me for a minute would want to make love to me. I should have been flattered by this, but it got to the point where he was convinced that I had seduced the teenage boy who came to fix my washing machine. I found it very irritating.

I enjoyed living alone and got Wojtek to agree to an arrangement where he picked me up on Fridays after work and spent the weekends with me until the appointed time for him to leave on Sunday night. I never saw him during the week.

Looking back, I treated him very badly, but I felt these were the restrictions I needed, and I never led him to believe that I would have a change of heart. He deserved a woman who was able to accept his complete love and attention and it wasn't me. I hope he has forgiven me.

⌒

When I was arranging a big party to celebrate my fiftieth birthday on 10 June I planned to do something a little bit off the wall. While deciding whom to invite I saw at a glance that I had far more women than men on my list. This would never do. In my experience, for any party to be a success, there have to be enough opposite hormones running around to keep up everyone's interest. Many of the male guests were gay men in longstanding relationships, and so were not in a position to keep my varied group of single women friends entertained in the way I needed them to be!

These fifteen women were a wonderful group of females over forty. They were attractive, well-groomed, intelligent, independent, interesting, witty and employed. Some were academics, businesswomen, self-employed; some were divorced, widowed, in between affairs or just happily single through choice. I was determined that they were going to have a bloody good time at my fiftieth.

But where was I going to find fifteen men who could match all my friends' qualities?

In the 'Singles Wanted' advertisements in the *Sydney Morning Herald* newspaper. Here Sydney's tall, short, fat, thin, young, old, neurotic, well adjusted, over- and under-sexed, and much more, wrote a few lines to describe what they wanted in a partner, and sat back waiting for the replies to flood in. I can still remember what I wrote: 'Wanted: Fifteen single men required on 10 June to provide injection of testosterone for elegant, harbourside, Formal 50th Champagne Birthday Dinner Party. Audition to be held at the Ritz Hotel at a time to be announced prior to the event. Employed, articulate applicants with wit, intelligence and class, please call for details.'

I was bowled over by the quality and quantity of messages I received on my answering machine. I stopped even playing them after they numbered 100. I narrowed down the field to twenty men I had spoken to on the telephone and by whose sense of humour, confidence or honesty I had been delighted. The deal was that they meet me, and about six of my close friends, at the Ritz Hotel a week before the party. If we liked them we would give them the address for the night itself.

Sandra was going to attend. This was by far the most outrageous thing she had ever done in her life, and she could hardly sleep waiting for the audition day to arrive.

What a raging success the audition was, too. I must admit I had been having a few misgivings about the whole plan, but that night we handed out printed invitations to a lawyer, a vet, a published poet, a musician, a taxi driver, an accountant, a clairvoyant, a self-employed businessman, a computer project manager, an artist, an investment banker, a plumber, the owner of a book store, a masseur and a fitness class instructor.

The only man who behaved badly was one who got really drunk and flirted with the waitress all night. Sandra was given the unenviable task of telling him he hadn't made the grade. He was still drinking when we were all leaving.

I gave the successful applicants a briefing. 'Look, guys,' I said, 'my eighty-year-old mother and some aged relatives will be there, and they will die with their legs in the air if they know where I got you all from. So when you are asked the inevitable question "And how do you know Geraldine?", you all say, "Oh, I met her at the Ritz at a cocktail party recently." And that's the truth. Deal?' That settled, I buried myself in plans for the party, and knew I was going to have a great success on my hands.

I was costing the night at somewhere between $2000 to $3000, not including my new cocktail suit with a black and gold lace jacket. It was a definite spanner in the works when my boss at Chase and I had a final showdown.

Our working relationship had never been made in heaven as he had inherited me when he was sent from New York four years before. And to be fair, although I considered myself a top-drawer personal assistant, the standard of my work dropped dramatically once the children came into my life. I wasn't really interested in it any longer and wasn't doing much to try to remedy this. After a long talk I walked out knowing that no matter how I interpreted what he had said, I was basically out of a job, although it was agreed I would stay on until a replacement was found.

Being fired days before my fiftieth birthday was some gift!

I told no-one in my family as I knew they would only worry. (But, like always, I called Trish, who was by my side immediately.) I pushed my looming unemployment to the back of my mind, promising myself that I would give it serious thought after my fiftieth.

⟜

The party was a raging success, with loving family and friends, dinner-suited old, present and could-be lovers all over the place and girlfriends flirting openly with very willing admirers. There was also scrumptious food and champagne flowing. I couldn't have asked for more.

The funniest thing was that my big mouth had caused me to tell my family about the singles ad, and all night they were accosting men they didn't know and asking them how they knew me. Each one replied as instructed, 'I met Geraldine at the Ritz Hotel at a cocktail party recently'. My mother and old aunts would reply by pointing at them, shrieking with laughter and saying, 'Oh, so you're one of the men who replied to Geraldine's ad in the singles column!'

If I had to do it all over again and spend that much money on my fiftieth, I would.

⌒

Several short-term and long-term love affairs resulted between the singles ad guys and my girlfriends, and I gained two close platonic friends, Paul, the clairvoyant, and Peter, a Swedish businessman. But with my new unemployed status just around the corner, I had no idea what I was going to do with my life. The rent on my much-loved apartment was far too high for me to stay there without a good income. I hated the thought of having to leave it.

I looked in the newspapers for jobs, but there was nothing. I faced the fact that I might have to go to the Commonwealth Employment Service, as I had nearly spent my final pay packet from Chase. I caught the bus to the nearest office, wearing dark glasses and a scarf, hoping I would not run into anybody I knew.

The interviewing officer was a woman of around twenty-five. She told me that as I was over fifty it was highly unlikely there would be any work for me. She advised me to go home and keep myself interested in some sort of hobby, and even asked me if I liked gardening!

I had to restrain myself from inflicting physical harm. She talked as though my life was over.

Little did I know what the fickle finger of fate had in store for me.

Yoth Riddth,
Man on the Moon

Sydney, September 1995 – March 1996

My involvement with Cambodian orphans was about to become the most important thing in my life. This was due to the entry into it of Yoth Riddth.

Princess Marie had sent me a message in August 1995 that one of the teenage boys in the orphanage was very ill, and needed so many blood transfusions that the Red Cross was refusing to give him any more. The doctors in Phnom Penh didn't know what was wrong with him, but he was clearly in danger. Could I do anything to help by getting him to Australia for diagnosis and treatment? She said she would arrange his passport, which would not be a simple matter. The orphans didn't possess such valuable documents, and passports cost several hundred dollars.

I wasn't even sure if I could wangle a medical visa for him. Embassies are careful about issuing visas for ill people in case they attempt to overstay them, using their health as a reason to remain indefinitely. An orphan with no familial ties to his country was an even greater risk. But I like a challenge, and I used all my contacts and filled in some forms. Much to my surprise, his visa was issued and he was on his way.

❧

Karen Soldatic was a young Sydney woman who taught English at the orphanage in time she had spare from her regular work as a language teacher in Phnom Penh. She was the one who had first brought Riddth's condition to Princess Marie's attention. During one of her weekends with the children, Karen had seen him languishing in his bed in the boys' dorm, barely able to speak, let alone get out of bed and feed himself. She took him to town by strapping him to her on the back of her moto, but couldn't find any doctor who could say what was wrong with him, except to confirm that he was in desperate, constant need of blood transfusions.

Karen took Riddth on, and became quite famous around town for picking up men in bars for no other reason than to coerce them into going with her and Riddth to the Red Cross Blood Centre to donate blood. In Cambodia you can't be given blood unless you turn up with someone willing to give their blood to the centre to replace what you have received! Unknown to Karen her nickname among Australian expats was the Vampire Lady. She was a particularly attractive woman, and it was easy to understand why so many men went off quite happily to be bled, with her hand gently, but firmly, propelling them through the gates of the blood centre.

Riddth came to depend upon her efforts to help him survive from one day to the next. If it hadn't been for Karen, no-one would have known how ill he was, and nothing would have been done to get him to Australia.

Karen even paid her own fare to Sydney to travel with Riddth, as he was far too sick to travel alone. I had no idea how I was going to raise the money for his airfare, though. Princess Marie had paid for his passport and Karen had paid for his visa, but there was nothing left for his ticket. Then Karen told me about an Australian man, Steven Briggs, who had offered to help after already giving over two pints of his blood to Riddth. At the time, Steven was in Phnom Penh working for Reuters as a television news cameraman. He was a damned fine one, too. He had won a Logie award for his coverage of the America's Cup race in 1983, and his peers in the media in Cambodia had high praise for his work. He thrust the money for Riddth's ticket into Karen's hands before she knew what was happening. I knew I was really going to like this guy if I ever got to meet him, and I wasn't wrong.

Even when I was so deeply involved in all the arrangements to get Riddth from Phnom Penh, I had no idea of how my life was about to change forever. I had thought that perhaps he needed an operation and that after a week or so in hospital I would be able to send him back to Cambodia, and that would be that. I would have done 'something nice'.

But there was something in particular that made me feel I had to help Riddth. On one of my visits to Cambodia in late 1994, I had been able to talk the local Telstra office into taking on one of the orphanage boys as a trainee. Riddth was the one selected for the job. The orphanage staff and I had left him in no doubt about what an opportunity this was for him and that we were relying on him to do his best. We drummed into him relentlessly that if he worked hard, maybe, just maybe, Telstra would give more of the children jobs. We laid it on fairly thick, the poor little bugger.

Then six months later, on my visit in April 1995, I found that Riddth had left Telstra. I tried to find out why, but there were so many versions of the story that I gave up. I was told he had reported sick so many times that Telstra became fed up, especially when their doctor couldn't find anything wrong with him.

I was furious. I dragged a translator with me to the orphanage to give Riddth hell. I told him he had let everyone down and ruined any future chance of others getting work at Telstra. I really let him have it. I remembered that he took all I was dishing out with his head hanging low and his eyes downcast. He didn't even try to defend himself.

Now I knew why he hadn't gone to work. He really was sick and no-one believed him because they could not diagnose his health problem.

I had treated him so harshly. I had to do something to make it up to him.

I think I fancied that others would see me as a modern-day Florence Nightingale when I helped Riddth. I was even secretly looking forward to playing the role.

On the day Riddth and Karen were to arrive, a friend drove me to the airport. It was early on a cold September morning. I remember that the wind was violently strong and I had difficulty walking against the gale into the airport building.

When the passengers emerged I recognised Karen first. Then I saw Riddth.

He was leaning weakly against her shoulder, trying hard to put his hands together in the traditional *wai*, the Cambodian greeting, bending low to me as a sign of respect. He almost fell and we got him into the car as quickly as possible. He was so exhausted after the long flight that when he backed into the car, we had to lift his lifeless legs in one by one. I was shocked into silence by his physical state and even wondered if he might die in the car before we got him home.

He was shivering with cold by the time we reached my apartment and I knew that buying him some warm clothes would be a must. I had booked him into the Royal North Shore Hospital for a checkup later that day, but at this moment he was in need of a hot bath, a sleep and a good meal.

At the hospital he looked so small and forlorn sitting there with people buzzing efficiently all around him. I could see his tired, intelligent eyes taking everything in with great interest. Just the cleanliness of the place would have been an eye opener for him after Cambodia.

Within twenty-four hours, after a barrage of tests, his disease was diagnosed by Dr David Ma, a highly respected and compassionate haematologist. Riddth had acquired aplastic anaemia, a life-threatening blood disorder that could only be arrested by a bone marrow transplant, preferably from a donor who was a close family member. The hospital translator explained all this to him in Khmer, but he shook his head sadly, saying, 'I'm an orphan, I have no living family. I'm all alone in the world.'

A course of Cyclosporin steroid treatment was ordered in the hope that the drugs would at least slow down the development of the disease. Then we went home together on the bus, as I didn't own a car. Riddth always loved these bus journeys that I found a real chore. As the weeks passed, he explained to me in his amazingly good English, 'Mum, they are so clean and comfortable and everyone can get a seat and they always come when the timetable says they will. We don't even have public buses in Cambodia. I love the buses, and the trains are even better!'

One of the most poignant questions Riddth asked me came after about a week of travelling to the hospital every day. 'Mum, there were no soldiers at the airport, no soldiers in the streets, no soldiers in the hospital and no soldiers even in the bus. Where are all your soldiers?'

I looked at his worried face and told him, 'Riddth, darling, Australia isn't at war, so we don't need lots of soldiers like you do in Cambodia.'

He looked at me incredulously and said, 'No war here, Mum? Really? No war?'

I took his hand and shook my head to confirm what I had said. He turned his head to look out the window of the bus, his face a study of sheer wonderment.

Riddth often unknowingly showed me in countless ways what a wonderful country Australia is and how lucky I was to be born here. There was so much I took for granted: no armed presence on our streets, regular rubbish collection, constant water and electricity supply, a reliable telephone network, a public transport system, social security, a high standard of medical care, diverse entertainment, and so much more.

I began to see Sydney through his eyes, and fell in love with the city in a way I hadn't when I first went to live there.

⌒

We settled into a domestic life together very easily. It was like we had always known each other. Riddth spent most of his time resting, and studying English by reading anything he could lay his hands on. He was almost manic in his desire to learn more and more so that he could express himself better and communicate with me on a deeper level.

His disease meant that his stool had to be checked every day for blood and he soon got over his embarrassment at having me peer into the toilet to examine his morning offerings. It became a joke between us, and often he would open my bedroom door and wake me saying, 'Mum, my shit is ready for you!' There are better ways to start the day.

But despite our comfort with each other I could see he was lonely. There were no teenagers where I lived, and if he went for walks in the beautiful harbourside park, he would return complaining, 'There's no people there, Mum!'

I knew what he meant. In Phnom Penh the streets were teeming with people going about their business, hanging out of windows and sitting outside their apartments. Old men would be sitting on rickety wooden stools, smoking pipes and talking about the old days; mothers would be cooking over charcoal fires and handing out plates of aromatic food to the children playing at the edge of the street; stall vendors would be pushing their rickety carts selling all kinds of fruit and cooked food; and teenage boys and girls would be cruising the streets on their motos, checking each other out as teenagers do in every city in the world. So, what was, to me, an idyllic little garden apartment, in one of the most elegant suburbs of Sydney, was for him like being marooned on a desert island.

But there were many things he loved about Sydney. His first visit to a Woolworths supermarket was unforgettable. He was like a child in a candy store, but trying to look very cool as though he wasn't really very impressed at all. After a few visits we had it all worked out. I would walk in front, and he would walk behind me with the trolley as I chose items and put them in. He would practise his English by holding my list and reading out each item I needed one by one. He liked being in charge and looking as though he was telling me what to do – something few people can lay claim to.

There was so much I didn't understand at first. I remember being irritated when I would ask him if he'd like chicken, beef, pork or fish for dinner. He would simply stare at me without answering. It took me a while to realise that never in his life had anyone asked him what he would like to eat. In the refugee camp and the orphanage he, like everyone else, simply ate what was put in front of him. He couldn't handle making these kinds of decisions. The first time I took him to a restaurant and handed him a menu, I stupidly still didn't realise he had never been shown one before and that it only confused him.

Riddth's first day in my kitchen was quite an adventure for him. He found the microwave oven the most mysterious item, closely followed by the dishwasher. He thought the dishwasher was a huge waste of money, and showed me how he could wash up ten times faster than it could.

He was very suspicious of frozen food and hated it when I put leftovers in the freezer to use another day. In the orphanage, each meal was prepared fresh and eaten on the spot, as there was no way of freezing food because there was no electricity. Riddth believed eating old food would make him sick and he couldn't understand why I would cook more than I wanted to eat at the time, only to freeze it. After a while I, too, wondered why, when freshly cooked food undeniably tastes better and is much more nutritious.

Prepackaged food worried him too. If he even saw me attempt to open a tin, or tear the top off a packet of a cardboard box, expecting him to eat the contents, he was off like a flash.

Sometimes his innocently wise statements knocked me out. I told him that Western people often didn't have the time or inclination to cook fresh food as they could get it already prepared and simply had to heat it.

'Why don't they have time, Mum?'

'Because they work long hours and often don't get home until it's too late to cook dinner.'

'So, even though they work long hours and get paid a lot of money, they still have to eat stale food?' he would argue.

But there was worse to come. He started to read the labels on tins in the supermarket.

'What are preservatives, additives and artificial colourings made of, Mum?'

'Look, Riddth, I just don't know!'

'You eat food without knowing what's in it, Mum?'

After a few of these question-and-answer sessions, I knew which country Riddth thought was 'Third World', and it wasn't his. I was starting secretly to agree with him.

But in some ways he was so damned easy to please it was sad. His idea of heaven was a Big Mac, large french-fries and a Coke. (He had no problem with takeaway!) He would religiously pick out the pickle, though, and was always too shy to ask them not to put it in in the first place.

He may not have liked my dishwasher but he was in love with my washing machine. At the orphanage clothes were washed by hand. After a few disastrous attempts by Riddth to use the machine, throwing in whites, black and coloured clothes together and seeing the results, he learned to sort everything and set the dials on the washing machine. He would grin all the way through these exercises, lifting the lid impatiently and getting flustered when the cycle automatically stopped.

We spent a lot of time rugged up on his bed watching television and videos. He felt the cold terribly and was really too weak to go out much. One night I put on the film *The Killing Fields*, after explaining to him that it was a movie about what had happened in his country. He was completely enthralled by it. When bombs were dropping and people were screaming, he would stop the movie, saying, 'Mum, Mum, it was just like that. This is about my life! I remember the bombs falling and hugging the ground. One day, I must have been very little, there was shooting all around me and I was face down on the ground with my eyes shut tight, trying to cover myself with the branches of a tree. It was just like this movie.'

Riddth had been born some time in 1978 in one of the Pol Pot labour camps and didn't remember, or more likely chose not to remember, anything about his early years. But the movie certainly prodded his memory as I had hoped it would. I knew he wouldn't have any pleasant memories, but it was important for him to face his past so that he could get on with his life now.

He watched *The Killing Fields* over and over again, asking me questions about politics. 'Why did the Americans bomb us like that? Why didn't the rest of the world do something? Surely the world knew what Pol Pot was doing between 1975 and 1979. And why were there no war crimes trials for guilty Cambodians?'

The questions spewed forth and I had no answers to give him. Indeed, I still have no answers for those Cambodians who ask me similar questions today.

The armed conflict and bombings he remembered would certainly have taken place in 1979, when the Vietnamese invaded Cambodia and 'liberated' the Cambodians. Fighting went on for years in the jungles, and especially around the border of Thailand, where the Vietnamese were bent on killing Cambodians who were trying to escape the 'liberation'. They were not safe from the Thais either, who were less than keen to let in hundreds of thousands of starving refugees they regarded as being a drain on their economy. Shooting Cambodians coming over the border became a weekend sport for many members of the Thai military and policemen, in much the same way that men in outback Australia go on kangaroo-shooting weekends.

Riddth's very real hatred of both the Vietnamese and the Thais was founded on actual experience. No matter how I tried to talk to him about how damaging racism is, there was no budging him on the subject. 'You don't know anything about it, Mum,' he would say earnestly. 'They want to kill all Cambodians until there is not one left, so they can take over all of my country.'

He told me that there were organised 'Resistance' groups loyal to King Sihanouk and his son, Prince Ranariddh, within the refugee camps, and that he and other boys as young as twelve slipped out during the day and at night to take part in raids on Vietnamese and Thai soldiers, who were never far from the camps. I couldn't bring myself to ask him if he had ever killed anyone.

He did tell me that being in the Resistance taught him that all soldiers can be bad. Even the Cambodian commanders were often cruel to young boys like him, using them as servants to carry heavy ammunition and ordering them over landmined areas to collect hidden caches of guns and hand grenades from caves. Riddth said some of his friends never returned from these manoeuvres, and after he had worked out what might have happened to them, he decided to stay in the camp, where he thought his chances of survival were much higher.

The staff at the Royal North Shore Hospital were so kind to Riddth, he couldn't believe it. 'Mum, at the Red Cross Blood Centre in Phnom Penh, they just told me after a few months not to come back. They said I was dying and it was a waste of time giving me transfusions. I should just go home and wait to die.'

In Sydney he endured many painful bone marrow extractions done by needles being inserted into the base of his spine, so that the doctors could examine his platelet levels and determine the next course of treatment. These were torture for him and I would hold his hand tightly while the procedure was being done. Sometimes he would choose to take gas to control the pain, but not always. The days he had to have these tests exhausted me emotionally, and on the way home on the bus, I felt I looked as sick as he did!

But our time then wasn't all misery and hospital visits. As well as bus and train travel he adored riding on Sydney ferries, and in particular getting off at Circular Quay at the weekend and walking around, looking at all the free entertainment. The buskers especially were a real delight to him. Nothing like that existed in Cambodia and he soaked up everything that was on offer.

⟺

Still, Riddth could be so exasperating sometimes. One day as we were leaving the hospital, I sat down in my seat on the bus and saw that he was still outside on the pavement, making no move to follow. I urged him sternly to get on and he did so reluctantly. He sat sulking beside me. He was a good sulker.

'Why didn't you want to get on the bus, Riddth?' I asked.

'Look, Mum, can't you see? There is a woman driving!' he snarled at me through clenched teeth.

He spent the whole trip on the edge of his seat, watching the traffic left and right, convinced that the woman driver could only be incompetent, and could not understand why Australians would let a woman do what he saw as a man's job. He couldn't get off the bus fast enough, and from then on I noticed him checking out the sex of all our bus drivers.

Germaine Greer, or any feminist, would slash her wrists within a week of arriving in Phnom Penh. Women are very far down the scale in Cambodian society. There is a Khmer saying: 'A man is made of gold. A woman is made of cloth.' If a woman is not content to be a wife and mother, her only possibilities are slaving away in a garment factory, as a promotion girl for a beer or cigarette company, or in a shop. Of course, there are also always the massage parlours and brothels, from which a pretty girl is never turned away. From the few whose families can afford it, there is a small emerging group of women learning professions in the universities and learning computer skills, but their numbers are very small in comparison to those of the men being trained.

A Ministry for Women's Affairs has recently been created and the minister overseeing it, Mu Sochua, is an American-educated returnee who is passionate about changing the lot of Cambodian women. If more women like Sochua come back to the country, the miserable lot of the Cambodian woman might, in time, change for the better. But for Riddth, and for most Cambodian males, women were not designed to drive buses, or do much else except raise families.

But as the months slipped by I could see his horizons begin to broaden when we would visit female friends of mine in their places of business and he could see for himself how many women had successful careers in Australia. I could see how he was growing to respect women when he saw them working and studying.

⌒

Riddth was developing new interests all the time.

I wanted to take him to a performance at the Opera House and I gave him the program for the Festival of Sydney, saying he could choose any event he wanted. I suspect his choice to attend a performance by the African Dance Troupe just might have had something to do with the advertisement showing dusky topless women. In any case, the show was so spectacular, with the musical and dancing talents of all the performers being of such a high standard that the women's bare breasts hardly registered with him on the night. After that he was hungry for information about Africa. He had never heard of the continent, and devoured every documentary on it I brought home from the video store.

Trish was living in Sydney now and was always there for me when I needed help to keep Riddth amused and occupied. He called her his Auntie Trish. She gave him a book called *The African Encyclopaedia* and he read it from cover to cover. It was always by his bed. One morning before dawn broke, he woke me, sitting on the side of my bed with the book in his hands.

'Mum,' he said, 'what does "a host of chattering monkeys" mean?'

His finger was pointing to a story in the book about monkeys in which he had come across the word 'host'. At around 5.00 a.m. I didn't feel like explaining it to him, and told him to get back into bed or else I would throw the bloody book into the harbour!

Riddth was forever combing his hair and practising his disco technique in front of my full-length mirror when he thought I wasn't looking. He had just discovered Michael Jackson and became an instant fan. He was really keen to copy his moondance steps. One night there was a Janet Jackson special on television and I told him she was Michael's sister.

Big mistake.

'No, Mum, that can't be right. Janet is black and Michael is so white. They can't be brother and sister,' he said.

I decided to quit while I was ahead. Trying to explain the Jackson family was something I knew was far beyond my powers.

⟞⟝

The first time I took Riddth to the cinema was a night I won't forget in a hurry. He had never been to a cinema and we were seeing the latest James Bond movie. When James jumped from the wing of one plane into the cockpit of another, at around 36,000 feet, Riddth jumped up from his seat, yelling, 'Never happen, never happen!'

I managed to settle him down until the steamy sex scene where one of the inevitable femme fatales was quietly eliminating one of her enemies by crushing him to death between her thighs. This was too much for Riddth, who leapt to his feet again, shouting, 'Tiger Woman!' at the top of his lungs.

I gave up, and just sank lower and lower into my seat. I knew that half of the people in the cinema were going to want to see who this crazy person was when the lights came on so, as the credits were still rolling, I grabbed his arm and said we had to leave straightaway so that we could catch our bus.

One of Riddth's greatest enjoyments was a bubble bath. When he was well enough to enjoy his first, I prepared one and called him. When he saw it his eyes grew wide with curiosity, and he cupped the bubbles with both hands, looking at me questioningly.

'You figure it out, love,' I said, and closed the door behind me. Two hours later I thought I had better check if he was OK. He was.

They became weekly events. Our trips to the supermarket usually concluded with the purchase of some variety of bubble bath for him to test out for me.

As the weather became warmer I thought about taking Riddth to the beach. I hesitated, knowing that it would be difficult to find a beach where some young thing wasn't prancing around in only one piece of her two-piece bathing suit. But I decided I couldn't protect him from the whole Western world, so we set off for Manly Beach. On the bus I tried casually to get across to him that Australian girls were not as shy as Cambodian ones and that showing their bodies was quite a normal thing for them.

He fixed a disbelieving eye on me, and said, 'No, Mum, you're joking with me. I don't believe you.' I shrugged and decided to let the day take its course.

He was too weak to swim and we couldn't risk him catching a chill, so I planned that we would just take a walk alongside the beach. It started out uneventfully, but after two sets of teenage girls jogged towards us topless, Riddth ducked his head down and was in danger of bumping into oncoming people. I felt for him, and suggested that he sit at a table and wait for me while I went to buy us some fish and chips for lunch. Before I left him, I handed him my sunglasses so that he could hide his discomfort. By the time we went home he had got over his initial horror and composed himself.

But then when I told him that there were beaches where people were completely naked in family groups, even the old men and women, it was too much for him. 'Horrible, horrible!' he said, covering his face with his hands and laughing. He was such a delightful innocent.

⌣

In Cambodia it was usual for me to squat back on my haunches to talk to children and old people. This is normal practice there, but I would never dream of squatting like that in a Sydney street. One morning when Riddth and I were waiting at the Cremorne Point ferry wharf, he simply dropped down on his haunches by my side like a faithful dog. There were too many people around for me to make a scene by asking him to get up. I simply stood there as though what he was doing was the most normal thing in the world.

But then he decided to mortify me further by loudly 'hawking'. He cleared his throat and spat out an impressive wad of colourful saliva, which only just made it over the edge of the wharf. It narrowly missed the highly polished shoes of an elegantly dressed middle-aged businessman, who was far from amused.

I was saved by the arrival of the ferry.

It didn't take me long to tell him that these two acts were definitely not acceptable behaviour in Australia and that he should try to remember this. No one squatted and no-one spat. Often after this he would clear his throat to catch my attention, and when he had, grin and swallow at the same time.

He liked to keep me on my toes.

Then there was the day in a park when two teenagers with shaved heads, nose rings, blue singlets and cut-off jeans, their arms covered with tattoos, were busy having a spitting competition with each other as they were walking along. Riddth nudged me so hard I nearly fell over. He pointed at the two young men and said cheekily, 'Maybe, Mum, you should tell them that they should not spit?' The mere prospect of even addressing these two hardened cases was beyond me, and I just hurried Riddth along the path and ignored his amused suggestion.

⌒

Riddth suffered from severe depression at times. Part of it was caused by the drugs he was taking and part of it by the turmoil in his life. Also, he was afraid to sleep with the light off.

On those days when he was very weak physically and depressed, he often talked about the refugee camp and the orphanage inside it. This was where he had spent his entire life until returning to Cambodia in 1993. The food there was only just enough to live on and he had been surrounded by people suffering from untreated TB or cancer, and amputees who were not receiving proper medical treatment. All the time there was the threat of the Thai police and military taking random shots at those who ventured outside.

He missed the other children from the orphanage keenly and spoke often of Tek Lak, his best friend. He told me that when he was too sick to go to the dining-room for meals, Lak would load a plate for him before eating himself and run back to the dormitory to feed him, often missing out on his own meal altogether.

He told me the story of the day he and Lak had stolen a chicken from a village after they had escaped from the refugee camp for a day. They ran into the jungle and cooked it over an open fire. 'Mum, I've never tasted a chicken so delicious,' he said, smiling at the memory.

Then he told me about his love for Koey Goey, one of the orphanage beauties. He said she was only thirteen, and that when he got better, and when she was old enough, he would like to marry her.

Before he got sick, though, Riddth had been in love with a girl from a village near the orphanage. He had tears in his eyes and his voice caught when he said her name: Vee.

He told me that Vee's parents had sent her to the countryside. They hadn't wanted her to marry a boy from the orphanage. No families in Cambodia want their children to marry orphans; they can't check the orphans' horoscopes because they don't know their birthdays, and they have no family history they can check. Vee's parents had sent her away before they had a chance to say goodbye and he knew he would never see her again. That was why he wanted to marry Goey: to protect her. He knew that no boy outside the orphanage would want to marry her.

He also said: 'Goey is very dark. We call her "khmau", which means "black" in Khmer. But I like black skin, Mum. I don't like the girls here with pale skin and eyes with no colour and blonde hair. Goey has dark skin and black eyes and shiny black hair, and when she is a few years older she will be very beautiful and I will be her husband.'

I wanted this for him too. I daydreamed about how beautiful their children might be if they ever got the chance to marry.

⌒

I wanted to give Riddth some responsibility and I also wanted him to know that I trusted him. So I asked him to carry and be in charge of my wallet at all times. He was with me one day at the hospital when I got money from the automatic teller machine. Well, I thought he was going to explode with curiosity. He walked up and down, tapping the area around the machiné.

'How did you do that, Mum? Where did the money come from?'

That night I sat down with a pen and paper, and wrote, 'education, job, salary, bank account, credit card, ATM, cash', with a chart and little arrows pointing from each item all the way down to the dollar sign.

'Riddth, without the education, job, salary, you can't have the bank account, credit card, ATM, cash.'

He simply drew a line through all I had written, saying, 'Can't I just borrow your card, Mum?'

From then on, when the money in my wallet got low he would say, 'Time to go to the wall, Mum.'

And off we would go.

⌒

His drug treatment contained strong steroids, which had side effects. The skin on his face and back was covered in angry acne, with pus-filled pimples that caused him considerable pain. You could almost see them throbbing on his face, and he had to try to sleep on his side or his back would be a mess of oozing, burst pimples in the morning.

But the side effect he hated most was the hair that was growing profusely all over his body, including the lobes of his ears. 'When I sit in the bus, Mum, the person sitting next to me is looking at my hairy ears,' he would complain sadly. It was too dangerous for him to shave any part of his face, as his blood disorder meant that if he cut himself he would very likely bleed to death. So every few days I would smear his earlobes with my hair-removal cream.

Aside from his embarrassment on the bus, the endless trips to and from the hospital were tiring for me, so I could only imagine how exhausted he was at the end of the day when we reached my apartment. He should have been a full-time, overnight patient, but as he was not an Australian citizen this wasn't possible without paying over $700 a day.

⌒⟶

I was grateful I was no longer working at Chase Manhattan. It's strange how fate works; I had thought losing my job was catastrophic, but it allowed me the time to care for Riddth. I lived day by day on my payout money from Chase and kept on putting off having to decide how long I could keep on paying $350 a week rent on my apartment. I tried to get the State Transit Authority to give Riddth a free travel pass. The hospital trips almost every weekday were becoming a financial burden, as we had to catch four buses every day. No amount of pleading worked, though; we had to pay the full fares. Kind people had donated some money towards Riddth's costs but it was inevitable that I would be dipping into my pocket for all kinds of reasons. But it was such a joy to have him in my life that it didn't even occur to me to put a cost on his living with me.

As time went by I could see he was really homesick for Cambodians, so I arranged with the local Cambodian community to take him to the Buddhist pagoda at Bonnyrigg. This meant two hours each way of ferries, buses and trains, but I knew he would enjoy being with his own people and speaking his own language. Privately I told the abbot at the pagoda that Riddth was very homesick and that I was trying to raise money to help pay for the treatment to cure his disease.

Once Riddth was sitting with me on the floor, the monk introduced him and asked him to stand up. He told the people gathered that Riddth was a very ill orphan from Phnom Penh, who lived with me on the other side of Sydney. Within minutes a silver plate materialised and was passed around. From a small community of working-class Cambodians over $600 was raised in cash. Some of the people who gave money were old Cambodian widows, survivors of the war years, who had shaved heads and were dressed in white mourning clothes for their dead families. Tears ran down Riddth's face as he knelt and shook the hands of his compatriots.

When we got home Riddth handed me the money to put into the bank. His face was full of emotion and disbelief. 'In Cambodia, no-one would ever think to help me like this. I can't believe they gave me all this money and they don't even know me, Mum,' he said, before he fell into his bed, fatigued from his long day.

⟜

Now, I have always been a mail-order catalogue freak. At least, I was before Riddth came into my life.

He would shriek with laughter at such luxuries as electric carving knives and toothbrushes, exercise bikes and beds for dogs and cats. He practically fell on the floor when I showed him gadgets to fry chips so that all the sides were cooked evenly, and a pet bag you could buy to put your wet dog in so that it didn't mess up your car.

Paying money for plastic garbage bags to put our rubbish in was anathema to him. He hated to see me buy something that was going to be thrown away. When I had to sit him down and go through my apartment building's rubbish disposal and recycling regulations, it was like getting him to understand Einstein's theory of relativity!

However, Riddth liked to be in control. I could relate to this as I am a bit of a control freak myself (which I know has caused me lots of problems in my personal life). I think recognising this in each other was one of the reasons we loved each other so much. So I put him in control of the rubbish. He actually grew to love sorting the bottles from the plastic, the tins from the food waste, and bundling up the newspapers for the rubbish collection days. Woe betide me if I tried to slip an orange peel into an empty tin. His look could kill!

⟜

One night when I thought he was settled down in front of the television, I was in my bedroom trying to read a book.

Riddth came rushing in, breathlessly saying: 'Moon, moon! Man walking on the moon! Come and look, quickly!' Old footage of Neil Armstrong's moon walk was being shown, the first inkling Riddth had ever had that humankind had reached the moon. In the refugee camps there was very little schooling in anything, and this was a piece of history that he had missed completely.

So off I went to the video shop to bring back everything I could find on space travel for him to watch. His eyes never left the screen. He had more questions than I could answer, so I bought him another book, *The History of Space Travel.*

In the end, the book just led to more unanswerable questions. 'Mum, it says here in the book that the satellites in space in the 1970s could actually read the headlines on a newspaper anywhere in the world. If they could do that, then the satellites would have been able to see what Pol Pot was doing in Cambodia. It would have been easy to see the forced labour camps, the piles of bodies. Everything. And if they could see that from the satellites, why didn't the world do something to stop him? Why didn't someone do something?'

At that moment, he made me so ashamed of humanity that I had no words for him. I was melancholy for the rest of the day.

Even if it sometimes made him think about disturbing things, Riddth loved to read. It was as though he was trying to catch up on what had been happening in other parts of the world that he had never known existed. He had never heard of Europe, the Middle East or the South Pacific. He had known of most Asian countries, India and America. That was about it.

One of the tragedies of the Pol Pot era that continues to affect Cambodians is that very few young people have the desire to read. Pol Pot killed all the poets, novelists and other literary people and there is not one living author in the country today. The children growing up don't have any books in their own language besides textbooks. I can't imagine my life without books, and it's sad to think that most Cambodian children won't know that lovely feeling of anticipation readers have when they open a book at the first page.

During one visit to the orphanage in 1994 I proudly presented the children with an atlas. They were all over it, showing great interest in Australia and the little spot that was Adelaide. But I had neglected to tell them that the world was round, and they thought it was flat because the pages were. Riddth was thoroughly pissed off with me when I went through 'the world is round, not flat' business with him. He felt I had lied to him when I had brought the atlas to the orphanage. I very quickly learned that Riddth did not forgive a lie very easily, even if it was a tiny one about whether his dinner was freshly cooked or a frozen leftover.

⸻

Riddth's passport showed his birthday as 1 January. I told him that he would be able to see the fireworks over Sydney Harbour on New Year's Eve and that I would like to give him a birthday party.

He thanked me but said that wasn't his real birthday. None of the children at the orphanage knew the date they were born and if they had to have any identity papers for school they put 1 January for all orphans. 'It's also another way of knowing if someone is an orphan or not, as generally anyone with a birthday of 1 January is branded as being one,' he said, in a very matter-of-fact voice.

On New Year's Eve he watched the fireworks spectacle with the enjoyment of the child he really was, despite his age. I had a birthday party for him, and staked out the stretch of lawn near my apartment that had a spectacular view of the Sydney Harbour Bridge and the Opera House. I knew Riddth had never experienced this kind of celebration; he wore a silly grin all night. Trish presented him with an expensive silver chain, telling him that it carried her energy, and that when he wore it a little bit of her would always be with him. She told him that if he ever wanted to give it to someone he loved, his energy would also be passed on to them. He wore the chain from that day on. When I put him to bed he was exhausted, as he wasn't used to such late nights.

'Thanks, Mum, for letting me stay up for the fireworks. It was the most beautiful thing I have ever seen. I just wish all the kids could have been here to see it with us. Good night, Mum.'

〰

As the weeks and then months slipped by, I could see Riddth was getting weaker. I didn't need the hospital reports noting low platelet levels to know that the drug therapy was no longer working as it had when he first arrived. He had built up an immunity to his medicine and was slowly slipping away.

The doctors knew it, I knew it, his Auntie Trish certainly knew it, and had gently tried to prepare me. And I think, in his heart of hearts, Riddth knew it too.

One day his doctor arranged to get a Khmer interpreter so that he could be absolutely sure that Riddth understood what he would say to him. I knew what was coming and steeled myself. I tried not to look at Riddth as the translator told him that the only drugs available for aplastic anaemia had been tried on him, and that although they had worked in the beginning, they were not working now.

Although he could be put on a course of stabilising drugs, if he had the slightest accident – bumped himself, fell over, or harmed himself in any way – the internal bleeding that would surely follow would kill him. He was also told that any infection, a cold or virus of any kind, could be the end of him. He would have to watch his every movement, keeping away from anyone with a slight head cold, or infection of any kind. If he was very, very careful he could live a few more years, but it was really up to him and to those around him as to how long he would survive.

He was told again that his only chance was for a blood relative to come forward and offer their bone marrow for a transplant. Again, he shook his head slowly and firmly, saying he had no-one to ask.

'I only have you, Mum,' he said sombrely.

Over the months of treatment Dr Ma had grown to feel genuine affection and admiration for Riddth, and I knew it really hurt him to give up on his patient.

'Riddth,' Dr Ma asked kindly, 'if you knew you didn't have long to live, would you prefer to live your life in Australia or in Cambodia?' What a loaded question. I held my breath and waited for the answer.

Riddth lifted his eyes slowly and gazed out the window deep in thought, trying to put his feelings into words. He looked at me directly, and then at the doctor and the translator, and said in perfect English: 'I love Australia, but Cambodia is my country, and when I die I want to be among Cambodians. Mum, will you take me home?'

The translator was wiping her eyes and blowing her nose quietly. Dr Ma, I knew, was used to giving patients bad news, but even he was having trouble controlling his emotions. He patted Riddth on the knee and rested his hand on my shoulder, squeezing it gently as he left with the translator, leaving us alone in the sterile hospital consulting room.

It was there that I made my commitment to be by Riddth's side for as long as he lived. I hoped we would have at least a year together.

We didn't speak all the way home on the bus. I knew he was trying to make sense of what the coming months might bring for us both. But I also knew he understood that whatever might befall him, he would not have to face it alone.

I spent the next couple of weeks holding myself together through sheer willpower, hiding my desire to weep. I was busy selling my furniture and packing up my personal effects for storage, and a friend lent us her apartment for the last weeks before our return to Cambodia. My personal funds were dwindling, and to be able to get my hands on my superannuation money (which I am still living on), I had to provide paperwork proving that I was moving permanently to another country. When this was complete and I had transferred my superannuation to my cheque account, we were finally free to travel. We set off for the airport, with Riddth proudly clutching a state-of-the-art radio/cassette player Trish had given him as a farewell gift.

Shelter in Death's Shadow

Phnom Penh, April – July 1996

O n the plane from Sydney to Bangkok, I watched Riddth sleeping. To the casual observer, there would have been absolutely nothing special about him. The most noticeable thing was that the drugs that were keeping him alive had made his face a mass of painful, angry pimples.

I wanted to scream: 'This boy is dying and he hasn't even lived. He's dying and he's not even eighteen years old!'

I placed my hand gently on his knee. He stirred slightly in his seat and I knew that he was aware of me sitting beside me. The trust and love that had grown between us in just eight months was amazing.

I must have dozed off. The next thing I knew the aircraft lights were coming on in the cabin and breakfast was being served before we made our descent into Bangkok. There we would make the last leg of our journey back into Cambodia.

In Phnom Penh we were met at the airport by friends of Princess Marie, who had booked us into a cheap hotel. I had told them that Riddth would need to rest before going back to the orphanage. The Hotel Tsai Teng turned out to be a real fleapit. I am sure that Princess Marie's people had not known about the corridors full of young teenage girls running around half-clothed, knocking on the doors of male foreigners in an effort to ply their trade.

I had an extra bed put in my room for Riddth, and we made our plans for our return to the orphanage the next day. He was so excited that he could hardly sit still. He had missed them all so.

A car came for us the next morning. I had planned the trip so that we would arrive at lunchtime when all the children would be present before going back to school in the afternoon.

Riddth dressed with the attention to his appearance of a rock star. He put on his best bought-in-Sydney jeans and a crisp, colourful T-shirt, and teamed everything with a pair of the finest Timberland walking shoes. He wore his much-loved Mickey Mouse waterproof watch and the silver chain that his Auntie Trish had given him. He combed his lustrous black hair back over his forehead and stepped into the waiting car with the grace of a film star about to attend a gala performance.

As the black limousine bumped and wobbled down the rough track through the orphanage gates, the children started to gather at the entrance to the dining room. When Riddth opened the door and started to step out, he was mobbed by all the children, who shouted his name and frantically tried to grab him. Some of the older boys and girls started to cry and laugh at the same time. He was king for a day.

Riddth was home.

After the hugging and kissing was over, he went into the boys' dormitory and dumped his bags on his empty bed. He then started to thump his chest like Tarzan and stamp all around his little space, as if to mark out his old boundary in the dorm. He was genuinely touched to see that his bed had been kept empty and tidy for his return.

We called all the children together for a meeting in the dining room and Riddth explained his disease in great detail and about how he could not play soccer or any games in which he might be accidentally hurt. The children, even the toddlers, listened intently, and I could see that they understood exactly how serious his physical condition was.

It was reassuring for me to see how much they had missed him and how whole-heartedly they welcomed him back into their fold. There was real love and affection for him, and I realised anew how lonely he must have been without them in Sydney, despite the comfort and luxuries I lavished on him.

Just being with them again I could feel the strange magic the children seemed to weave around almost anyone who got involved with them.

⸻

He was weary, but surrounded by friends who were hanging on his every word about his experiences in Australia. He was the first among them to have travelled so far away and return to tell them what the world was like beyond the borders of Cambodia.

After kissing him goodbye and getting a warm hug in return, I left for the city, telling him to come back to me when he was ready. I had to find a job and somewhere for us to live as, although the hotel was cheap, I had no intention of staying there for one day longer than I had to. His health was far too delicate for the rough-and-tumble conditions at the orphanage, and he knew I would look for a small place where we both could live so that I could take care of him properly.

Before I left the orphanage, I handed him his Cyclosporin medication in a chilled wine bag from Australia. I reminded him that he would have to get the orphanage cook to buy ice for him so that he could keep his precious capsules cool. These drugs ($10,000 worth, and donated by Sandoz, a sympathetic pharmaceutical company) were the only things keeping him alive from one day to the next.

As I drove back to town I felt as though I was leaving half my heart behind. I wondered how I would get through the night without waking to feel his forehead or to cover him in his sleep.

⸻

I returned to the fleapit of a hotel and spent a restless night worrying about Riddth. I was tired and grumpy the next morning, but brightened up immediately when I ran into an American woman, Lauryn Galindo, I had met on an earlier visit. Lauryn was from Honolulu, and was an adoption agent. She had travelled in her business to many developing countries, but had the same sympathy for Cambodia's children that so many of my friends had.

Lauryn had the figure of an Hawaiian hulu dancer, because that was what she was whenever she had time. Her hair was light brown and wavy, and she wore it to her waist or tied up in many different kinds of twists and buns that I wished I knew how to do with my own hair. She wore clothes that would not have been out of place in 1960s San Francisco, but always looked neat and feminine. She was a Buddhist and had the serenity of those who meditate regularly.

She could afford a better hotel but had chosen the Tsai Teng because of its proximity to the Nutrition Centre Orphanage just across the road. There she was able to select orphan babies for her adoptive families.

Lauryn invited me to lunch, and I found she was easy to talk to. I told her all about Riddth, and how worried I was about him being at the orphanage; it was such a relief to have a sympathetic ear. By the end of lunch she had invited me to share her room, which cost the same whether she was alone or not, and I moved in later that day.

It's rare to find such friendship after just a couple of meetings, but life in Cambodia is like that. Some people seem to be especially kind to others in the midst of so much poverty, and Lauryn didn't have to be told that I was watching my pennies. She made me feel that I was doing her a favour by sharing her room and providing her with company.

⌒

I spent the next couple of days reacquainting myself with Phnom Penh. During my brief visits over the previous couple of years I had not had the time to be a tourist. I didn't like what I saw.

There were beggars, rubbish in the streets, dangerous traffic with motos being driven recklessly by twelve-year-old children, drunk soldiers, threatening armed soldiers and menacing policemen. I saw potholed streets, bullet-ridden houses, empty hotels, ostentatious houses built by military arms dealers and casinos full of addicted Chinese and Muslims who were forbidden to gamble in their own countries.

But to me, the most disturbing problem facing the country was the rapid spread of HIV/AIDS. After Africa, Cambodia was the country with the highest rate of infection in the world, with a totally inadequate system of information and training. Experts were saying that in twenty years, this deadly disease would kill more Cambodians than did Pol Pot's regime.

During my time in Phnom Penh, I discussed Cambodia's many problems with Martin Flitman, a friend who was arguably the best professional portrait photographer in the country. He had lived there for nine years and was fast reaching saturation point.

'I've had enough, Geraldine. I'm off to South America as soon as I can get enough money together,' Martin said to me one day as we were going out to the orphanage so that he could take photos of the children for me.

'How can you leave Cambodia after all these years? I know you love it here,' I asked him.

He replied, 'I love the people, Geraldine, but, let's face it, as a *nation* they are beyond help.'

I hated it when friends I thought were going to stay on in Cambodia indefinitely decided to leave. I did not consider Cambodia to be a 'basket case' and had high hopes for vast improvements in the future. But I knew that many ambassadors and international investors put Cambodia in the 'too hard' basket.

⟳

What I had expected, happened. After just three days Riddth came into the city and found me in Lauryn's room.

'Mum,' he said, 'I can't stay at the orphanage. It's too hot and the mosquitoes are really bad and the bed is hard, and I can't sleep with all the boys mucking around all night. I want to stay with you in town. Can I please, Mum? Please.'

Living in the same apartment in Sydney where we had our own bedrooms and space to move around was one thing, but sharing a hotel room with a teenage boy was something else again. I had spent the previous days looking for cheap housing with at least two rooms so we could be together when Riddth had had his fill of being at the orphanage. He had got used to his creature comforts and had forgotten about the conditions there. But everything I had looked at was far beyond my budget.

Then Lauryn told me about a friend of hers who owned a house in which older orphans who had come to live in the city stayed while they were looking for jobs. He had told her that he had two rooms available and she was sure he would give us a room each until we were able to get ourselves sorted out. All I would have to pay for would be any phone calls.

The house had once been on stilts and the upper floor was completely wooden, but the ground floor had been concreted in and divided into lots of little bedrooms. Riddth had one to himself downstairs and I had one (about the size of my bathroom in Sydney) above Riddth's bedroom.

Anyway, I certainly wasn't complaining. We set off to buy some beds and a few other bits and pieces of furniture. Riddth was thrilled to be able to chose his own, and settled on a canvas navy-blue soldier's bed with a mosquito net, a round bamboo table and a matching set of chairs with dark-blue cushions, and a set of bamboo shelves.

I enrolled Riddth at the Australian Centre for Education, where he had English lessons three times a week. He spent a lot of time in bed studying and reading. However, part of the deal at the house was that all the males living there had to do night-guard duty for a rostered week at a time. Riddth was fit enough to do this and quite enjoyed the responsibility. One night when he was on duty I came home with a belligerent cyclo driver who insisted I pay him US$3, more than three times the normal price for the journey. I refused and left the driver screaming at me in the street.

'I'm not going to be taken advantage of like that, Riddth. It's robbery!' I said, as I walked up the stairs to my bedroom.

'I'll pay him what he wants, Mum,' Riddth said. 'I know his type. These cyclo drivers can be dangerous. If he thinks you are rich and you don't pay him, he could come back and throw a hand grenade into the house. I will take care of it,' he said and paid him out of his pocket money.

He was quite the man looking after his mum.

⌒〉

I hated the bare wooden walls, floor and ceiling of my room and decided to brighten things up. I asked Riddth to take me to a paint shop. He was riding a *Chaly* motorbike that belonged to the orphanage and that he was allowed to use in town so that he didn't tire himself walking around. (He took me wherever I wanted to go, but hated it when people laughed at us because the bike was very small and I hung out all over the place. Still, one night I found him rolling around on his floor laughing his head off. He showed me a photo someone had taken of us as we were driving away from the house and all you could see was me, and my bum hanging over the seat. Riddth was completely hidden in the driver's seat. He loved that photo of me.)

After our visit to the paint shop I painted my room purple. I knew all the Cambodians in the house thought going into my room was quite an adventure. As I was the only foreigner in the house, they expected me to be a bit strange.

But even with my colourful room, living at the house was no picnic. There was one toilet and shower in the same room, and in the morning there were as many as eight of us lined up waiting to use them. If you left your place in the line to get something from your room, you lost your turn. Those were the rules.

It was not possible for the bathroom to be clean. The plumbing hardly ever worked, and it was usual for the toilet to be full of what toilets are for, so sitting on it was not an option. (When the toilet got too bad, one of the older boys would tackle it with a rubber plunger.) Also, the drain didn't work and the shower water didn't run away. If you were not first in the shower in the morning you had to stand ankle deep in all the previous bathers' dirt, with what they had cleared from their noses and bits of their hair floating on top. The kids weren't dirty, it was just the old plumbing.

I never wanted to jump the line, as we were living there for free. But one day I had diarrhoea, and there was no way I could wait for five other people to shower before getting to the toilet.

I rushed back to my room and scrounged around for a couple of plastic bags that I kept in a drawer for when I did my shopping. As I squatted awkwardly over the spread-out bags I hoped there were no holes in them; there were many cracks in my floorboards and if the bags leaked, the people below were definitely going to know about it.

⟲

For the Cambodian New Year in mid-April Riddth and I were together at the orphanage. I was about to have a wondrous experience that would more than make up for any little inconveniences in my lifestyle.

'Mum, go and take your clothes off and put this on,' Riddth said, handing me a sarong he had got from the girls. 'You are going to have a bath.'

'But I've had a shower, Riddth. I don't need another one.'

'Just do it, Mum,' Riddth said with a shy smile. 'It's a surprise.'

The children grabbed my hands and sat me on the steps of the office in an old wooden chair. They had decorated it with green vines and flowers from their small garden. On each side of the chair they had placed two large buckets of water with gloriously scented jasmine flowers and lotus flower petals floating on top.

'In Cambodia it's our tradition that all children bathe their mother to thank her for taking care of them during the previous year,' Riddth explained. 'And most of the kids have never had mothers for long enough to have done this ritual, so we decided to all do it for you today.' He was beaming, so pleased with himself for arranging this for me.

The children lined up in single file. Then one by one they came and took water from one of the buckets with a little dipper, and washed some part of my body with the water and soap. I was covered from head to toe in water and petals, and they were giggling as they fought with each other over which part of my body they would be responsible for. Even my feet were lovingly scrubbed. It was such a touching experience that I didn't know where the bathwater began and my tears ended. Riddth was the last one to perform the ritual. He cupped his hands in front of my nose.

'Blow,' he said.

'What do you mean, "blow"?' I asked, not understanding what I was supposed to do.

'I'm your eldest son, and I have the honour of you blowing your nose into my hands so you will be completely clean for the new year,' Riddth said quite calmly.

I did what I was told amid great clapping and cheering by everyone enjoying my embarrassment. How could I ever live without these children?

⌒

In late May I was offered the job of a lifetime.

I visited Princess Marie regularly to keep her informed of Riddth's declining health condition and to give her the monthly cheque for the orphanage that came from the foundation in Sydney. One day, while waiting in the Cabinet office building to see her, I got into conversation with Kong Vibol, a handsome young Australian Khmer from Melbourne, who was working for Prince Ranariddh. When he found out who I was and that I was giving money to Princess Marie for her orphanage, he dragged me upstairs and introduced me to Ly Thuch, the Cabinet director. Within a day I had been cleared by the prince to work in the Cabinet as an assistant to Ly Thuch and I was put to work immediately.

I loved it! It was like being back in Foreign Affairs. I answered a lot of the English correspondence addressed to the prince in his capacity as the First Prime Minister. The replies could be standard National Day messages from him to heads of state, answers to foreign companies wanting to know how to go about investing in Cambodia, or responses to inquiries from the local English press. I also prepared press releases on a wide range of subjects and helped out with speeches for the prince and other senior members of the Cabinet staff. Both Vibol and Thuch knew that the Cabinet was in dire need of a good administrator as none of the staff had clear job descriptions, and even answering the telephone and sending faxes was a feat for some of them. I did what I could to give telephone etiquette training and made simple office procedure suggestions, but to no avail.

I was aware that some of my Cambodian colleagues at the Cabinet had mixed feelings about me. Some thought I was a spy for the Australians. Some resented my presence as a foreigner in their midst, no matter how much I tried to fit in. Some were jealous, because I was granted access to Princess Marie at any time.

I didn't always know who my friends and enemies were. No-one wanted me to learn of their disapproval, in case I used my (largely perceived) influence against them. I thought if I just worked hard, was polite and helpful to everyone, and continued to show my love and knowledge of all things Cambodian, eventually I'd become more accepted. I wanted Cambodians to understand why I felt so much passion for their country.

The scariest thing was the complete lack of security. People came and went without identifying themselves to anybody. Often visitors were left alone in a room with classified documents. There were no passwords on any of the computers. Most worrying of all, there was only one way in and one way out; there was no fire escape or back door from the Cabinet, or from the prince's residence, which adjoined the Cabinet. I voiced these concerns to Thuch and was asked to prepare a detailed security manual. This was a doddle for me, as security and its maintenance was one of the things that had been drummed into me during my years in embassies. I loved putting that manual together and handed it over with immense pride.

Unfortunately, none of the precautions I mentioned were ever taken.

Next, I was asked to devise a set of protocol guidelines, which I tackled with the same zeal as the security manual. These guidelines were later followed, and mainly concerned the preparations to be made prior to a visit somewhere outside the city by the First Prime Minister.

I was truly surprised at the shabbiness of the Cabinet offices: a few dusty rooms, mostly without air conditioning, and poor quality furniture. The computers and fax machines were often out of order and there were no funds to call in technicians. The toilets often did not have water. Soap was not provided and toilet paper was worth its weight in gold if you were lucky enough to find any. Coffee was made in the same room as the toilet was located in, and the drinking water often ran out.

I shared a room with five other people and there was barely enough space for us to walk sideways between our desks. There was no air conditioner or fan in our room. After my second day, I showed a colleague how sweat was dripping from my chin onto letters waiting for the prince's signature, and I explained that I could not work without at least a fan.

'Ah, a fan! Yes, yes, I will get you a fan,' a young colleague said eagerly and rushed out purposefully.

Within minutes he returned, beaming with satisfaction. In his hand was the flap from a cardboard carton of fish sauce, carefully cut off with a pair of scissors. He presented it to me with great pride.

'Here is fan for Madam,' he said, as I tried to cover my mixture of disappointment and merriment at his resourceful gift.

'Thank you,' I said, 'but I meant an *electric* fan.'

'Ah, so sorry. No have electric fan. Only cardboard fan. Is not good?'

'Yes, is good. Thank you,' I smiled. I put the fan away in the drawer, after writing on it with a large black texta, 'The Cabinet Fan' and the date.

Friends sometimes came to visit me and half the time none of the guards outside knew my correct name so they could not show them to my office. But if other soldiers overheard, they usually solved the problem by telling the guard on duty to show my visitors to the office of 'Madam Big', 'Madam Australia' or 'Madam Carrot', because of the colour of my hair.

Despite everything, I thoroughly enjoyed my job and working alongside Cambodians every day. I also had time in the mornings to spend with Riddth so that he never felt neglected. He was so proud that his mum worked for the prince.

⟨⟩

Riddth was always on at me to gather my voluminous skirts around me more securely when I rode the motos. I should have listened to him. One day I was on my way to a friend's house for lunch when the hem of my skirt got caught in the spokes of a moto that had no guardrail. Within a split second my whole skirt, which I had bunched between my legs, had been caught up in the spokes and was torn away completely from the waistband. This sent the moto, the driver and me sprawling into the street, directly into the path of traffic behind us. How we weren't killed is still a mystery. After concerned passers-by had helped me up, the main problem was that my skirt had been ripped off me. I was standing in the street wearing nothing but a bra and a long T-shirt which only just covered my crotch (just as well it did, as I never wore knickers in Phnom Penh because of the heat).

I slowly bent my knees so that I could wrap what was left of my skirt around my nakedness. I then limped to my friend's house with blood pouring from the wounds on my inner thighs.

When I finally got home I was reprimanded severely by Riddth.

'Please, Mum. Don't take motos anywhere. They are too dangerous. I'll take you anywhere you want. If anything happens to you, who will take care of me?' He said this almost angrily, although he was very sympathetic about my injuries.

⌒

Riddth was happy to be living in the house with kids his own age who were all orphans too. He felt less separate from other Cambodians, and enjoyed to the hilt his status with me as his 'mother' living there watching over him. I adored watching him flower. He loved his English lessons, was getting high grades and tackled assignments with the enthusiasm of the young.

I often saw him sitting with the other teenagers, talking animatedly in Khmer about his life, and I wished so much I could understand and be a part of it. However, my Khmer was lousy and having him explain things to me would have spoilt the spontaneity of these moments. He traded unashamedly on his experiences as a travelled person, and spoke proudly about his time in Australia.

Late one afternoon he came to me, his face flushed with excitement.

'Mum, Mum! I've got a letter from Vee. You know, the girl I loved in Ampil whose parents sent her away because I was an orphan? I am too scared to open the letter. Can you open it for me and stay with me while I read it? I feel like a pig who has got drunk on leftover rice wine.'

Vee had heard he was sick and had written to say she was sorry that she was in the countryside and could not visit him. It was a long letter and he didn't tell me everything in it. He smiled at part of the letter, and put it away in his shirt pocket, patting it into place.

'It's good, Mum. I know how she feels. She says she loves me still but can't go against her parents. But at least I know now not to expect to see her again. Don't worry, Mum, I'm not sad,' he said, stroking my arm as he left my room whistling.

But I was worrying. He was getting weaker every day, and battled with a cold that a healthy person could have shaken off in a day or two. He was getting through a huge bottle of peroxide every week when he brushed his teeth. The brushing always made his gums bleed alarmingly, he hated the taste of blood in his mouth and the peroxide helped lessen it.

One Thursday night when he was on guard duty, I sat talking with him as he lay down, resting.

'Mum, I want you to promise me something.'

'Anything, darling, you know that. What is it?'

'When I get really sick, even if I can't talk, promise me that you will *never* take me to a hospital in Phnom Penh. I hate them all. Please promise me that you will stay with me and let me die here with you.'

I couldn't speak. I wrapped my arms around him and hugged him as gently as I could, and nodded my agreement through my tears. I left him there reading his English lessons by torchlight and went to my room to try to sleep.

⟨══⟩

A week later Riddth came to my room to show me his foot, which was swollen, and almost black with congealed blood under the skin. He had dropped one of his peroxide bottles on it and within minutes his foot had started to swell. We both knew there was nothing we could do. The bleeding had already started internally. I moved a woven mat into his room downstairs and took what I would need to stay by his side. No one could tell how long he would live.

I called the Cabinet to say I wasn't coming in and why. The next few days and nights I spent in his small, hot room. At night he would drop his arm over the edge of the bed and I would reach up and hold his hand all night. If I got up to go to the bathroom he would wake, feeling my absence.

'Mum, Mum, where are you? Don't leave me.'

'I'm here, Riddth, don't worry,' I would say, taking his hand as I lay down on the floor by his bed.

Toeub, one of the older boys from the orphanage, for whom I had found a job, was living in the house with us at the time. He had seen death many times in the refugee camp. He came in to talk to Riddth while I was there.

'Riddth, do you have the receipt for your next term of English lessons?' he asked, standing at the foot of Riddth's bed. 'You won't be needing it and if you give it to me I can attend the classes in your place.'

I couldn't believe my ears! How could Toeub be so insensitive, and see only an advantage for himself in Riddth's death? I dragged him out of the room by his ear before Riddth could reply and told him what I thought of him.

⟜

I could not manage to carry Riddth to the toilet by myself so I asked for two of his friends to come in from the orphanage. This was so they could help me take care of him and so he would have other people to talk to during the day.

Tek Lak and Eng Sophea came, and were there when Riddth said he had something to tell me.

'Mum, I know I am very sick and will die if I don't find family to give me a bone marrow transplant. I lied to you and Dr Ma in Sydney when I said I have no mother. I have a mother and two brothers in Siem Reap, and Lak says he will go and find them, and they will come and give me the bone marrow transplant and I will be OK.'

I wanted to shake him until his teeth rattled, and would have if he hadn't been so ill.

'Riddth,' I screamed, 'why didn't you tell the doctor in Australia this? We could have done something about it then, but now it is too late. They can't do this kind of operation in Cambodia. Why did you lie about such an important thing that could have saved your life?'

'Because I was afraid that if you knew I had a mother, you wouldn't want to look after me,' Riddth said, actually ashamed to make eye contact with me.

Jesus wept, I thought. The poor little bugger was actually afraid I would reject him because technically he wasn't an orphan.

'How could you think that? You know how much I love you,' was all I could say.

We were both silent for a long while. Riddth spoke first.

'Mum, I'm glad I got so sick.'

'What on earth do you mean, Riddth?'

'Because if I hadn't been sick I would never have gone to Australia, and you would never have loved me like your son. You are my real mother and I am your real son. I know that now.'

How much I needed him to say these words to me.

'Hush, now. I know. I know. All that you say is true. I *am* your mother. Now try to rest.'

Tek Lak still went to see Riddth's family with money Riddth gave him and details of how to find them. I didn't try to stop him, as I knew he would not understand why his mission was futile. I was still hurting from the knowledge that Riddth had been so unsure of my love that he had kept this secret from me for so long.

It had only been a week since the night I had promised not to take him to the hospital, when his vital organs started to shut down one by one. He could no longer eat anything and could only sip water. He didn't go to the toilet at all. But he was still studying his English! On the Friday morning I woke and started to wash him, and there was a lot of dried blood around his lips. I knew how he hated the taste of it, and started to wash it away using a bowl of warm water and a towel.

'What's all this, darling?' I tried to baby him.

'It coagulated during the night, Mum. Sorry.'

'Coagulated! Coagulated! Where did you learn a word like this?' I asked, joking with him.

'You were asleep when I woke up this morning and I knew you would ask me about it so I looked the word up in my Khmer dictionary.'

I turned my head as I washed his face so that he wouldn't see how moved I was that he was still trying to study English in his condition.

That night his stomach became very hard; I could feel the mass of blood slowly hardening internally. He said he didn't feel pain but he started to hiccup, and this distressed him as well as making him dreadfully tired. He hiccuped all night and so was deprived of sleep.

I knew the end was very near.

On the Saturday morning, Karen Soldatic, our old friend who had flown him to Australia, dropped by to visit with a pot of fresh food she had made. As she came into the room and saw us her face became ashen. She sat down and talked to Riddth, who was starting to lose his sight. Karen brushed his hair back from his forehead, and said she would come back when he was better. He nodded and smiled in her direction. Karen hugged me and left sobbing, promising to return later when she had composed herself.

Word spread and soon that day I had other friends – Australians, Americans, French, Japanese and Khmer – visit us, and I brought them to sit in Riddth's room. I was barely aware of their presence as I sat by Riddth's bed, holding his hand and talking to him. He could no longer talk, but he could hear, and responded to my voice by squeezing my hand.

'Darling, don't fight against death. Let it come. You can go to Africa now. You will be healthy and strong and free from disease in the next life. And you will have a father and a mother who will love you and keep you. And you will marry and have lots of children and be a wonderful father. You can see all the animals in Africa that you have read about. Please let go, darling. I am right here. I will not leave you. Press my hand if you can hear me.'

His mouth made an ugly grimace, but I knew he was trying to smile at the thought of Africa, and he squeezed my hand weakly. His hands were swollen and the skin was stretched tightly across them. It must have been painful for him when I held his hand, but I needed him to feel my touch.

As I was talking away about all the animals in Africa, the radio, which had been playing softly in the background for days, started to play Michael Jackson's 'I'll Be There,' Riddth's favourite song. I turned up the volume so that he could hear it and I sang the words as best I could. I could see that he heard me.

He was only unconscious for about thirty minutes when he stopped breathing. Seconds before he died at 3.30 p.m. on Saturday 26 July 1996, a storm broke, and before the rain started, a gentle wind stirred the curtains around the window by his bed and swung the shutters open. It was almost as though Buddha had reached into the room and gently taken Riddth's soul in his hands.

That's what I like to think happened.

Ashes to Ashes,
Dust to Dust

I wasn't prepared for the grief I felt; I was desolate and unable to function properly. I had seen death close up many times but this was so intimate and personal. My father died in the nursing home. We sat in the antiseptic-smelling waiting room until a nurse came and told us he had passed away. Comparing Riddth's death in the arms of someone who truly loved him with my father's death in a hospital room surrounded only by nurses and medical equipment, I know which way I want to go, given the choice. My grief was mixed with the joy of knowing I had kept my promise to be with him to the end. This was my final gift of love to Riddth: the knowledge that he wasn't alone.

How blessed I was to be surrounded by so many friends at this time. One group of friends spent their own money, and called in monks from a nearby temple to chant the customary Buddhist prayers to help Riddth pass into his next life. I wasn't even aware that monks had to be paid to chant and pray over the dead. Every Buddhist must have these rites as soon as possible after death. My Cambodian friends knew I didn't know what had to be done and handled all this for me. My friends and the monks crowded into Riddth's shabby room, where he was lying on the bed. Before the ceremony started, one of the monks asked if he was an orphan and I was able to save Riddth from this final insult. He hated being described as an orphan.

'No,' I said to the monk. 'He was *not* an orphan. He was my *son*.' What pride I felt as I said those words.

Eng Sophea hurried off to the orphanage to tell everyone that Riddth had died. Other friends reported the death to the local police so that the death certificate could be issued, enabling a cremation to take place. Again I was completely unaware of the requirements and would have been unable to make these arrangements competently.

Friends helped me prepare Riddth's body for the cremation that would have to take place the next day. Together we washed him and shaved him. I knew that in the incredible heat the smell of decay was inevitable. We had to make do with what we had in the house to pack his rectum to prevent any leakage, so we used some chopsticks from the kitchen to poke the filling from his pillow inside him. We closed his eyelids firmly, and stuffed his nose and ears with cotton wool.

When I was finally alone with him I gazed at his handsome face, knowing this would be the last time we would be alone together. I felt he knew I was there and I experienced a painful joy in brushing his thick black hair. It still shone, and insisted on falling over his forehead just as it did when he was alive.

Toeub relinquished a pair of his cherished white trousers and a shirt; all Buddhists have to be cremated wearing white and all of Riddth's clothes were either black or coloured. Toeub redeemed himself in my eyes as he offered me his clothes before he hurried away to hide his tears. He and Riddth had grown up together in the refugee camp and were like brothers.

Night was falling when the orphanage car pulled up. Ming and most of the older children had come and they all filed into the room, crying. Goey was the most affected and threw herself on his body to kiss him. She knew she had lost her future husband and protector.

The children carried Riddth on a mat to the orphanage's pick-up truck.

They stretched him out on the floor, to take him back to the orphanage. A wake would be arranged there for the morning before he would be taken to the village pagoda for cremation.

What happened next was horrible for me to watch, but I was too tired and confused and sad to try to stop it.

The children returned to the room with Ming, and systematically and quietly stripped it of everything. Into his suitcases went his clothes and books. They had brought plastic bags and they filled them with every personal item they could lay their hands on. They figured everything in the room that had been his now was theirs. They would have taken the bed and the other furniture if there had been room in the car.

I was saddened at the heartless way they packed all that was left of Riddth and hurriedly shoved it in the car before driving in the dark back to the orphanage. They had even taken my alarm clock and hairbrush, and other personal toiletries I had taken to Riddth's room. My mind flashed back to the scene in the movie *Zorba the Greek* in which the village women broke into the room of a dying woman and emptied all her drawers before she had even died. On the other hand, the children were simply being practical; nothing should be wasted or left for strangers to steal.

Ming said she would arrange everything for the cremation ceremony and told me to go to the orphanage in the morning. It was late by the time all my friends had left me, and I went to bed feeling an emptiness I knew would take a long time to diminish. I would need all my strength for the next day.

⌒

I woke with the sun, and dressed in a white skirt and blouse; white is also the Buddhist colour of mourning. My friends tied a small square of black cloth to the sleeve of my shirt and tied a white scarf around my head, and we set out for the orphanage.

In one of the empty buildings there Riddth had been laid out on the floor on a mat and covered with a white sheet. His arms were crossed over his chest. Goey was sitting next to him with a fan, keeping the flies away from his exposed face. The children had placed empty Coca-Cola cans with burning candles and incense stuck in them at his head and feet. The girls and women from the village had fashioned arrangements of fruit and flowers for him to take on his journey.

The large room was full of children and families from the village, and many of my friends, who had heard about Riddth's death in the inexplicable way that news travels in Phnom Penh. There was even a wreath of flowers from Princess Marie and Prince Ranariddth. Ming had found a large photo of Riddth and put it in a frame amongst the flowers.

On the verandah men from the village were busy making Riddth's coffin out of old plywood, and the younger children were pasting brightly coloured paper to the outside of it. Everybody seemed to have a job to do, and I didn't try to stop crying and neither did the children. Even the little ones seemed to understand what was going on and why.

After the village monks had finished the chanting, the elders lifted Riddth into his coffin and loaded him onto the truck that had been hired to drive him the short distance to the pagoda. The truck had been wrapped in white cloth with black bows linking the material together, and was the traditional vehicle used by the local people to carry the bodies of their loved ones to the cremation point. Only the closest family members travel with the body and I was asked to climb into the back and sit with Riddth. I saw Goey's grief-stricken face, and I took her hand and helped her up to sit beside me. Through my tears I noticed with a joyful satisfaction that she was wearing the silver chain Trish had given to Riddth. It was rightly hers.

The truck set off at a sedate pace with all the people walking behind. It was fitted with a loudspeaker that blared funeral march music. The road was lined with many farmers and their families wishing Riddth a final farewell. Some of the older girls and boys walking behind the truck threw handfuls of fake paper money to keep evil spirits away. The farmers' small children ran laughing to pick the money up as fast as it was being tossed away.

I was so grateful to Ming, who had been up all night arranging the truck, flowers, food and monks for the cremation. I had given her some money the night before and I found out later that many of my friends had donated money towards the cost of the funeral. Ming had asked me if I wanted Riddth to have a Christian funeral, as she knew I loved him like a son. I was touched by her thoughtfulness but assured her that Riddth should have a Buddhist end to this life.

The truck stopped outside the pagoda, where a funeral pyre had been hurriedly built from large bamboo trunks. It was a large rectangular box filled with a mixture of charcoal and kindling wood. The elders of the village lifted Riddth out of the coffin and placed him on the pyre. It was just a little too small for him, and they had to push and poke him to make him fit.

After a short chanting session by the monks, everyone was invited to pass by for one last look. The children walked slowly past leaving Goey and me last in line. After Goey had said goodbye, I knelt down and brushed his shiny black hair back from his eyes and kissed his cold forehead. I then placed a closed lotus flower on his chest. I felt a wave of weakness and was afraid I was going to faint, and in a second Toeub was at my side to help me stand up. He took my arm and led me to the grass where all the children were sitting quietly several metres from the pyre, and sat me down next to them. The elders poured kerosene all over Riddth's face and body and threw in a lit match. The flames crackled and leaped high into the air. It was that simple.

For the next few hours I sat with the children, who were amazingly well behaved, and we all waited for Riddth's body to burn. They were really quite surprised to see the extent of my grief, and I could see that now they really believed how much I loved him and them.

As the smoke and fire started to die down, Toeub told me that now we should search the embers for those bones that had not completely burned. These would be placed in a jar called a *chedi*, which would be placed in one of the stupas in the pagoda grounds.

Toeub said that Ming had forgotten to buy a chedi and had returned to the orphanage to bring back something suitable. When Ming returned I was not happy that the container she had brought back to carry Riddth's bones was the green plastic strainer used to wash vegetables in the kitchen. But I knew there was nothing I could do.

I didn't shrink from joining the children leaning over the pyre looking for bones. The charred remains still had the form of Riddth's body, although the intense heat had pulled his legs up into a bent position. The children hit the remains with sticks to make them crumble, so that they could more easily look for the bones that had not been turned to ash. When enough bones were lying in the strainer, ready to be transferred to a more fitting chedi the following day, the children and I packed up, and began the trip back to the orphanage for dinner.

I slept in the girls' dormitory that night, and they fussed over me like little mothers, giving me back rubs and preparing my bed and mosquito net. They sat around my bed until I fell into a fitful sleep.

I woke the next morning to the normal sounds of the children getting ready for school. I had breakfast with them, and saw the green plastic container that had a few hours ago held Riddth's bones, full of freshly washed vegetables to be cooked for lunch. It made me think about how I would have to get on with my life.

When the children had gone to school, I went and lay on Riddth's bed. I knew Tek Lak would return soon from trying to find Riddth's mother and I dreaded telling him he had missed the cremation. I thought about Riddth's life and all the things I would never know about him. I had not had time in the last few days to ask him why his mother had put him in the orphanage. I wished I had some photos of him as a little boy. I thought about how intelligent he was, and what a difference he might have been able to make in Cambodia if he had lived. I recalled the months we had spent together and was so thankful for all he had taught me about Australia, Cambodia and myself. I was emotionally and physically exhausted, but I began to feel calmer and more accepting. I started to understand how Cambodians accepted grief and loss as part of life, and just got on with the business of living.

I returned to my little purple room in town, content in the knowledge that this chapter of my life with Riddth was part of my destiny in Cambodia. I was also comforted by my honest belief that Riddth's next life was going to be full of all the things he had lacked in this one.

Cambodian Memories

Phnom Penh, August 1996 – June 1997

It was good to be able to throw myself back into my work at the Cabinet. I had always used work as a way of coping with my problems and it never failed me. But the first day I returned I was still teary. A woman I worked with in the same room asked me why I was crying. She was new, and didn't know about Riddth and me. She was a princess but preferred to be called by her nickname, Moit. She and her husband both worked for Prince Ranariddh's party, FUNCINPEC (National United Front for an Independent, Peaceful, Neutral and Cooperative Cambodia). She had a handsome, strong face that reflected her intelligence. We were alone and I blew my nose loudly.

'You don't know what it's like to have someone you love die in your arms,' I said, feeling very sorry for myself.

Moit took her reading glasses off and lay them down on the desk.

'Oh, you are very wrong, Geraldine. I watched helplessly while two of my babies slowly died of hunger and thirst in my arms in the labour camps of Pol Pot. You are not alone in your sadness.'

I felt so ashamed of myself. I was surrounded by people who had lost every living relative, their homes, their livelihood, their youth and their hopes. How could I have been so stupid.

⌒

I needed to spend more and more time with the children. They seemed to sense my need, and responded by coming to me with all their little cuts and bruises. They must have thought that as I didn't have anyone to nurse anymore I would feel better if they let me be their own special doctor. In between the regular visits by a doctor that Princess Marie arranged, I took care of any accidents and all kinds of illnesses and fevers. When I took the children into town to the hospital for treatment, they always stayed overnight with me in my room. It saved another trip on the tortuous road that was wrecking my car, but I was really seizing the chance to keep the kids with me to give them some extra love and attention.

I would take them for a good feed at one of my favourite food stalls, and then we would all snuggle in my big bed for the night. I always had two children at a time; if a sick one was alone they would be bored just with me, especially as I had no television, so they were always invited to bring their best friend with them.

One day I returned to the orphanage with two ten-year-old boys, Chaab and Sopheak. The kids greeted them as they got out of the car.

'Where did Big Mum take you to eat? What dishes did you eat? Tell us.' They were always obsessed with food.

I was picking up a lot of Khmer through my work in the Cabinet and through the kids, but kept my growing vocabulary to myself. I saw an advantage in letting everyone think I didn't understand what was being said. But this day I understood more than I wanted to.

'Oh, we had beef and big prawns. It was delicious,' said Chaab.

'But why didn't you tell us that Big Big Mum snores and farts in bed? It was so loud we couldn't sleep!' said Sopheak, giggling.

'And she squashed us up against the wall and we couldn't get out to go to the toilet!' chipped in Chaab as they ran off with the other children to play.

All this was a rude shock. I wondered how many of my lovers had been too polite to complain about my sleeping habits. Now I knew what I would be putting any child through if they stayed overnight with me. But a few days later when two more children needed to be taken into town, they didn't need any coaxing to come with me.

'I'll count how many times she snores, and you count how many times she farts,' one said to his friend on the way into town, not knowing I understood every word. I couldn't resist a smile. God I loved the little rascals.

⟜

I knew I couldn't continue to stay on in my purple room; there were too many memories of Riddth that I didn't want surrounding me any longer. I asked Vibol if he could do something about getting me into one of the free rooms the government sometimes gave to employees who were being paid low salaries. I could certainly put myself into that category; my salary was a source of great amusement to me, and I enjoyed telling my friends what my 'package' was at the Cabinet of the prince.

I was paid US$130 a month for a five-day week, the going rate for foreigners who offered their services. I, like all other Cabinet staff, was given a seventy-kilogram bag of rice every quarter and nine bottles of soft drink a month. All the soft drinks would appear one day on my desk and could be a motley mixture of Coca-Cola, 7-Up, and various brightly coloured Cambodian drinks with jellied coconut or cooked beans floating around in them. Each month I was given coupons for 100 litres of gas which I sold to others who had cars. I couldn't rely on my salary being paid on time, and when I did receive it I was given a handful of grubby US dollars that weren't even in an envelope.

Despite everything, I wasn't complaining. I was working where I wanted to be. I believed that Prince Ranariddh was the answer for Cambodia's future, and I wanted to be a part of his FUNCINPEC party, which would help him win the elections scheduled for July 1998.

Within a few weeks Vibol found me a room in the government staff hotel called Sakal Two. It was only five blocks from the Cabinet. I had merely one large room with a bathroom and toilet, but it was heaven to have my own bathroom. I was thrilled. I felt rewarded by being given this room as it meant that Vibol, Thuch and Prince Ranariddh took me seriously.

I was the only foreigner in Sakal Two and was allowed a few renovations. I added a ceiling fan, a bath, ripped up the black, red, yellow and green striped carpet, and laid cool ochre-coloured tiles on the floor. It felt like home when I had bought some wooden furniture and added other personal touches. Riddth would have loved my room. I could sometimes feel him grinning all the way from Africa when I brought some little treasure home from the markets.

This room became all things to me. I slept, ate, bathed and worked there. I was even able to seat six people around a bar I had built so that I could entertain a little. So what if my refrigerator, toaster and electric cooking ring were in the bathroom, right next to the toilet? When in Cambodia, do as the Cambodians do, I always say.

I was a constant source of curiosity for the other occupants. I soon learned that it was no use tying my rubbish up in plastic bags for the cart downstairs. I would see the women in the building quite openly going through my rubbish to see what I was throwing out.

I did have to fight off some of the women who lived in Sakal and who wanted me to pay them to clean my room and do my washing. I told them that I did all these things myself and could see they were horrified that a Westerner was doing housework. However, I had to admit I didn't enjoy handwashing my sheets by slapping them around in the bath. In the end I agreed to have a woman come twice a week to clean and do the washing and ironing, for the ridiculous sum of US$20 a month.

In March 1997 I met Geoff Edwards, a Queenslander who offered me a job trying to build up a business by securing aviation insurance in Cambodia. I was still working at the Cabinet but, like so many other Cambodians, I needed two jobs to keep my head above water. It was a trial to see if it was worthwhile, and I was judged to be a good person to hunt for business in government circles, which controlled most of the aircraft. I was to be paid a quarterly retainer, which would make a huge difference to my lifestyle. But the best part was that the company was supplying me with a four-wheel drive car, which would be registered in my name and remain mine no matter whether the aviation business was successful.

I was getting tired of travelling on the motos. The thirteen kilometres to the orphanage were particularly taxing. It was funny in the beginning when the moto drivers made jokes about there not being enough room on their bikes or that they would have to stop and get more air in their tyres, but it was beginning to get annoying. In time I managed to find a phrase in Khmer close to 'Just drive, needle-dick', but this didn't always have a good effect on the moto driver.

But now I would finally have wheels. I couldn't believe my luck. Things were looking up at last.

The Cambodian newspapers provided me with all the entertainment I could wish for. They had recipes for bat soup, advertisements for dog restaurants, where you could eat at a discount if you BYOD (Brought Your Own Dog), directions to the best marijuana sellers, and stories about the refusal of the male population to wear condoms and about countless sightings of Pol Pot, as well as a what-to-do list prepared by the UN on how to survive if kidnapped by rebel Cambodians. And all this would be in one issue!

On a more serious note, I became a member of the Foreign Correspondents Club of Cambodia (FCCC). It was an old building right on Sisowath Quay that oozed character. It was the kind of place where you half expected Humphrey Bogart to come out of a back room, but it needed a good paint job. The food was excellent if a little expensive and I could always be sure of seeing other Westerners. There has been a lot of political information passed around the FCCC as journalists from all over the world gather there.

The FCCC had a permanent group of cyclo and moto drivers stationed outside hoping to get fares from the tourists when they left the club. I had noticed an old man with lines of suffering and hard work on his face. I was drawn to him, and asked him to be my permanent cyclo driver. He then showed up every morning to take me shopping. I couldn't believe that he was actually younger than I was; the years in the labour camps had taken their toll. In his excellent French and halting English he told me how his fortunes had changed through the years of war and genocide. He told me to call him Ba.

Ba was a young man when Lon Nol had deposed his beloved Prince

Sihanouk in 1970. He had started a small wooden furniture business and made enough money to marry his childhood sweetheart. Together they had built a house and started a family, and Ba had opened a bank account and had a chequebook. He wore an expression of wonder at ever having had these things.

When the Khmer Rouge drove everyone out of the city he lost everything. His wife and children died because they were not strong enough for the hard work in the fields. The children were taken from him when they got sick and put with all the others, who were just left without medical attention to die slowly. The Khmer Rouge would not even let him visit to show them he still loved them. He said he had not wanted to live after this, but somehow he continued to wake up each morning.

Ba returned to Phnom Penh when the Vietnamese emptied the camps in 1979, and hoped that he could live again in the little house he and his wife had built. However, he found out other Cambodians had moved into it. The Khmer Rouge had burnt all the legal records proving ownership. Ba said he still often walked by to look at his old family house from the street.

After a while a friend took pity on him and gave him enough money to buy a cyclo. Ba said he had been a cyclo driver since 1980. His cyclo was his home; when he was not working in it, he slept in it. He made enough money to eat twice a day and that was sufficient.

Ba said he tried not to think of the days before Pol Pot, because this was his life now. He always had a smile for me and sometimes he would not take money from me. 'I had a good day today and my stomach is full. I know you are working for the royal family and that you help orphan children. Please allow me to drive you for free when I can afford it. We are friends you and I, because I know you love Cambodia.'

⤳

I met many exceptional characters like Mr Ba over the next twelve months. I listened to stories sad beyond anything I could imagine and they all deserve to be told. I cannot tell everyone's stories, but some were so exceptional that I could not put them out of my mind.

Samnang Siv was a woman to whom I became very close. She was also a friend of Roland's, and worked as an advisor in the Ministry of Tourism. Samnang was a returnee from the United States, where she had escaped after the Pol Pot years; she was a gorgeous woman of about forty and her Western style of dress gave her away instantly as a returned Cambodian. We liked each other from our first meeting and she had already heard about me from Roland. We spent a lot of time together and she never let me pay for my dinner at restaurants.

Samnang, like me, supported Prince Ranariddh. After the 1993 elections she decided to resign from her job in a medical research laboratory in Massachusetts, and return to Cambodia to give something back to Cambodian society.

One night while Samnang and I were having dinner in a Thai restaurant, I finished my pork spareribs and left the bones on my plate. She stopped the waiter from taking the plate away and scraped my leftovers onto her empty plate. She proceeded to eat the bones I had had in my mouth, stripping off the little bits of pork that remained, crunching the bones up until nothing remained. I tried not to look shocked.

'Sorry, Geraldine,' Samnang said. 'I don't do this with everybody, just people I trust and like. You see, I can't bear to see any food wasted. I was so hungry for four years in the Pol Pot camps that now I have this terrible habit of finishing off food that other people leave. I know it's very bad manners and I control myself when I'm with people who wouldn't understand. But I know you won't think I'm disgusting.'

I wanted to jump across the table and hug her there and then.

She said it had been a long time since she had spoken about her ordeal and was very definite that she didn't want sympathy or admiration. It was just time she got it off her chest.

She described herself as a survivor, having survived in conditions where others had died like flies around her. Sometimes she felt very guilty that she had survived when so many 'more worthy' people hadn't. That was why she had come back in 1994 – to try to get rid of the guilt.

Samnang's family was well off, and she attended a private school in Phnom Penh before being married off to a young military man she barely knew. She accepted this, as arranged marriages were part of society. She didn't remember much about her husband, but did know that he was one of the military men killed in the first few days of the Khmer Rouge takeover in April 1975.

A week before the Khmer Rouge marched into Phnom Penh, she asked permission from her parents to go to Sihanoukville to celebrate the Cambodian New Year; they said it was too dangerous and refused to let her go. She disobeyed them and went anyway, and never saw them again. She was cut off from them when the population was forced out of the city on 17 April 1975. It tormented her that she didn't know how they died, or where, but she did know that if they were alive they would have found each other. Samnang said it was many years before she was able to accept that they were all dead and lost to her forever.

Samnang stayed in Sihanoukville and was forced to work eighteen hours a day in the rice fields with everyone else. After a couple of months she realised she was pregnant but didn't believe she would survive long enough to have her baby. She worked in the rice paddies next to women who miscarried while they worked. She heard that women fought over these dead foetuses, hiding them in their clothes until they got back to their huts at night, where they cooked the babies in a soup. They saw the foetuses as protein that would give them strength to stay alive another day. Samnang didn't want that to happen to her baby.

She was afraid when her time came to give birth, as she had already seen one woman bleed to death after delivering a baby. She shared a hut with many others and the woman had gone into labour in the middle of the night. There was no water for her to drink and no knife to cut the umbilical cord. Finally, an old woman bit the cord with her teeth, but the woman and baby still died. In the end, though, Samnang's baby came in the daytime; many other women helped her deliver a beautiful boy she called Samiti. Samnang's eyes glowed with pride when she mentioned his name. I had met him at her home in Phnom Penh and he was a very good-looking young man, who was completely devoted to his mother.

Samnang went on to say that the Khmer Rouge took all the babies from their mothers and gave them to trusted Khmer Rouge women to nurse. They wanted to cut family ties and this was how they started the process.

But some of the Khmer Rouge women didn't agree with this system, and the old woman taking care of Samiti always found ways to let Samnang visit him and hold him. Samnang started to steal food to give to the woman taking care of Samiti as she knew that if she helped her she would take good care of Samiti. Samnang stored food she saved from her one daily meal, as she knew the old woman and Samiti needed it more. She stole sugar palm juice from an old man who was in charge of extracting it, and passed it on to pregnant women who needed this extra sweetness for the babies growing inside them. Whenever Samnang felt strong enough she gave the small bits of meat she received as a person working in the rice fields to Samiti's nurse for her to share among the other women and small children. Samnang knew that what she was doing was very dangerous. The Khmer Rouge were watching her closely as they had sensed she was not a peasant girl and were looking for a reason to kill her.

She never forgot Buddha, even though they were told they were not allowed to practise their religion and she often saw monks being slaughtered. She prayed every day for strength to go on, and she said that Buddha never abandoned her.

When the Vietnamese liberated her camp in 1979, she was able to get Samiti back, and took him with her to Phnom Penh to look for her family. She searched but no-one could tell her anything about their fate, and she cried every night.

The Vietnamese gave her a job working as an administrator in a high school run by the government and she thought her life would improve. But very soon she saw that the Vietnamese were indoctrinating all Cambodians into communism and she knew that her family would never want her to become a communist.

She often prayed to her dead parents for guidance, and to her grandmother, who had loved her deeply. In her dreams they told her to take Samiti and run away to Thailand. The dreams were so vivid that she and a friend took off one dark night through the jungle, with Samiti tied to her back with a cotton kroma.

Samnang said she had taken some rice with her for the journey. They rested in the jungle during the day and at night ran for as long as they could. She lost count of how many days she travelled like this. She had run out of rice and was afraid that she and her son would starve to death when she saw the smoke of the refugee camps in the distance. She and Samiti had survived.

Samnang had a much older brother who had gone to America to study when she was a little girl. Miraculously, through the tracing agencies, she was able to find him. He was living in America and he sponsored Samnang and Samiti to go and live there. She put all the bad memories behind her and began her new life in the United States. Within a year she was working with the Cambodian community in Massachusetts, knowing she had survived so that she could help others when they arrived in America from the refugee camps. Samnang was rewarded with an honorary degree from Endicott College in recognition of her humanitarian work with Cambodian refugees. Working with her people in America gave purpose to her life, but she wanted to do even more. Samnang said, with a determined toss of her head, that she had to face her old ghosts and work to make Cambodia a better place.

She loved being back in the country of her birth. Samnang said that in her dreams her parents and grandmother told her that they were very proud of her, and this alone made her content. In one dream her grandmother reminded her of an old Cambodian fable: 'When the rice stalk is straight, it bears nothing. When the rice stalk bends, there is plenty.' Samnang said she liked to think she resembled the rice stalk that bends when it has to. She believed that's how many people in similar situations to hers survived the Pol Pot years.

⟳

Meanwhile, back at the Cabinet things were not good. Many of Prince Ranariddh's advisors were very corrupt but no-one was brave enough to tell the prince. Many FUNCINPEC members were giving the party a bad name because they were lazy and did not carry out their duties efficiently.

Although I did not think much of the Cambodian People's Party (CPP) and shared the view of all my FUNCINPEC friends that Hun Sen was a thoroughly evil person, I did notice that his advisors were working hard and getting things done. The CPP was attracting Cambodians who had the necessary qualifications to build the party back from the US, Europe and Australia.

Very simply, FUNCINPEC had large numbers of the rural population as members; they always had and always would vote for the royal family. The CPP had as followers that section of the community happy with what had resulted from the Vietnamese-led liberation. They believed that Cambodia required a strong man like Hun Sen to make the drastic changes required to improve their lives.

Admittedly, things were much more difficult for FUNCINPEC, because they had very little money to pay decent salaries. Also, they had to rely on cash from the government for their programs, and the Council of Ministers, where the money came from, was controlled by senior CPP members. The Council of Ministers refused to pay what we needed to keep the Cabinet office supplied with drinking water, soap and toilet paper. One day I complained to Vibol that I was thirsty and wanted to use the toilet but there was no water, soap or toilet paper, and that I was going home until these minimal requirements were supplied. Most of the time Vibol or Thuch personally bought these items for the staff. The CPP controlled everything even though the prince was legally the First Prime Minister.

The media didn't help the situation either. Every public and private disagreement between Hun Sen and Prince Ranariddh was blown up out of all proportion. It was evident to everyone that the shaky coalition between the two men was becoming untenable, and that it was just a matter of time before one of them would have to go. But no-one knew who would go or when. Every day there were new stories of corruption allegations against both prime ministers, and many members of both parties. In June there was a fierce battle outside Prince Ranariddh's home between the royal bodyguards and Hun Sen's ferocious crack bodyguards.

As if all this wasn't enough, the floods during the monsoon months of 1996 were among the worst since the war. Most of the country's rice crops were ruined and the peasants in the provinces were facing famine.

Cambodia's pot was well and truly at boiling point.

I was busy planning to take all the children for a weekend at the beach in Sihanoukville, where Lauryn had arranged for us to stay at a friend's house. The children were very excited and I was also looking forward to a weekend away from all the tales of woe in Phnom Penh. After our holiday the bus returned on Sunday night and deposited a sleepy but happy bunch of children at the orphanage.

I wanted to get a good night's sleep as I knew the next week was going to be more hectic than usual at the Cabinet. The Friday before going to the beach, I had spent a day helping some senior generals complete applications for their families to go to America on tourist visas that were to be hurriedly processed. It didn't take too much imagination to work out that something was in the wind.

The Coup No-one Dared Call a Coup

Phnom Penh, 5–7 July 1997

I never slept late in Phnom Penh as the dawn sounds of the city were impossible to shut out. That morning I did; the noisy truck that delivered the small mountains of green coconuts, fresh chickens and vegetables to the noodle restaurant next door hadn't arrived.

No Cambodian worth their salt would consider starting the day without a belly full of spicy noodle soup or rice porridge. The restaurant was a popular centre for locals to meet over breakfast, and to gossip and compare the rumours that were flying, especially since an unprovoked attack in June on Prince Ranariddh's bodyguards by Hun Sen's elite bodyguards. When I finally awoke, I also wondered at the absence of the mournful music from Wat Lanka's crematorium. Usually, the first Buddhist cremation of the day started at dawn, with the family and their hired loudspeakers going slowly down my street.

I couldn't hear the tooting of the ever-present moto drivers seeking pillion passengers to take to work or to the markets. And where was the familiar sound of the friendly chattering and giggling of the hotel maids on the balcony and staircase? Also missing were the usual early morning sounds of the cleaners and security guards downstairs, who every morning vigorously swept the dust from the day before to a different corner of the hotel's entrance, ready to sweep it back the next day.

Silence. All-encompassing, ominous silence. And it was already eight o'clock!

I dressed quickly and carelessly, impatient to go outside so that I could find out the reasons for this strange start to the day. Nothing would have surprised me.

⌒

The day before, Thuch had asked me to represent FUNCINPEC at the American ambassador's 4 July reception at the Cambodiana Hotel as all senior Cabinet officials were busy. I usually loved these opportunities to socialise. But that night I had felt embarrassed. Most of the guests were ambassadors or senior diplomats, and my relatively junior status in Prince Ranariddh's Cabinet could have been seen as insulting to the Americans. If so many of the other guests had not been friends, I would have felt like a gatecrasher.

A journalist to whom I often gave cleared information, approached me with the grin that journalists reserve for those they think might just be stupid or drunk enough to tell them something worthwhile.

'Ah, Geraldine! You can confirm this, surely. Everyone here says that Prince Ranariddh flew out to Bangkok this afternoon. It's a strange time to leave the country, don't you think? What could possibly be more important than being in town now, after last month's attack on his bodyguards?'

I didn't know anything about this. A trip out of the country was certainly not on the weekly agenda of the prince's movements I'd been given.

Shit!

Why hadn't someone briefed me on what to say? They must have known I'd be asked for confirmation of some kind. I felt very angry that I'd not been regarded as trustworthy enough to be told of these important developments. It put me in a position of having to pretend I knew more than I did, a skill I had picked up when working in Australian embassies. It often came in very handy in Cambodia.

'Yes, this commitment in Thailand has been on his schedule for some time and it's something that couldn't be postponed,' I said, with an air of authority I certainly didn't feel.

A senior Asian diplomat brought me a glass of champagne. Everyone knew what I liked to drink. People were known to hide bottles of champagne when they saw me coming.

'Geraldine,' he said, 'perhaps you can tell me why no-one can get a statement from FUNCINPEC officials about when Ranariddh will be back? What's the story? I can't even get anyone to answer the Cabinet phone!'

'Sorry, I've just seen someone I promised to have dinner with tonight. I'm sure Protocol will answer the phone in the morning. Excuse me,' I said, as I smiled and escaped across the crowded room.

I listened to Ambassador Quinn's standard 4 July speech, grateful that at least no-one could ask me any questions while he was talking. Then I left as inconspicuously as I could. I was furious. How dare Thuch use me like this!

The distance from the Cambodiana Hotel to my room was only a few short streets. I didn't notice that the traffic was much less than usual on a Friday night.

Once home, I did what I always do when frustrated or annoyed – I buried myself in a book. I was halfway through *A Hundred Years of Solitude* by Gabriel Garcia Márquez, for the third time, before it fell on my face. This told me that perhaps I had drunk enough champagne after all and it was time for me to sleep.

⌒

I had arranged to take my friend Bill Grant to the orphanage in the morning. Bill was a Scot, close to fifty years old, who had lived in Cambodia for years, and had his own landscaping business. We'd discussed with him what could be done about planting some shade trees for the children, as the land was painfully barren and there was no escape from the glare of the sun. That morning he was going to see the land for the first time. He lived around the corner from me and, as he didn't have a car, usually walked to my place.

'Sorry I'm late,' he said, 'but my housemaid didn't come this morning. Very strange. She's usually very reliable and today is her payday. But I must say, the street was deathly empty on the way here. Anything I should know?'

'That's OK, Bill. I slept in too. I've never known it to be so quiet. Do you mind if I stop by the Cabinet on the way to the orphanage? It appears that the prince left the country yesterday and there may be something brewing,' I said.

We got into my dilapidated old four-wheel drive and drove to Norodom Boulevard, the most prestigious street in town. On the way I was struck by the fact that never had I seen the city's streets so ghostly. Not even in the 1970s with the Vietnam War at its zenith, had they been so deserted. The usual collection of characters was nowhere to be seen. The local mangy dogs were skulking about with their tails between their legs. The noodle shop was locked up like Fort Knox, with the steel grille concertina gates securely padlocked.

I cautiously drove the few short blocks to the Cabinet, with Bill sitting calmly at my side. He had been part of the UN task force during the lead up to the elections in 1993. He actually knew Cambodia much better than I thought I did. Neither of us spoke. We didn't need to.

Norodom Boulevard was swarming with Hun Sen's blue-helmeted soldiers, stationed in pairs at every intersection. The few people who were in the streets were all hurrying along the footpaths, obviously frightened and desperate to reach their homes.

'Jesus, Geraldine, drive carefully,' Bill said. 'That last lot of soldiers were very interested in your car registration plates. What plates do you have?'

'They're green government plates, but I don't think anyone can tell where I work just from looking at them. But you're right; the bastards did look interested in the car. Don't worry, Bill, we are close to the Cabinet,' I said, sounding much more confident than I felt.

I had to double-park outside the Cabinet. There were dozens of military commanders' cars and four-wheel drives everywhere. They were parked on the footpath, haphazardly across driveways; anywhere their drivers had found a spot.

I left a very tense Bill in my car and walked through the Cabinet gates. Never had the Cabinet been so crowded and busy. I felt in the way, out of place, in my own office. But I damn well wanted to know what the hell was going on. I cornered Thuch in his office across the hall from mine. It was the first time I'd seen Thuch's chic Parisian business suits and tailored safari suits replaced by army fatigues; his regular bodyguard was armed to the teeth and unusually alert.

'What the hell is going on, Thuch? Why did you send me there last night when you knew the prince had left? How the hell was I supposed to explain why he had left? Why don't you trust me?'

Thuch's fear had reduced him to a quivering wreck. He was incapable of making sense in any of the languages he normally spoke fluently.

'Go home, Geraldine! Stay there. Don't go outside. We call you. Airport road, many tanks. Very bad, very, very bad. Not good, not good. Shooting! Too much shooting. Tanks. Big tanks! Many tanks. Too many soldiers. Very dangerous! Everyone afraid. Go home. Killing, killing! Again killing. Nothing to do here. Go, go, go,' he almost rasped, in a mixture of Khmer, French and English.

Soldiers were all screaming on their mobile phones. Every desk telephone was ringing and no-one was picking them up.

After leaving Thuch's office I had to flatten myself against the wall on the stairs as more soldiers ran up. They were all asking for their orders. Thuch yelled in Khmer for the commanders to come in, and slammed the door behind them, shutting me out. I was definitely not wanted.

When I got back to the car, I said, 'Well, Bill. I think the visit to the orphanage is off, for today anyway.' I tried not to sound nervous.

I told Bill that Thuch couldn't give me a coherent explanation of what was going on, but that it was obvious that Hun Sen was mounting some kind of coup. I put Bill in the picture by telling him that any coup was going to be easy to mount as it appeared that Prince Ranariddh had in fact left the country the day before, and FUNCINPEC didn't seem to be prepared, as we could see by the mayhem outside the Cabinet gates. I told

Bill that I thought we should both go home and then try to get advice from our embassies. Bill agreed on the spot. He wanted to get home to call around his friends for a reading on the situation.

I drove back slowly, through the side streets this time, and took Bill home. We passed no-one.

It had only been fifteen minutes since we had left my place.

A fever to reach safety started to affect me once I was alone in the car. Having Bill with me had been a comfort, but now he was gone.

Just seconds after I had dropped Bill, I saw the tanks and heard their loud portentous rumbling as they made their forbidding way down Norodom Boulevard, just a few houses away from where I had stopped the car. I was immediately transported back to the 1970s. Tanks were a common sight then and were often used as a mode of travelling around the countryside and outskirts of the city.

Today they were instruments of violence and aggression. The stern faces of the CPP soldiers sitting and standing on the tanks with their weapons held in attack positions, spoke volumes. They knew what was expected of them and heaven help anyone who got in their way.

The hotel was only about 300 metres from Bill's place, but it felt as though hours had passed before I parked my car inside its gates.

Many of the hotel's permanent guests were FUNCINPEC party members working in government ministries. I'd observed previously that they were intimidated by the CPP public servants or military officers living in the hotel. They far outnumbered the FUNCINPEC members.

The CPP soldiers and party members in the hotel were now strutting around like peacocks. They were watching with amusement some FUNCINPEC residents who were in a panic, gathering their families and frantically packing their belongings so that they could escape from the city.

No one greeted me as I passed by. I might as well have been invisible.

Once inside my room, I locked the door and leant against it, noticing for the first time, how thin the plywood was and how useless the locks would be if forced.

My old Foreign Affairs wartime background was beginning to kick in. I checked the electricity and water. Strange that these services hadn't been cut. But I wasn't going to complain! Then I remembered something.

Fuck! Fuck! Fuck!

My passport!

I'd got it back with my renewed residency visa from Immigration the day before and it was still in my desk drawer at the Cabinet. How could I have neglected to get it when I was there? I knew how dangerous the situation was going to become. How could I have been so unprofessional and careless?

Well, it was much too risky to return now.

I examined my water and food situation. It looked as though this was going to be a wonderful time to start a serious diet. I ate most of my meals at Cambodian street stalls and restaurants, and the only equipment I had was an electric jug, a small refrigerator and a sandwich toaster for making my famous toasted sandwiches. The only edible food I had was half a loaf of bread and some rather stale cheese.

But wait, that's not all. Last, but not least, was a jar of Vegemite.

See, there is a God.

To complement this gourmet banquet was one bottle of drinking water, an unopened bottle of gin and six bottles of tonic water.

I could almost have had a dinner party!

I realised that my real lifeline was going to be my mobile phone and lost no time in recharging it. I couldn't be sure how long the electricity would stay on. It rang and startled me.

'Hello, Geraldine Cox speaking.'

'It's Russ, are you OK?'

Good old Russell Walker. He was Prince Ranariddh's personal pilot and Julie, his wife, and their children, Amelia and Julian, were my closest Australian mates. Russ had read the writing on the wall weeks earlier. He had heard a lot of military talk from his Cambodian counterparts in the air force, and had told me several times over the last few weeks that things were coming to a head. He had decided to send Julie and the children back to Australia and to stay on himself until he was paid his salary, which was very overdue.

Russ summarised the situation for me as he saw it from driving around town and talking to Australian embassy officials. The embassy confirmed that a coup was in progress and the shit was definitely expected to hit the fan. He was told that the word on the streets was that embassies were busy arranging to have their staff and expatriates evacuated, and this included the Aussies. He was concerned that I didn't have my passport. He knew I was aware of the drill in a situation like this and made me promise to stay in my room. I asked him when he next called his wife to get Julie to call my mother to tell her I was not in danger. Not yet, anyway.

Russ agreed I should keep my mobile phone open for incoming calls, and was maintaining his sense of humour sufficiently to laugh when I told him I had a bottle of gin if he could make it to my room.

My stomach was telling me I hadn't had breakfast, but the noise of the shelling pretty much destroyed my appetite. More memories of the 1970s in Phnom Penh came flooding back. Then the shelling came from everywhere and hit homes at random all over the city. Today, unless you were caught on the streets, or were close to the key target points, you would most likely be all right.

The phone rang and I could barely hear it through the shelling. I still don't know who called.

'Call back later. I'm fine, but I can't hear you over the bombing!' I yelled into the phone.

I hoped it wasn't my mother. Poor Mum.

I'd really given her a bad time of it one way or another. During one of the worst night-time rocket attacks in 1972 I had the bright idea of recording the war, calling the tape 'Sounds of Phnom Penh'. I proudly sent it to my mother, not appreciating how much it would worry her back in peaceful Adelaide. She had never let me forget that.

My radio was permanently tuned to the BBC and within two hours it was confirmed that Hun Sen had launched a coup to overthrow Prince Ranariddh from his position of First Prime Minister in the coalition government put in place by the UN-brokered elections of 1993. What everyone in FUNCINPEC had feared had finally happened – more Cambodian blood was going to be shed. And again, it was going to be Cambodian against Cambodian. The sheer lunacy of it all filled me with despair.

It was Orwellian to be sitting in my room, with the rockets and bombs going off all around me, listening to the BBC reports. What they were reporting sounded much more dangerous than the shelling just outside my door.

It appeared that most of the action was concentrated at key target points around the city. It seemed to me that the loudest shelling was around Prince Ranariddh's residence and the Cabinet office just down the road, and, from what friends told me by telephone, at FUNCINPEC's headquarters, radio and television stations, the airport and the homes of prominent military generals loyal to the prince.

There really wasn't much I could do when there was a raging battle going on outside and I was trapped inside.

Did I say trapped?

My God, how lucky I was to have a room to hide in. What about the wretched street people who had nowhere to go? The street children, and whole families sitting on the side of the roads with fathers and husbands who had lost their arms and legs with the help of a landmine or two. What would they do? Where could they go? I hoped the monks in the pagodas would take them in.

I'd seen from the short drive in the morning that all, and I mean all, shops and houses on the streets were shut as tight as a drum. No one was going to open their door to give shelter to a homeless person.

Mr Ba, my dear old friend. He slept in his cyclo in the streets.

It was impossible not to think about my kids. I kept telling myself that they were thirteen kilometres out of the city and that although the noise of the battle would frighten them, they were in no real danger.

I tried calling many of my Cambodian friends. I wasn't that worried about my Western friends, as most of them lived in solid houses with walls and locked gates. My Cambodian friends, though, were so vulnerable in their little wooden houses, and many of them lived in the city centre at street level.

My mobile worked, but all the landline phones and other mobile telephones I called were not working. Either the lines were congested by thousands of calls made by Cambodians trying to get news of the situation, or the Ministry of the Interior had pulled the plug on some of the communication services. However, I was getting lots of incoming calls on my mobile. I became paranoid about it ceasing to work. I would pick it up every minute or so, even when it wasn't ringing, just to make sure it was still operating.

The shelling and rocketing continued on and off all day, but around midday it was a little quieter. Chow time for the soldiers. Living a few short blocks from the Cabinet, I could hear that the heaviest fighting was taking place around there. Did Thuch and my friends get out in time? Were they dead? Had they been captured?

Jesus Christ! What about Chong Wa?

Wa was one of the oldest boys from the orphanage. When I had first met him in 1993, he had been about thirteen or fourteen years old. I remembered clearly that out of the toys we had taken to the children, Wa had chosen a soft white rabbit with long ears, and a pair of pink plastic heartshaped sunglasses. I took a photo of him holding his presents; I still have it.

He had turned eighteen a few months ago and I'd got him a job with Prince Ranariddh's bodyguard unit outside the residence. He'd been thrilled to be working for the prince and wearing his new smart soldier's uniform, and I'd been glad to have him close to where I worked, so that I could see him every day. He hadn't even been trained to use a gun when I had spoken to him the week before.

The radio continued to report that FUNCINPEC soldiers were not militarily prepared; they were poorly trained, heavily outnumbered, and strapped for cash. All the power, experience and, most importantly, all the government money, was in the hands of Hun Sen and the CPP. FUNCINPEC would need a miracle to survive, let alone win.

⌐⁓

How could I be hungry at a time like this? But I was, so I had a toasted cheese sandwich, just as if it was any ordinary Saturday afternoon, and washed it down with a good slug of cold gin and tonic. And then another. And another.

By 3.00 p.m. the bottle was half-empty and I only had two bottles of tonic water left. Normally that much gin would render me completely legless; I couldn't remember ever having drunk that much gin in one day. But I was cold sober.

The phone, the phone! I could only just hear it ringing over the rockets.

'Hello, Geraldine here. Hello.'

'It's Bora. Are you OK?' Bora was my Khmer teacher.

'Bora, where are you?' I asked.

'I'm home with my family. We are all safe. We worry about you. Are you in your room?' I could hear the concern in his voice.

'I'm fine and in my room. Don't worry about me, Bora. Stay together and don't come over the bridge to town.'

'My mother said you should try to come and stay with us when the shooting stops. Can you drive your car?'

'Yes, Bora, but I will stay here. It will all be over soon.'

But Bora insisted. He said his mother had begged him to get me to come to them. She had said too many CPP soldiers knew where I lived and that I worked for the prince; she was sure they would round all his people up and shoot them, just like before. Bora said his mother would be angry with him if he could not convince me to go and stay with them. He was using a friend's telephone and would not be able to call me again. He made one last plea that I come to their village, telling me they had plenty of rice and that there was fish in the river next to his house.

Bora hung up before I could say anything, which was just as well, because I was crying. How could they have the heart to worry about me when the nightmare was happening to them again?

I had many long talks with Bora after my lessons, when we would discuss all kinds of things. I remember asking him once if there was anything he was still afraid of. I knew he had faced starvation, torture, seen loved ones die, fled through minefields as a refugee, been homeless and unemployed. Cambodians usually dislike answering personal questions like this; Bora would never have asked me a similar one. He took a long time to reply, but finally spoke: 'Only one thing, Geraldine. I am afraid of being alone. Only of being alone.'

When Bora called me he knew that I was alone in my room and to him that was terrible.

(It's almost impossible to make most Cambodians understand the common Western desire for solitude. The bigger the family, the more noise, the better they like it. My Khmer friends, who know I live alone by choice, think I'm a very eccentric lady. They may well be right.)

I thought about what Bora's mother had said. Would Hun Sen's soldiers really come for me? Why would I be a target? I had no power, but I was known to be close to the Norodom family as well as being employed by them. In the weeks to come I would learn that FUNCINPEC people had been tortured and murdered for much less than this. Just having a framed photo of Prince Ranariddh on their wall or a FUNCINPEC sign outside their house, had meant the torture and death of dozens of Cambodians, many of whom simply disappeared. However, I didn't hear about this for days and never seriously considered the advice to leave my room.

David Perkins, an old friend and Chase Manhattan Bank's company lawyer, called to say that everyone at the bank was worried about me. He advised me to get myself a media profile, as I would be safer if people outside Cambodia were following what happened to me. My family would have been worried sick when the news of the coup hit Australia. I remembered the warning Trish had given me just before I left Sydney with Riddth, when I had needed her powerful intuition. She had warned me very strongly that I should not, under any circumstances, become involved in Cambodia's politics. Too late to think about that now.

Fuck!

The information on my computer at the Cabinet could certainly get me killed if anyone from the CPP saw it.

I had advised Cabinet officials over and over, verbally and in the security manual I had designed for them, that the minimum security requirement for any government computer in which sensitive information was stored, was the installation of password-protect software.

How I wished they had acted on my advice, but for reasons unknown to me they hadn't. As a result, the information on the Cabinet computers was as free as that in a public library. Just switch them on and it was all there.

Most of my work had consisted of speechwriting, answering correspondence and preparing press releases. There was nothing very covert about any of that.

But after the attack on the Cabinet bodyguards, I'd been asked to help translate into English the contents of a bugged telephone conversation between a very senior CPP member and one of his military commanders. (In Cambodia spying is normal practice.) On the tape, the CPP commander was seeking orders from his superior about a planned attack on a village where it was thought a FUNCINPEC leader was hiding. The commander confirmed that arrangements for the attack were in place, but said that the villagers were loyal FUNCINPEC supporters and were hiding the man they sought. He said that he was expecting the villagers to resist them and was asking advice as to how the soldiers under his command should handle such a situation.

The barked order in response is burnt into my memory.

'Kill them!'

It wasn't just the words themselves that were so horrifying; it was the sinister tone in his voice. He followed this order with an angry tirade at the subservient commander about how he should have known better than to ask such a stupid question when everyone knew CPP's policy in these matters.

What if the Cabinet office building was captured and the files on my computer analysed? This document had the potential to identify me as being more involved with politics than would be good for me.

⌒

Despite such distractions, I still couldn't stop thinking about the children. Just how safe were they at the orphanage? The older ones had already suffered so much and had seen too much fighting and killing. On the other hand, those who were toddlers would be experiencing bloodshed for the first time. I knew they must be terrified.

The road to the orphanage was off the main road that led to Pochentong

Airport, and the reports from friends and on the radio confirmed that the road to the airport was coming under extremely heavy tank and artillery fire, including B40 rockets. Hand-to-hand fighting was taking place between CPP and FUNCINPEC soldiers. Many innocent civilians were being killed and wounded in crossfire. I knew it would be stupid to try to reach the kids. I tried to put them out of my mind, but their little faces kept floating in front of me whenever I closed my eyes.

The gin helped me through the rest of the day. At dusk the sounds of the battle faded when it was time for the evening meal. After the last sporadic noises of B40 rockets, AK47s and M16s stopped, I carefully opened my door and ventured out to the front balcony overlooking Pasteur Street. People slipped out of their shelters, hugging the walls as they ran down the streets to who knows where. No one uttered a word and everyone avoided eye contact.

'Where are you going?' I called out in Khmer.

No one answered me. They just scampered away to their destinations for the night. Everyone knew that Sunday would bring more death and destruction.

I was suddenly filled with an overwhelming sense of sadness that almost took my breath away. I watched a pitiful scene in the street below. A husband and wife who worked in the hotel were trying to get all their family and belongings onto their moto. We had always smiled at each other on the hotel stairs and I would give the children some sweets from time to time, but I never knew their names. The father was a junior clerk in the Ministry of Commerce and a card-carrying FUNCINPEC member. I went down to help them. They said they were going to try to get to Takeo province, which was only about thirty kilometres from the city. They thought it might be safer for them to stay with relatives there.

The husband sat forward with his bony backside resting on about one inch of the bike's seat. A large sack of rice attached to the handlebars was making it difficult for him to have a firm grip. His frightened young wife, wearing all her clothing in layers, sat behind him, with a small boy and girl of around three and four years old balanced on each hip. It was impossible for her to hold on to her husband.

Next, an older girl, aged around seven, sat tightly up against her mother's back, plastic bags of assorted clothes, bottles of drinking water and diesel for the moto, clutched in both hands. The girl's brother, aged around twelve, pressed himself onto the already heavily loaded saddle behind his sister. Then I lifted another small girl up onto the shoulders of her father; a younger boy sat on his brother's shoulders, hanging on to his hair with both hands.

Just when I thought the eight of them were about to take off, their wizened grandmother came out from the hotel, her arms full of more plastic bags of belongings. I didn't think it was possible for her to get on, but she did. She could have been anywhere between fifty and eighty years old. She had seen everything: French colonialism, Lon Nol, the American carpet bombing, Pol Pot, the Vietnamese invasion and now Hun Sen. There was no way she was going to be left behind.

The family moved forward another centimetre and the old lady put aside her modesty, hitched up her sarong and let me help her onto the bike. She tried in vain to hold on to the plastic bags, but there was no way she could keep her balance without putting both arms around her grandson. She dropped the bags full of their lives in a bedraggled heap at the side of the road.

I wished them luck and watched the nine of them wobble off around the Independence Monument, into Norodom Boulevard and the road to the province.

⌒

The rest of the evening I spent either talking to friends on my mobile or clasping a pillow over my head when the bombing went off close to the hotel.

There were so many rumours. One was that Hun Sen had accused the prince of negotiating with the Khmer Rouge, that the prince had transported hundreds of armed Khmer Rouge troops into the city to mount a coup against him. Hun Sen had said he was just protecting the Cambodian people against the hated Khmer Rouge!

Stories of assassination-type murders of many FUNCINPEC figures, including Ho Sok, a secretary of state in the Ministry of the Interior, who was loyal to Prince Ranariddh, outraged everyone. The killing took place at the ministry by a well-known CPP official.

I was about to drop off to sleep, despite the din, when the mobile rang once more. It was Kamal Ismuan, the Malaysian ambassador, who was a special friend of the orphanage, often having sent gifts of food and clothes to the children. He had joked with me on Friday night at the American reception about the prince leaving the country. He now told me that Thuch, Yath and Vibol had escaped from the Cabinet by hacking their way through the back wall with a crowbar. They had gone into the garden of the Singaporean ambassador and from there to the Cambodiana Hotel.

Kamal said I should know that senior FUNCINPEC and Cabinet officials were literally heading for the hills, and urged me to get myself to the Australian embassy for the evacuation when it was announced. Any FUNCINPEC and Cabinet officials in danger who had second passports were trying to get diplomats to escort them to the Cambodiana Hotel, where a safe house had been created, guarded by US marines from the American embassy.

Kamal had seen CPP soldiers lurking on the street outside the hotel, obviously very disgruntled that some embassies were assisting FUNCINPEC leaders to escape from Cambodia. He thought the soldiers had been ordered not to take armed action in front of foreign journalists and photographers.

He told me as gently as he could that many of our mutual Cambodian friends from FUNCINPEC had not made it to the hotel.

⌒

That night sleep at first seemed impossible when I thought of what might be ahead the next day.

I was beginning to understand that there was a very real chance I might not get through this episode alive. I sat on the edge of my unmade bed, thinking. If I knew I was going to die, were there any fences I'd want to mend?

I'd been saying goodbye to Mum since she had turned eighty, but she was eighty-four now and still going strong. I'd told her I loved her and thanked her for being a wonderful mother so many times that she was getting bored with it.

And Lisa Devi, my daughter, and one of the most important people in my life? She and I would have to wait for another lifetime to be able to communicate. But even though her retardation was profound, I hoped that she understood my deep love for her. I had made my peace with Lisa too. I knew that she had forgiven me for not being able to take care of her for the rest of her life.

It didn't take too much soul-searching for me to admit that there was a lot of unfinished business between Mahmoud and me. I'd never really told him how sad I was that our marriage had failed. Our happy times had been very happy. I decided that if I died, he was the one person I'd like to say 'I'm sorry' to. I got pen and paper and poured myself another gin.

Fuck, no more tonic left.

It wasn't easy opening such old and sensitive wounds. But if it were Mahmoud in danger asking himself this question, I sure as hell would want him to decide to send me a letter.

'Dear Mahmoud,'

'My dear Mahmoud,'

'Mahmoud,'

Oh fuck, Geraldine! Just write the bloody thing!

My letter was only one page, but what a relief it was to see the words in black and white. I cried when I sealed the envelope. They were not tears of fear or anxiety about my situation, but bittersweet tears of grief and loss, for a love that once promised so much, but had withered. I would always be sorry that Mahmoud and I would not grow old together as we had planned.

However, writing it was one thing; posting it was an entirely different matter. I could hardly pop it in the mail between rocket blasts! I stood it up against my graceful statue of Buddha. If there was an Australian evacuation, maybe I could give it to someone to post in Australia.

The main thing was that I had written it. I should have done it long ago. I wasn't surprised when sleep then beckoned me like an old friend.

Whether it was the cleansing experience of writing my feelings to Mahmoud or just the gin, I was able to sleep through the night. I knew that the next day would be a momentous one, for me and for many people in Cambodia.

⌒

Sunday, bloody Sunday. Dawn heralded the unmistakable sounds of violence.

Amazingly, though, I still had power and water.

I ran a hot bath. As I lay in the soothing water, the telephone rang.

Fuck! I had forgotten to take the mobile with me to the bathroom.

I got out of the bath as quickly as a large lady can when she's slippery and wet, and slithered across the tiled floor to answer it.

It was my friend Dominique. When I met her, she was teaching English to landmine and polio victims without charge, so that they could get jobs. But what I would always remember most about her is that on the day Riddth died, she sat at the foot of his bed and sang lullabies to him until he left us.

Dominique lived in a French-run hotel near the roundabout across the road from the French embassy and the FUNCINPEC military headquarters. She told me that all the guests were trapped inside the hotel and that bullets had been flying around all day. But she was safe. Was I?

I told her that I'd had better days, but my telephone still worked, I had power and water and even a spot of gin.

She told me that most of the hotel guests had to lie on the floor all day. However, she had been able to see out of the top-floor window when Hun Sen's soldiers attacked FUNCINPEC headquarters. She had been horrified to see so many people caught in crossfire. Old men and women were killed, and mothers were running for their lives with their babies in their arms.

While she was talking to me she was looking out her window, and saw the hotel staff trying to cover the body of a teenager with some cardboard, to keep the flies off him. The soldiers would not let them go anywhere near the corpse. She was crying when she said that somewhere in the city, his mother would be worrying and waiting for him to come home.

To get her mind off the dead boy in the street, I asked her if she was going to try to make it to the French embassy.

She said she had watched with shame as Cambodians with French passports had tried to get into the embassy only to have the French staff lock the gates in their faces. She said nothing would induce her to go there for help.

After my conversation with Dominique, I went back to the bathroom to run more hot water to reheat my now cold bath.

Now there was no water. Well, it was only to be expected and at least I was clean.

Sunday afternoon dragged on. BBC radio seemed to know more about what was going on at the end of my street than I did. If journalists could walk around out there, what the hell was I doing hiding in my room?

Get off your fat bum, Geraldine. Get yourself out to the orphanage. Just do it. Go!

Self-loathing consumed me. How could I sit in my room when God only knew what the kids were going through? I wanted to bang my head against the wall with rage at my inaction, but the thought of trying to brave the streets continued to fill me with dread.

I was a despicable coward. The children meant everything to me, but here I was, hiding.

I looked at my face in the bathroom mirror. I hated the weakness I saw.

⌒

I knew I should eat something. The bread, cheese and Vegemite I ate tasted like cardboard, but I forced myself to finish my lunch, and made a strong black coffee from the little bottled water I had left. That was all I could manage to keep down.

Telephone calls from friends spoke of relentless looting by the victorious CPP soldiers. I was told they were even looting from their own party followers. The Chinese, in particular, were a target and in one hotel the soldiers went from room to room, raping all the Chinese maids they could lay their hands on.

Russ told me that heavy fighting and looting continued in and around

Pochentong Airport, which the soldiers had stripped of everything. The city's car showrooms had been among the first places the soldiers had gone. Tanks drove right through the plate-glass windows. Soldiers broke into cars and jump-started them, filling them with petrol from the pumps, which they later ripped from their moorings. Huge garment factories, set up by Malaysians and Chinese, were also looted and vandalised. The streets were full of CPP soldiers on tanks loaded up with household goods, motos, refrigerators, even kids' bikes! If it wasn't screwed down, they took it. Russ warned me to stay inside.

The CPP had control of the airport, radio and television stations, all government ministries and the FUNCINPEC headquarters. Prince Ranariddh's residence and Cabinet were occupied by high-ranking CPP soldiers, busy taking stock of their spoils.

Russ confirmed reports that FUNCINPEC's royal bodyguards had either been killed, or had deserted or defected to the victors. I could only hope that Wa had had the opportunity to escape or the sense to defect and survive. All of Prince Ranariddh's senior advisers who had not been killed or had not fled to the countryside, were either hiding in their homes, too afraid to leave, or had made it to the Cambodiana Hotel. There they trembled in fear, waiting for foreign embassy officials to give them safe passage to the airport, so that they could join the evacuation flights on their governments' military aircraft. Friends urged me to get myself to the Cambodiana, too.

I could tell Russ was concerned about his own fate as well as mine. He had spoken to Julie and she was out of her mind with worry. She had already called my mother and Sandra, but there would have been little she could say to put their minds at rest. I knew that both of them would be trying to call me.

Later Russ called to tell me he had been near the airport and seen that the sky close to the orphanage was black with smoke. The CPP soldiers had hit the military barracks near the orphanage pretty hard.

My imagination started running a grisly movie. I saw myself unharmed, surrounded by the bloody bodies of all my children, their faces twisted in agony and death. The ground was damp, and stained dark brown by their blood, soft and spongy with their bodies' juices. My movie had no sound and it was shot in fast split-second takes. One child's face flashed before me, and then another and another.

Ry Pros was only nine years old and totally alone in the world. Nhem Kea was ten. She had seen her mother step on a landmine. Her father's new wife had not wanted her in the house and had forced him to abandon her.

The gin, cheese, Vegemite, and more gin, rose in my throat. I only just made it to the toilet and threw up the lot.

⤙⟶

As night fell the power supply still had not been tampered with. The soldiers wanted to be able to see at night, to catch those they were seeking.

Anyway, thank God, I could keep my mobile phone charged. (For a usually non-religious person, I had been talking to God a lot during the last couple of days.)

The phone rang again. I snatched it up halfway through the first ring.

'Geraldine, it's Mum and Sandra. We're on a conference line. Darling, what's happening? Are you OK? It looks really bad on the news here.'

Now I'd see what kind of an actress I was. I wanted to cry, but knew that if I did they would worry even more. I put on my breeziest voice and told them I was fine, and that I had loads of friends around me and we were supporting each other. I reminded them how journalists always liked to make things look worse than they were, and told them not to believe all they read or saw on television.

Sandra mentioned there was talk of a military evacuation for all Australians. She said I could be home in a matter of days.

I knew I couldn't let them think I would leave. It would be too cruel. I said I had known that sooner or later there would be trouble in Cambodia and that I was prepared for it. I said it was nowhere near as bad as it had been twenty-seven years ago, so I'd feel really silly running away. I hoped they would understand. I told them that the streets of Washington D.C. had been more of a threat. I tried to sound amused, praying that a loud rocket didn't go off while they were on the phone. I pointed out that surely neither of them would have wanted me to leave before I could find out how the kids were.

I could hear Mum crying. Shit, this was so hard.

I asked them to trust me to do what I thought was best. 'This will all blow over and everything will be back to normal,' I said. 'Just trust me.'

I explained that lots of people's telephones had been cut off and that this might happen to me soon. I told them not to panic if it did.

'I love you all,' I said, as I screwed up my face to stop myself from crying.

'Bye, Geraldine. We'll call again soon. We all love you. Take good care of yourself and please don't take any silly risks,' Sandra said before hanging up.

That conversation took a lot out of me. I loved them both so much. Mum had always supported me whatever I did, and had never tried to stop me from travelling. And Sandra was everything a sister should be and more. Back when I had been trying to have my own children, I had been jealous of her family life. How could I have known how content my gorgeous Cambodian sons and daughters would some day make me? Sandra could have been envious of my free lifestyle and international travelling but she never tried to make me feel guilty about not being home and available for the family more often.

The phone rang again just a few minutes later.

'This is Murray Nicoll from the ABC's Drivetime show in Adelaide. How are you, Geraldine? Your mother gave me your number. We hear you are in a bit of trouble there. What is really going on there? Hun Sen is saying it's not a coup and that Ranariddh started it all. What's your opinion, Geraldine?'

A 'bit of trouble', I thought. Understatement of the fucking year!

There was no stopping me then.

Instinct told me that the more attention I drew to myself in Australia, the safer I'd be in Cambodia. Hun Sen was fast losing the sympathy of many international governments, but thanks to Ambassador Tony Kevin and his glowing reports of what a wonderful job Hun Sen was doing in bringing peace to Cambodia, the Australian government was one of his staunchest allies. Hun Sen would not want to harm an Australian and upset one of the only governments friendly to him.

I quietly thanked Murray for his support; I wanted to sound calm. But I made it clear that I knew a coup when I saw one, and this was a coup – and a bloody one. I told him that it had started on Saturday and that anyone who had had a home to go to was in it. I said that I had seen Hun Sen's, not Prince Ranariddh's, soldiers on the streets on Saturday morning. I told him that it had been raining bullets and rockets for two days, and that the main attacks had been on places associated with Prince Ranariddh and FUNCINPEC, not the other way around. I thought I sounded pretty good for someone who had never spoken on radio before.

'You've convinced me, Geraldine. I'm told you have an orphanage there. How are the children faring?' Murray asked.

I said how worried I was about the children, but that the streets were full of tanks and looting soldiers and I hadn't been able to get to them. They had been expecting me on Saturday to take them their food money for the month, but I didn't know when I'd be able to get there.

Murray confirmed that the Australian government was organising RAAF planes to evacuate all Australians in a day or two, and he wanted to know if I would be on one of them.

'Look Murray, if I left now I'd never have a bloody night's sleep as long as I live. I won't be going anywhere until I know my kids are safe,' I said, already regretting that I'd said 'bloody' on radio.

Murray wished me luck, and promised to keep in touch on behalf of the people of Adelaide who were listening to his program. Calls from Murray would come in almost every day until the worst was over. I certainly felt a lot more secure knowing that if I didn't answer the telephone people in Adelaide would be asking why.

Just as I was trying to decide if I'd been incredibly stupid or incredibly clever by talking politics on the radio, someone banged loudly on my door.

'Geraldine, let me in. It's Nancy Boyd!'

Nancy was an American woman I had met through the Cabinet. She had run to my apartment from where she lived one street away, something I wouldn't have done that day. She urged me to pack a bag and go with her immediately. She was leaving on a plane to Bangkok with a FUNCINPEC minister and his family, and they had agreed to take me too. The minister had told her that anyone involved with the prince would be killed. Nancy had told the minister she'd be back with me in thirty minutes. He wouldn't wait longer than that. He had arranged a diplomatic escort all the way to the airport.

I told Nancy I didn't want to go, that I couldn't go. I didn't want to argue with her as she had so little time to get out herself, but she knew me well enough not to bother anyway. She gave me her address in America, and flew out the door to brave the street back to where her escape car was waiting.

I was so lucky.

I didn't know what I'd done to deserve such caring friends.

⌐

The kids have enough rice. They could always eat the chickens they're raising. They won't have clean water to drink, though. There is no way they could go to the local market near the airport to buy water, even if it were open. They would be so thirsty. Maybe they would drink the well water. That would make them sick, for sure.

Soth (the supervisor) would have gone to his little jasmine farm early on Saturday morning for his day off with his wife and two daughters. He wouldn't have been able to get back, even if he wanted to. There is no-one there to protect them.

They are so close to Taing Krasaing (FUNCINPEC's largest military barracks). That's probably where the black smoke was coming from. Russ was right. It would have been a major target.

Oh, sweet Jesus! Eng Supiap (another older boy and Chong Wa's best friend) is billeted as a soldier there. He has only been in the army for a few weeks. What would he know about defending himself from an attack of this magnitude?

How many of my kids have I lost these last two days? How many?

I just have to get out there. I have to see them. I must be with them. I must.

⌒

I woke up exhausted at around 6.00 a.m. on 7 July. My body was desperate for sleep, but my mind was working overtime, creating all kinds of scenes I feared would be reality outside the safety of my little room. I listened for more sounds of war, but it was quiet. No shooting at all.

I could hear some normal traffic noises outside. Could it really be over?

I was startled by a soft tapping on my door. It was rapid, urgent, but muffled to the point I could scarcely hear it. I crept softly from my bed to the door, and saw the shadow of a pair of feet in the crack under it. It couldn't be any of my friends. We had all agreed to stay in our homes and communicate by telephone. I hesitated, too afraid to speak or to open the door. The soft tapping continued.

'Who is it?' I whispered.

'Ming, Ming, Ming!' came the soft reply.

God! I threw a sarong around my naked body and ripped the door open; Ming fell into my arms, she was so relieved that I was home. She was definitely in shock. I sat her down and dashed like a madwoman up a flight of stairs to find someone to help translate her story for me.

I found Syavouth, a Cabinet colleague I had known only briefly who was quite fluent in English. Months before, he had complained that my music was too loud, so I avoided him whenever I could. Now I was praying he was still in his room. I pounded on his door and probably scared him shitless. He and his wife Vanda opened the door slightly. I grabbed them, said nothing and dragged them back down to my room. The four of us sat on my floor while Syavouth translated Ming's story. It confirmed my worst fears.

I listened with my head in my hands and wept. I hardly knew Vanda, and she didn't speak any English, but she put her arms around me and rocked me like a baby. Syavouth, Vanda and I have been fierce friends since that day.

Ming said that on Saturday afternoon fifty to sixty CPP soldiers had stormed through the gates of the orphanage. They had come again on Sunday afternoon, armed with B40 rockets, AK47s and M16s. She said the soldiers had screamed at the children, and pointed guns at their chests and heads; they accused them of harbouring some of the prince's deserting soldiers and helping them escape. They could see that Ming was the only adult and that there were no men to protect them as Soth had already left early in the morning. Her eyes were still wide with fear.

The soldiers had stolen so many things. They took a lot of their chickens, clothes and some of the toys and books. They forced open the locks on the storeroom and took a lot of the rice and canned fish. One soldier had taken plastic watches from the kids' arms and even torn off the photos of their families some of them had on the walls by their beds.

They had taken Soth's files and papers on the children and the accounting records.

Ming was beginning to compose herself now that she had someone to listen to her.

The dozen or so war widows who lived at the orphanage working on a weaving project of Princess Marie's, had fled on Saturday at the sound of the first shots. They were all survivors of the Pol Pot years. They were afraid they would be singled out for arrest, as they were known to be Princess Marie's 'women'. They had advised Ming to leave too, as they were sure the soldiers would try to get everyone off the land. But she had no money and nowhere to take all the children, and decided to stay and try to hang on. She knew that the minute she walked out of the compound with the children, the soldiers would occupy the buildings and they would never be able to go back.

Ming started to tremble again but she wanted to finish her story.

On Saturday night the children all slept outside, afraid that rockets would hit the buildings. Many of them were so stupefied with fear that they hadn't spoken a word since the fighting had broken out. And since the terrifying visit by the soldiers many of them were wetting themselves, even some of the older kids. Ming said this with a touch of embarrassment.

A smaller group of soldiers came again on Sunday, to tell them they could no longer count on any protection from Prince Ranariddh and

Princess Marie. They said that the prince had run away and that the land was being returned to the military. Then they rounded up the older boys, Supiak, Ros and Saboeun among them, and accused them of being deserters hiding in the orphanage. Ming told the soldiers they were children from the refugee camp in Thailand and that they attended the village school in Khmougn. They demanded proof of this, but she told them that the day before the soldiers had stolen all the paperwork from the office. Some of the girls and smaller boys came running up, and begged the soldiers not to harm their friends. They fell on their knees to the ground and begged.

My heart sank. I recalled that the week before Supiak had had his hair cut short in the new military style, which was all the rage among the teenagers in Phnom Penh. I had laughed at him and said he looked like a soldier. I wasn't the only one who thought that, apparently. And Ros was very tall even though he was only fourteen. Saboeun was very proud of his strong body and worked out every day to develop the muscles in his torso and upper arms. Of course he, too, would be mistaken for a soldier.

Words were gushing out from Ming's mouth. She said the soldiers had told her they would be back and if they didn't leave they would be bombed out. They said the land wasn't Prince Ranariddh's to give away, that it belonged to the Ministry of Defence, and they were going to take it back. They also said that if there was no written proof that the boys went to the local school, they would arrest them until evidence was produced. Ming started to cry again. She didn't know what to do or where to go. She said the radio was full of talk of foreigners leaving Cambodia and that the children thought I would fly out with the other foreigners soon. Some thought I had already gone. What was she to do? What instructions could I give her? How could I help? Ming was pleading now.

We sat and held each other's hands, and tried to communicate our pain with our eyes and our tears.

I knew she would have almost no money. I had been going to give her the money for food for July and for salaries on Saturday. She had been feeding the children rice and chicken, and had been boiling water over the gas burners all day so that they had clean water to drink.

All I had was US$80, kept in my bra. I had intended going to the bank on Saturday, before the pandemonium began.

'Syavouth, what shall we do? Can you help us? You know so many high-ranking people. Isn't there anything you can do?' I pleaded.

He said through his tears, 'If I am going to die because of an Australian woman, I might as well die helping her save Cambodian children.'

He and Vanda took Ming and me upstairs to their modest room. The three of them were chattering together and I couldn't make out a word. Syavouth was now in charge; when he wanted me to hear the plan he would tell me.

He and Vanda were arguing, and Ming didn't want to be involved; she kept shaking her head. Whatever Syavouth's plan was, she didn't like the sound of it.

Syavouth was a Director of Information at the Cabinet and worked closely with both the foreign and domestic press.

'Geraldine, do you have your Cabinet ID card?' he asked.

'Yes, I carry it all the time,' I replied.

Syavouth outlined his plan. It was a long shot, and dangerous. The CPP military commanders who were directing the coup had set themselves up in the Juliana Hotel. General Tea Banh, the CPP Co-minister for Defence, was in charge, and Syavouth's sources had told him that the hotel was completely occupied by CPP soldiers and high-ranking FUNCINPEC people they had arrested. They wouldn't let journalists near the hotel, so if we went there and didn't come out, no-one would know what had happened to us.

Still, our only chance was to go to the hotel and plead with Tea Banh not to force the children out of their home. Syavouth didn't believe the soldiers who had gone to the orphanage were acting under orders. He thought that perhaps if we told the general we knew he would never have ordered soldiers to seize an orphanage, he would take our side. Syavouth agreed to take me to the Juliana if I wanted him to, and that he would go in with me. But it was a risk – a big one.

I looked at Vanda. She took my hands and nodded. Then, with a beautiful smile, she put my hands into her husband's hands. What do you do with people like this?

'I'll go and get my ID card and let's go,' I said.

'You might want to put some clothes on,' Syavouth said, grinning.

I was still only wearing the sarong I had thrown on, that just covered the area between my knees and chest. Vanda and Ming thought this was incredibly funny and we all had a great laugh, which did us a lot of good. It was decided that Ming, who badly needed to rest, would stay with Vanda. She had put the older boys and girls in charge of the orphanage until she returned.

I dressed in minutes and met Syavouth downstairs by my car. He took the keys out of my hand and got in the driver's side; this was his plan, after all.

'I've got my chequebook. When we have finished at the Juliana I need to go to the bank to get food money for the kids,' I said.

'*Oui*,' said Syavouth (he had been educated in France), 'but let's get in and out of the Juliana first.'

It was still early, not even 8.00 a.m., and Syavouth drove around the city so we could see what damage had been done. We could see that the Cabinet had a rocket hole through the roof; it was right above where I had sat just three days ago. A chill went down my spine.

'*Merde*,' muttered Syavouth through the cigarette dangling out of his mouth. I have a strict rule that no-one smokes in my car, but Syavouth could do just about anything he wanted that day as far as I was concerned.

Many of the motos and cyclos were back on the streets and some of the markets were slowly beginning to reopen. It was too early to see if the shops along the commercial section were going to open or not.

As we drove slowly down Monivong Street we passed the biggest moto-dealership in town. Only two days ago I'd passed it and noticed it was newly painted, chock-a-block with the latest Japanese motorbikes that were so popular with Phnom Penh's nouveau riche. A banner had been hung outside the shop that said, 'Buy Now, Before It's Too Late'.

Today, the banner was half torn off and riddled with bullet holes. The shop itself was completely empty. All that was left was a plastic chair with only three legs, lying on its side. (Days later I heard that the owner, who had lost everything during Lon Nol's time, again during the Pol Pot years, and a third time when the Vietnamese occupied his country, climbed the stairs to the roof of his shop and hanged himself.)

Then we passed a man walking the other way, towards the hospital. He was crying uncontrollably, and wheeling a rickety wooden cart. In it were bodies we presumed were those of his family. We could see a blood-spattered woman who was clearly dead, and two children I fervently hoped were dead, so horrific were their injuries.

'Why, why, why?' he was crying, to the people who hurried by him, trying to avert their eyes.

I'd seen almost exactly the same sights in Phnom Penh twenty-seven years before. At least then, the death and destruction were caused by the Vietnamese, not the Cambodians. I could only ask myself the same question as the man with the wheelbarrow.

No-one answered him either.

'Let's go to the hotel. We've seen enough,' said Syavouth.

⟜

Soldiers pointed their guns at the car as Syavouth slowed down and carefully turned into the driveway of the Juliana.

'Fuck,' I said, not sure if Syavouth knew the word at all.

I had never said the 'f' word so many times in one day! I had often, quite pompously, told others, that the English language was more than rich enough to describe any situation adequately, without resorting to filthy words. But today, 'Damn', 'Good heavens' or 'Golly' just didn't do it for me. 'Fuck!', on the other hand, encapsulated exactly how I felt.

'*Merde*,' said Syavouth. I was to learn that this was the only swearword he knew but that he used it frequently.

'Don't talk until I tell you to and don't speak Khmer at all,' he ordered.

He handed our Cabinet ID cards over to the soldiers. They had a long look at the cards, my number plates and at us. They then searched the car and my small bag, handed us back our cards and waved us through, while using their radio telephones to alert other soldiers to our arrival. We parked the car among countless military jeeps and walked to the hotel entrance. Syavouth looked neither right nor left, but I knew he was taking in every face he passed on the way. Once inside, a senior-ranking soldier stopped us; Syavouth and I showed our cards, and I again handed my bag over for searching.

In Khmer, Syavouth asked for an urgent meeting with General Tea Banh. When asked what he wanted it for, he said he was trying to prevent Cambodia from being involved in an embarrassing international incident I had brought to his attention. He said that CPP soldiers were threatening to force Cambodian orphans out of their home, and that I was an Australian involved with the orphanage who had been asked to intervene. He said that I had an appointment with the Australian ambassador that afternoon to advise him whether the problem had been solved or not.

God, this man was a bloody treasure! He was making it up as he went along, of course, but it sounded pretty credible to me.

We were then passed from one rank of soldier to another. Each time we repeated our story. We were led to the third floor, and asked to sit in the hallway outside a room with its door open. Several soldiers guarded us. Syavouth still hadn't told me I could speak.

More people escorted by soldiers were coming up the staircase. I saw with horror three of the maids from Prince Ranariddh's residence. I knew them well. They were trusted, loyal retainers whose families had worked for the royal family for generations, some serving King Sihanouk in the palace. They were obviously under arrest, but for what? Cooking and cleaning? Our eyes met as they passed; it would have been foolish of us to speak to each other. They were pushed into a room down the corridor and the door closed behind them. Were they going to be tortured? They probably thought we were under arrest – perhaps we were and just didn't know it yet!

Finally we were ushered into a room buzzing with activity: soldiers holding papers came and went, and whispering to General Tea Banh, and telephones rang non-stop. The general was very ordinary looking; he could have been an insurance salesman. Nonetheless, he was second only to Hun Sen himself. Syavouth explained the situation to him in Khmer.

Finally General Tea Banh assured me that he would do everything necessary to secure the land for the orphans. He said that obviously some local military rebels were behind what had happened and Hun Sen's soldiers would never have acted in this way. The general asked me to tell the Australian ambassador that they were arranging neutral military police to guard the area for as long as necessary. He then spoke to Syavouth and told him who he should contact about the security personnel. He apologised profusely for any misunderstanding and finished the meeting by explaining in English that he was extremely busy.

I just bet you're busy, buddy, I thought to myself, as I thanked him with all the false sincerity that I could muster.

Syavouth and I were handed over to more soldiers, and were asked to sit in the hall again. This didn't feel good; we should have been allowed to leave. I knew that I should have tried to call Russell before I left to let him know what I was doing, but I hadn't because I knew he would try to talk me out of it. I decided to let him know where I was, and took my mobile phone out and started to dial his number.

Whoosh! The barrel of a gun whizzed past my face, and closed the bottom cover of my mobile, cutting off the line.

'No call!' barked the soldier who was the owner of the gun. He was really angry. 'No call!'

Syavouth looked the other way and ignored me. He was as still as a statue. A soldier came and asked for our ID cards, and took them into another room that was across the hall from General Tea Banh. It was a radio-transmitting room, and I could see technical equipment and a table of noisy soldiers playing cards and smoking heavily. A commander came out, and stood in the hall with two other senior soldiers examining our cards. They were arguing and looking at us.

'*Merde*'! They think we are surrendering to them, that we have come here to defect to the CPP,' Syavouth said out of the side of his mouth.

There wasn't much I could say to that.

My mobile rang and I answered it on the first ring; the soldier who had been so angry with me for using my telephone was not around. It was the Australian ambassador, Tony Kevin. This was the only time he had ever called me. He had already heard about my comments on Adelaide radio and was very angry with me. His stress showed in his voice. He said

I was not helping my situation by making emotional public statements that it was Hun Sen who had started the coup, and said I was mad to have said that I was still a Ranariddh supporter. He told me that if I wanted to help the orphanage, I must stop making political comments, and wanted assurance from me that I would take his advice.

I reminded Tony that I didn't work for him, that I would say what I liked when I liked and that I was the best judge of how to protect the children. I would have said more, but Syavouth stood up in front of me to shield me from the soldier who had shut my mobile with his gun and who was coming back into the corridor. I hung up quickly, furious that anyone would tell me to whom I should give my allegiance.

However, I had more serious things to worry about.

The commander who had examined our cards took them back into the general's room, and this time closed the door.

'*Merde, merde, merde,*' said Syavouth under his breath.

After a few minutes the soldier returned, begrudgingly handed us our cards and got another armed soldier to escort us outside to our car. Syavouth drove cautiously out of the driveway into the street.

'You did it, Syavouth! You're a bloody marvel. I love you!' I said to him as we drove out of the temporary CPP headquarters.

'Next time, don't try to use your phone,' he said, grinning.

'There won't be a "next time". You won't be getting me to go there again, I promise,' I said seriously.

'Let's go to your bank now, Geraldine. It's 10.00 a.m. It should be open by now.'

When we got to the bank there were crowds of angry foreigners and Cambodians outside.

'What's the problem?' I asked a Western woman I'd met many times before in the bank.

'The bank's closed and no-one will tell us when, or even if, it will open. All our money is here and we have been told that all the banks are closed. No-one can get any money from anywhere!' she said.

Syavouth was anxious to get home to Vanda and he had to find out how to contact the military police commander General Tea Banh had appointed to help us. I looked at my watch and couldn't believe it was only 10.15 a.m. I was already worn out. We decided to go home.

The streets were starting to come alive again, but you could smell the fear and tension in the air. People were riding their motos all over the city like tourists, looking at the burnt-out houses and empty, looted shops. Although Hun Sen's soldiers were still on every corner, they had obviously been briefed that their side had won and was in control of the country. At least they no longer needed to shoot anyone.

I hoped Ming would be resting with Vanda and not worrying too much. I knew Syavouth would tell her what had happened when he got home. Syavouth drove us both there. We got out, and I gave him a huge kiss and hug before taking back the keys and swinging the car out into the road. He guessed where I was going.

Tired as I was, now was the time to go to the orphanage.

Now!

～

Pochentong Road was a mess! There were burnt-out tanks all along the road where FUNCINPEC soldiers had put up quite a fight. I passed a crowd of people gawking at the charred remains of a CPP soldier lying on the top of a bombed tank. There's one that won't need to be cremated at Wat Lanka, I thought! I felt no sympathy for him, but knew I'd better watch myself. When you stop being moved by tragedy, it's a little death of the soul.

All the gas stations along the road were stripped even of their plastic signs. Petrol was running in little rivers down the gutters of the road where one of the station's gas lines had leaked. The smell of burning rubber was strong because a mountain of new car tyres had been set alight. The fire would burn for days.

I turned off the main highway to the bumpy road leading to the orphanage; I could see the tanks' tracks on it. They had not improved the already bad road and the potholes were enormous. I knew I should drive very slowly. But I put my foot down on the accelerator and whizzed along as fast as the potholes would let me. I couldn't be sure what was going on at the orphanage and was afraid that if I didn't hurry, something dreadful would happen.

It was very unsettling to see the unfriendly faces of the villagers as I drove by. Some of them shouted abuse at me and shook their fists. I knew that many of them were CPP supporters, but I had had no idea they felt so strongly about me. I knew it was probably because the orphanage was patronised by Princess Marie, and that now Prince Ranariddh had been well and truly deposed they wanted to look as though they were on the side of the victor.

I kept my eyes on the road. Not far to go now; I could see the orphanage buildings in the distance. I started beeping my horn to let the kids know I was coming.

The dust from the road was so bad I nearly missed the open gateway. Then as I drove up they came from everywhere. There were children who were half-dressed from bathing at the well; children pulling their pants up on the way from the toilet. They came from the chicken farm, the dormitories, the dining room. Others came screaming and waving from the direction of the fishpond.

The noise of their cheers and shouting was louder than the racket of the coup. I stopped and turned the engine off. I couldn't open the door because they were all crowded around the car, hugging it.

The older boys jumped up onto the roof and bonnet, waving their arms high above their heads. They yelled out. Their shouts turned to tears and their tears turned to shouts. They screamed out in Khmer:

'Big Mum's here!'

'Big Mum didn't leave!'

'Come, come, see for yourself, she's here, she's here!'

'She loves us. She didn't leave us.'

'Hurry up, everyone. Come.'

'Big Mum's really here.'

'Come and kiss her.'

'Get everyone.'

'Tell everyone Big Mum's here.'

'She really does love us.'

'She stayed. She stayed!'

'Big Big Mum's here!'

'I told you she loved us!'

'I knew she would come as soon as she could.'

'Big Big Mum's here at last!'

'Big Big Mum will never leave us!'

They were laughing, crying, jumping up into the air, clapping. The boys were slapping each other on the back, and the girls were hugging each other and jumping around in circles. They were pushing and shoving each other to get to me. They were crushed up against the car door and I still couldn't get it open.

'Let Big Mum out!' shouted Kosal. He was only eleven but he was pulling the others away from the car.

I tried to put my foot on the ground, but I never made it. Together, somehow, the kids picked me up and carried me into the dining room. Then they sat me down on top of one of the tables, and smothered me with kisses and hugs. The little ones had taken my sandals off and were holding onto my dangling feet, kissing my toes and giggling. The girls were touching, patting and stroking me all over as though they wanted to make sure it was really their Big Mum. Everyone wanted to touch some part of me and there was plenty for everyone!

The relief and love in their faces was unforgettable. Their tears were those of unadulterated love and gratitude.

I've had some pretty euphoric moments in my life, but this was far beyond anything I'd ever experienced. It was like a thunderbolt in my soul. This was love – real love. I knew then that I could never leave Cambodia. It didn't matter if I couldn't explain this moment to anyone else. What was important was the truth and depth of the feelings flowing between them and me, like an electrical current that poured energy and strength into my brain and body.

It was a rebirth. For the first time in my life, I felt that I was the person I was supposed to be.

These children were my destiny. And I was their destiny.

We were one and nothing would ever separate us.

Ducking, Diving, Surviving

Phnom Penh, July 1997 – September 1998

I was a different woman when I drove my seriously damaged car back to Phnom Penh after staying with the children for the night. I now understood that their future depended on me, no-one else. Princess Marie and the others associated with the orphanage had run away to save their lives.

I knew I had to get some kind of plan together. I was more focused and clear headed than I had ever been in my life.

It was imperative that I arrange the military police protection with Syavouth. Then I had to get some money; the $80 in my bra wasn't going to last long and I only had quarter of a tank of gas left in the car. I also knew I had to do something about getting journalists out to the orphanage. By now many people had urged me to build a media profile, and I couldn't ignore the sense in this. I also needed to try to get my passport and the children's records back. Amongst these were copies of all the children's school attendance records, which I could use as proof of the older boys' identities as schoolkids, not soldiers. I decided to place a visit to the Cabinet at the top of my list.

First I went home. Years of travelling had taught me always to keep a photocopy of my passport and I pulled this out of a drawer as well as a large photo of myself with the children. I thought wearing the colour of surrender would be a nice touch of the dramatic, and changed into a pair of white pants and a long Indian shirt. I tried to call the embassy to tell the duty officer where I was going but all the lines were busy. I did get hold of Russell, though. I told him my plans and instructed him that if he didn't hear from me in an hour, to tell the embassy where I had gone.

'Geraldine, you are bloody crazy. The Cabinet is surrounded by CPP bodyguards. Listen to someone for once in your life,' Russell tried to reason with me.

'I know I will be OK, Russ. I have to go. I'll call you. Bye.' And off I went, feeling oddly calm.

I drove slowly the wrong way down Pasteur Street. As I got to the corner of Street 214 where the Cabinet office was, I slowed down even more as armed soldiers came out of the concrete bunkers with their guns pointing at me. I switched the engine off and left the car in the middle of the street. I got out, clutching the copy of my passport and the photo of the children and me.

The soldiers were confused and didn't know what to do. They were trying to get me back in the car, but I explained in my very bad Khmer that I needed to get into the Cabinet as all my files and money for the children were there, and that the children would starve if I couldn't get in. I asked to see their commander and went into the bunker and sat down in the only chair.

They said their commander wasn't there. I said I would wait. They argued loudly with each other again and said I was not safe in the bunker, that more fighting could start and they could not protect me. I said I would stay with them and take my chances. They finally convinced me that I should return at 2.00 p.m. when their commander was expected back. I left the copy of my passport and the photo for them to give to him.

'Please tell your commander that all I want to do is get the children's records and money to feed them. I will be back at 2.00 p.m.' I waved them a friendly goodbye, and they were still arguing with each other as I drove off.

I had a couple of hours to kill and visited some Australian friends. I got all the support I needed, food and lots of chilled white wine. By the time 2.00 p.m. approached I was feeling no pain. I called Ross to tell him the change of plans.

My worried friends waved me off as I went to keep my appointment with the CPP commander. I parked my car in the middle of the street again, and the two soldiers escorted me to meet the commander. He walked towards me, carrying the ever-present machine gun and with enough ammunition strung across his chest to start World War Three. My mouth was suddenly very dry and my lips were practically stuck together.

'G'day,' he said.

G'day? He even had a slight Aussie accent! Was I dreaming? I just stood there looking loopy. He held the photo of the kids and my copied passport.

'My men tell me that you have records of an orphanage in the Cabinet and that you want to get your records. Is that correct?'

'Yes, yes,' I stammered. 'But you speak like an Australian. How can that be? Sorry, sorry. I don't want to take up your time. Sorry.' I was making a real fool of myself. He was enjoying my confusion and we walked together through the Cabinet gate towards the stairs to my office.

The place was crawling with soldiers looting like there was no tomorrow. My heart sank as we entered my room. The top of my desk was wiped clean; the computer was gone, and even the silk kroma I covered my desk with had disappeared. The floor was strewn with papers, among which I could see dozens of photographs of the children.

'Where do you think your records might be?' the commander asked. He bent down and started to pick up the photographs. 'Are these some of your children?' Before I could answer he picked up a box of printed name cards lying on the floor. He looked at the cards and then looked at my passport papers. Shit, they were *my* name cards.

'You work here? You never said you were Cabinet staff,' he said, annoyed.

'No one asked me. I would have said so if someone had asked.' It was all I could think to say.

'So you work for Prince Ranariddh?' He was sounding very suspicious.

'Yes, but I am also responsible for all these children at Princess Marie's orphanage and there is no-one left in the country to take care of them.'

I held my breath. Some of his soldiers were speaking to him in Khmer, and I understood they recognised me and were confirming that I was FUNCINPEC. They were looking at me with distaste and I heard the word 'enemy' in Khmer. He put one of my cards in his pocket.

'Which desk is yours?' the commander asked without any expression on his face.

I pointed to my empty desk and noticed that my unlocked drawers were open and their contents strewn all over the floor. I opened the small locked drawer, knowing that all I had inside it was my passport, a small amount of jewellery, some personal letters, about $200 in cash and the orphanage chequebook.

The commander looked at everything in the drawer.

'You can take everything. There is nothing here interesting for us,' he said.

After I had removed the contents of the drawer, I started picking papers up off the floor.

'See, these are the school records from the orphanage, the master list of the children's sponsors and copies of our accounting details. Can I please take them?'

'Of course,' the commander said and started to help me find the English language papers on the messy floor. His soldiers were blatantly against him giving me any help, saying so with a lot of scowling in my direction. He ignored them, and when the soldiers left the room he continued to help me collect all the photographs and files for the orphanage.

He told me he had lived in Australia upon leaving the refugee camp a couple of years after the Vietnamese came. 'That's where I learnt most of my English and why I speak with a bit of an Australian accent,' he explained.

'Did you like the life in Australia?' I asked tentatively. I was taking advantage of his lack of attention, shoving anything I could get my hands on into a cardboard box he had given me to put my things in.

'Yes, but I wanted to come back and help my country.'

'And this is how you want to help your country?' I was getting really bold now. 'Do you have any idea how many dead Cambodians there are because of the last two days?'

'Don't blame my soldiers for that. They are uneducated. It is ignorance that killed people. They have known nothing but fighting, war and army life.'

He told me that he had been studying to be a doctor in 1970 when the war broke out, and he was put into the army to fight with Lon Nol's troops. His dream of being a doctor was smashed, then Pol Pot came and he nearly died. He lost everyone he knew and loved. He escaped to Thailand and then to Australia, but heard that Hun Sen was doing good things for the people; he returned and was given a senior army position. He had the utmost respect and admiration for Hun Sen, and believed he would bring real peace back to Cambodia.

He continued to help me pack boxes of paperwork and ordered some of his soldiers to carry them to my car. They gave him filthy looks as they walked out with my boxes. There were photos of Prince Ranariddh, Princess Marie and King Sihanouk on the walls as well as photos of my other friends on the floor – of their weddings and university graduation ceremonies.

'Please, can I take these photos for my friends and the prince and princess? They can't possibly be of any interest to you.' I had nothing to lose and hated to think of these items being treated as rubbish – they were important parts of people's lives.

'Take them.' The commander spoke begrudgingly, but with a hint of kindness.

He told me to bring my car closer to the Cabinet gates, where the soldiers were standing with my boxes. As I opened the back doors so they could put the boxes in, it dawned on me that I was actually getting away with this. I had to control the desire to laugh. The commander had allowed me to take much more than I had expected and perhaps would be severely criticised by his soldiers. His superiors might even reprimand him. I knew he was very much aware of all this.

Before I got in the car I wanted to thank him, but anything I could have said would not have been enough. I did something very un-Khmer instead. I threw my arms around his neck and hugged him, kissing him on the side of his cheek.

'Thanks, mate. From the children and me. From one Australian to another.'

He was grinning but looked embarrassed and I could feel the disapproval of all the armed soldiers standing around watching. They were muttering and spitting on the ground in my direction.

He took my card out of his pocket and looked at it again.

'I know where you live. Maybe I'll come and see you some time when this is all over,' he said with a small smile.

'You will be very welcome.' I can't imagine that ever happening, I thought, driving away as slowly as I had come.

I was laughing hysterically when I entered the Sakal driveway and turned around to see Russ right behind me in his car. He jumped out and rushed over to me, opening my door.

He told me he couldn't let me take the risk all alone, so he parked at the other end of Street 214. 'I thought you were a goner, you were there so long. I thought if you didn't come out, at least I could tell the embassy where you were last seen.'

We carried the boxes upstairs and both did a little jig around my room. I was as high as a kite.

Stage one of my plan was successful. I had the orphanage records, a little more money, my passport, my jewellery, and the chequebook to get money for the children's food. Also, I knew how much it would mean to my friends and to Prince Ranariddh, Princess Marie and the king to get their personal photographs back. But Syavouth and Vanda were horrified when they saw the photographs of the royal family lying around my room. They said that Sakal residents were almost all CPP now, and would not want these photographs kept there. Together we hid them behind my bookcases.

⌒

The next day the banks were still closed and I had to get more money from somewhere. I took my last bank statement to the embassy to prove the orphanage had money. I knew from past experience that embassies always had contingency funds, and I was relying on my powers of persuasion to get a few hundred dollars from them to buy food for the children until the banks opened.

I knew Tony Kevin's secretary and asked her for a chance to speak to the ambassador. I wasn't his favourite person but I couldn't imagine he would turn down a request for a few hundred dollars to feed orphans.

The secretary returned and tried to avoid my eyes.

'I'm sorry, but the ambassador is taking a nap right now and I can't disturb him.'

A few choice expletives escaped my lips but she ignored them, and I left the embassy.

I had time for a quick dash to the orphanage, and was saddened to hear that some of the local villagers had been looting. Some of them had broken into Princess Marie's stocks of rice, tinned fish, evaporated milk and other staple goods. I couldn't really hate them, as they were only trying to feed their families during bad times. But I knew I was never going to feel quite the same about them.

I needed money. What did I have that I could sell?

It came to me like lightning. The town was crawling with journalists from all over the world who were covering the coup and its aftereffects, and I had something they would pay money for. I grabbed the official government list I had been given by the Cabinet containing the personal mobile phone numbers of everyone from the king to every ministry's undersecretaries of state. The list had the king's numbers in his palaces in China and Korea, as well as in Phnom Penh; Hun Sen's private telephone and fax numbers at his offices and at home; all the CPP and FUNCINPEC generals' numbers, and much more. And they were not going to be sold cheaply.

When I have good ideas, I have bloody good ideas. And this one was a gem.

It was the cocktail hour and I knew the FCCC would be bursting at the seams with journos. When I got there it was standing room only; I climbed on a table, stood as tall as I could, and yelled out: 'Hey, guys! I have the government list of mobile phone numbers. I'm selling them so I can get money to feed kids at an orphanage. Who wants the Minister of Defence's personal telephone numbers? Who wants to talk to Hun Sen? Just tell me the name of the official you want and I'll sell you the number.'

There was a stampede. I left with several hundred dollars, which would be enough money to feed the children until the banks opened.

⟨⟩

Very early the next morning I was wakened from a deep sleep by my telephone ringing.

It was Princess Marie calling me from Bangkok. She had heard that CPP soldiers were trying to take the orphanage's land and was beside herself with sadness and frustration, as she could do nothing to help us from where she was. However, she was comforted by the knowledge I was there doing what I could and reminded me that there was still money in her account in the Indo-Suez Bank. She told me to take it all to use for the children.

I had spread the word at the FCCC the night before that my children were under threat from the CPP and that I would take any television journalist interested in covering their story to the orphanage. I would take many television teams to the orphanage to film the children over the next two weeks – certainly enough to show their plight to the world, and to Australians in particular.

Telephone calls would then come pouring in from friends I hadn't seen for years, and from people I hadn't even met, who had seen the children and me on television. They all gave me encouragement and support. I would certainly end up with the media profile I had been told I needed.

⟨⟩

Later in July my most urgent problem was that the orphanage boys over fourteen were still being accused by CPP soldiers of being FUNCINPEC deserters. We were afraid that they would be abducted and I had to find somewhere to hide them. Traditionally, the safest places in unstable times were the pagodas. I visited a monk I knew and told him of the danger my teenage boys were in. He agreed to hide five of them in his pagoda outside the city, as well as their smaller brothers who didn't want to be separated from their only family.

I squeezed the monk, the boys and their belongings into my car, and sped as quickly as my clapped-out car would allow to a quaint pagoda on the edge of the Mekong, surrounded by old boab trees. I left them money for food, hugged them goodbye, and promised to come back for them when it was safe.

The next morning I was woken up early by a telephone call from the monk. He was afraid, and what he told me scared me as well.

He said that plain-clothes officers from the Ministry of the Interior had come to interrogate him after I had dropped him off the day before. They accused him of collaborating with FUNCINPEC members and said they knew he was hiding deserters from the army in the pagoda. He had told them that the boys were from an orphanage but he didn't know which one. They demanded he give all details of the boys and their photographs to the Ministry of the Interior immediately. They had obviously followed me in my car and now his pagoda was under threat.

The monk apologised, saying he wanted to help the boys and me but could not put his pagoda and its people at risk. He asked me to give him a history of each boy and their photographs so he could comply with the demands. Before he hung up he advised me to take the green government registration plates off my car as they only attracted attention. He warned me that I was definitely being watched.

I cut the 'Princess Marie's Orphanage' heading from each of the boys' records, attached each one to The Australian Cambodia Foundation letterhead and delivered them to the monk.

I was paranoid after that, noticing that I was getting hostile looks from the new people who had moved into Sakal. Syavouth noticed it too.

I decided to ask the advice of someone I trusted. Steve Woodall was a senior police officer who was running an Australian government-funded project to improve the Cambodian prison system and to try to stop corruption in the police force.

'Let me drive you to Sakal and I'll get a reading from the reaction when you walk in,' Steve said.

When we got there, I walked to my room past the other tenants milling around outside Sakal. Steve watched from his car and followed me in a little later. He told me to pack a bag, saying he thought I should stay with his family until things settled down. 'You are not the flavour of the month in this place. Hurry up. I'll wait for you downstairs.'

I had hoped I was imagining things. I hadn't been.

⟶

Syavouth and I had arranged for the 'neutral' military police protection at the orphanage, but the kids were terrified of anyone in uniform with a gun. To them there wasn't much difference between CPP soldiers with guns and the military police soldiers with guns.

Also the soldiers expected to be paid and were eating huge quantities of food; some of them expected us to feed their families as well. When they left after providing less than a week's protection, we were a lot poorer, but wiser about the military police.

I was trying to see Hun Sen to get written confirmation that the children would not lose their home and that I could continue to run it as an orphanage, but my letters and faxes were never answered. He was busy with damage control as his international image was taking a bit of a beating. The press loved to make him look bad and he gave them plenty of ammunition, especially when he lost his temper in televised interviews with journalists who asked questions he disliked.

⟶

Si Kusol had left the orphanage about a year before, when I had got him a job in administration at FUNCINPEC headquarters. He was a bright kid and wanted to work in an office, as well as being an ardent admirer of Prince Ranariddh.

On one of my daily trips to the orphanage the kids dragged me into the boys' dorm, where Kusol was lying in bed with a bandage around his head and another dressing on his stomach. He had been at work when rockets started to fall near the headquarters. He was wounded, and didn't remember anything until he woke up in Calmette Hospital with a hell of a headache.

Somehow Soth heard that Kusol was injured and in hospital under arrest with other FUNCINPEC wounded soldiers. He went to the hospital and found Kusol. Then he waited until no-one was looking, and told a nurse that Kusol was not a soldier but from the orphanage where he worked, and that he had come to take him home. Kusol was very weak, so Soth had to carry him outside. Then he tied Kusol to him with a rope and took him back to the orphanage on his moto. I was worried about the potential backlash if CPP people found out we had kidnapped an arrested FUNCINPEC staff member.

⤚

When the banks finally opened the word spread like wildfire, and there were long queues outside all of them. For the purposes of crowd control armed soldiers were on the roof of the Indo-Suez Bank.

I wanted to laugh when I got inside. There were two signs: one said 'Deposits' and the other said 'Withdrawals'. I don't have to tell you which sign had the longest line of customers in front of it.

I wanted to withdraw the complete balance of US$15,000 and so decided to close the account altogether. Using a cheque account in the name of 'Princess Marie's Orphanage' did not seem sensible only days after the coup. I left clutching more cash in my hands than I had ever held in my life. I went to the embassy in the hope that I could leave it there for safekeeping. I was grateful that Tony Kevin agreed to this.

I went straight from the embassy to the Cambodiana Hotel to see how my Cabinet friends were faring. It was a madhouse. The Americans had provided FUNCINPEC government officials with US marines to guard them. The CPP soldiers outside the hotel were enraged by the presence of the marines, and it was only the presence of international journalists that was preventing them from going in and dragging people out.

Vibol was the only one of my friends calm enough to speak to me. He couldn't believe it when I handed him his framed graduation photo, which he knew I could only have got from his desk at the Cabinet. Thuch and Yath were obviously scared out of their minds, and were not sure if they would get safe passage to the airport to board the evacuation planes.

⤚

Cambodia has always provided me with the unexpected. But what happened the next day was really distressing.

Officials from the Ministry of Social Affairs came to the orphanage looking for me. They told Soth that I was charged with running an illegal orphanage, and that this crime attracted a twenty-year prison sentence. They told me that when the children had come to Cambodia from Site B refugee camp under the patronage of Princess Marie, she had not registered the children as orphans with the ministry. Consequently the children were not even considered to be Cambodian; they were illegal aliens because many of them had been born in the refugee camp in Thailand.

Friends told me that they thought this was really a ploy to get me to leave Cambodia so that the orphanage's land could become a military barracks again. I had to get the charges dropped.

I remembered that the temporary new First Prime Minister, hastily installed by Hun Sen to replace Prince Ranariddh, was the old FUNCINPEC Minister for Foreign Affairs, Ung Huot. Huot was an Australian–Cambodian who had been educated in Australia. He understood Australians and I felt sure he would remember me from when he visited the Cabinet. Surely if I could explain my problem to him, he would have enough power to get my charges dropped.

While I was waiting to see him, Soth and I got all the children's files together so that I could register them with the Ministry of Social Affairs. At least then the children would legally exist.

The meeting with Ung Huot went better than I had dared hope. He called the ministry on the spot and asked that the charges be dropped; especially as I had given them the documents to register the orphans officially.

'I have Miss Cox with me now,' the First Prime Minister said to them. 'And she is far too *old* for us to consider putting her in prison for twenty years.'

I smiled sweetly, like the old woman he thought I was, and made a mental note that Huot was not over-endowed with tact. But, hey, he could have insulted me all day as far as I was concerned. I had been looking at a twenty-year prison sentence in one of the most God-awful prisons in existence. I would have quite happily pleaded insanity.

⟶

Things were finally beginning to settle down a bit, and I was getting daily phone calls from Murray Nicoll in Adelaide. What I wasn't getting was something in writing from Hun Sen guaranteeing that the orphanage would not be taken over.

Steve Woodall wanted to take some fruit to the orphanage and to bring his young son with him. I told him I was not sure how safe the orphanage was. Soldiers had been there for over a week, but I still didn't have anything official saying the orphanage wouldn't be taken over.

'She'll be right, love, let's go,' Steve said, loading the car with hundreds of bananas.

The children were happy to see Steve and his son, and the bananas were scoffed down in a matter of minutes. We had said goodbye and were about half a mile down the road from the orphanage when Murray's call for the day came through. I got out of the car to get a better reception and while I was talking, a car full of armed soldiers came towards us. I knew it could only be going to the orphanage, as the road leading to it is a dead end.

Mid-sentence I got back into the driver's seat, tossed the mobile to Steve, told him and his son to get out of the car, and asked Steve to finish the interview for me.

I took off alone after the carload of soldiers. I caught up with them just outside the orphanage gates, and beeped my horn and motioned for them to stop. About six of them got out with their machine guns and I wondered what on earth I was going to say. Some of the kids were watching from the orphanage.

I wasn't being brave; I was past being scared. I was just bloody angry that soldiers were still intimidating the children.

Sometimes, when it's absolutely necessary, Khmer comes out of my mouth.

'I'm sorry but you need permission to enter the orphanage,' I said. 'You should get permission from General Tea Banh. He has told me that Hun Sen has protected the orphanage and that no CPP soldiers are allowed to enter without his knowledge.'

I hoped that if they didn't understand anything else I said at least they would recognise Hun Sen's name. They ignored me, and started to walk to the entrance of the orphanage. I walked in front of the one who looked like their leader, and who would have weighed all of fifty kilograms wringing wet. He could have been one of my older boys in the orphanage, except that he had a cruel face for someone so young.

I touched him on his chest to make him stop and listen to me.

'You can't go in. I'm sorry, but they are Hun Sen's orders; please leave.' I smiled and tried to turn him around as I walked back to their car. The other soldiers were confused and looked to their commander for orders. We all just stood there and looked at each other, and I smiled and smiled.

The leader shrugged and ordered the others into the car, and I stood there until they drove away. I drove back to where Steve was standing. He was very pissed off.

'Murray asked me what you were doing, and I couldn't bloody tell him, could I? Why didn't you tell me what you were going to do? You should never have left us here like that,' Steve said grumpily.

'Sorry Steve, but I couldn't tell you what I was going to do because I didn't know myself. I've just got to find a way to stop these goons from going in and scaring the children.'

I went back to the orphanage the next day, and the older kids said that they had been watching me and the soldiers from one of the buildings. They had been afraid I would be killed.

'But Mum, we know why they didn't shoot you. It's because of your red hair!' they said.

'My hair? What about my hair?' I asked incredulously.

'In Cambodian folklore there is a very powerful witch. She can put spells on you and turn you into stone if she doesn't like you. And she has red hair!' Soth explained, laughing. 'They think the soldiers thought you might be the red-haired witch reincarnated and so were too afraid to go against you. All the children want you to promise to keep your hair red.'

'That's good enough for me. If my red hair can protect me I don't care if people think I'm a witch,' I told the children, who were all laughing and hugging me.

Before I left them that day the children dragged me around to the chicken house. They showed me a big hole they had dug under it. They wanted me to promise to go to the orphanage if I was in danger and they would hide me in the hole. They said they would cover me with chicken shit and the soldiers would never think to look there. For kids, it was a pretty good plan, but I hoped I would never have to put it into action.

⌒

Morale was very low in the orphanage after the July 1997 fighting. I remembered advice I had been given that one way to increase self-esteem and heal people's suffering was through exposure to the arts.

I asked around and found an old man, Eb Chea, who was teaching traditional music in Phnom Penh's School of Fine Arts. He was being paid only US$15 a month and was barely able to feed himself and his wife. He jumped at the chance to earn a decent salary, and immediately started working for the foundation. He helped me buy the necessary musical instruments for us to set up our own orchestra.

Eb Chea was a national treasure. He was the only surviving member of the Royal Palace Orchestra, and showed me photographs of himself playing for Prince Sihanouk in the 1960s. All his contemporaries from the orchestra had been killed during the Pol Pot years.

While he was in the refugee camp, he knew it was just a matter of time before someone recognised him and pointed him out to the Khmer Rouge cadres. One night soldiers came to take him to the camp commander's hut and he knew he was going to be killed. He kissed his distraught wife and children goodbye and went quietly, knowing it was useless to fight. When he came face to face with the commander, he pointed his finger at Chea, accusing him of being a musician and a lackey of Prince Sihanouk. Chea confessed and knelt down waiting for death.

But then a bowl of delicious-smelling hot rice was placed under his nose, and the commander told him to play for them on some instruments they had found. From then on Chea played every night after working in the fields and was given extra rice. He explained that music was not *only* his life, but had *saved* his life.

Soon after he started teaching at the orphanage, he came to me very excited about the progress the children were making.

'Ban Sey Ha, one of the ten year olds, will be a great drummer one day, and his sister, fourteen-year-old Ban Srey March, is also very talented. They all just need to be taught,' Chea said.

It was true! I could see the change in the children almost overnight. Instead of lying on their beds in their spare time, staring at the ceiling, they were lapping up their two music lessons, one in the morning and one in the afternoon. Even the children who were not learning crowded into the music room and listened intently.

The obvious next step was to get a dance teacher, and I found Saam Monytha in the same place I had found Eb Chea. Her reports on the lessons were even more encouraging. The boys as well as the girls were learning dances faster than she could teach them. Later, I also employed Chea's daughter, Thierry, another musician.

We were getting to be quite famous in the village; the children were so good that it wasn't long before the elders from the pagoda asked if the children could play music and dance for religious and traditional celebrations. They were even paid small sums of money by the villagers to perform, and to see their faces when they had their own pocket money was a joy to behold.

Thanks to Pol Pot and his suppression of the arts, the children had never given a thought to learning anything about them. But now at the orphanage the mornings and afternoons were filled with the happy clangs and tinkles of Cambodian music, and the laughter of the children dancing as others watched and clapped. Chea, Monytha and Thierry were embraced and respected by the children, and I thank them for what they are doing.

⟵⟶

In the days just after the coup I had wanted to get all the children uplifted in the Australian evacuation. They were all sponsored by Australian or

Cambodian–Australian families who had supported them financially since 1993, they had received all the necessary health vaccinations, and were learning English and would assimilate if given the chance. I had had every reason in the first week to believe that they would be thrown out of their home at best, injured or killed at worst. Even as I appealed to the Australian government I knew it was a shot in the dark. I even told the kids not to count on it too much. Still, I was touched by the hundreds of Cambodian families in Australia who petitioned the Department of Immigration, signing undertakings they would take my children into their homes so that they would not be a drain on the Australian social security system. However, my plan came to nothing.

I still felt I hadn't done enough to ensure that the children wouldn't be harmed or turned out of their home. I decided to go to the top. The king was quoted in the local newspapers as being very disillusioned with recent events, and said he would not come to Phnom Penh until the government was more stable. He remained at his residence in Siem Reap.

I referred back to my trusty list of Cambodian government officials' telephone numbers, and sent a fax to the palace chief of protocol, requesting an audience with His Majesty King Sihanouk. I explained that most of the children I was trying to protect were originally the sons and daughters of soldiers who had fought and died for the royal family; that they came from Site B refugee camp, which was also known as Sihanouk's camp. I asked the king to grant me an audience so that I could tell him my fears.

In the middle of September when I received notification that the king would see me in Siem Reap no-one was as surprised as I was. I had to rush around and scare up a suitable Cambodian outfit to wear, and scraped the airfare together and flew to Siem Reap.

I knew that Sihanouk had little power politically and much less militarily. But if he supported the children and me privately, it was bound to be heard of in political circles; this would, if nothing else, raise my profile, which was, of course, necessary for my personal security.

I spent an hour with the king, with only his chief of protocol present. He was distressed when I told him all that had happened, but confirmed that he was politically powerless to help and couldn't give me the physical protection for the children I needed. However, he did give me a donation of US$5000 towards their care and said he would make sure part of my audience with him appeared on television so that Cambodians would see he appreciated what I was doing for those he called his 'grandchildren'.

King Sihanouk asked me to keep some of the political comments he had made to me in confidence. I got the impression it was a pleasant change for him to talk to someone who was not going to report his comments back to a foreign government or to different Cambodian political parties. From what he said, and how sad he looked when he said it, I left convinced that he was a man who lived only for his country and his people. Sure, he had made some decisions that had resulted in disaster, but I believed he had only wanted the best for the Cambodian people.

I had seen immense sadness in his eyes and despair in his voice when he had said he feared what lay ahead for Cambodia.

⌇

One day Syavouth and Vanda drove me to a village pagoda. There I was to meet an old nun and monk, both famous for the blessings of protection they gave. But the highlight of the day was when the nun sang for us. Out of that wrinkled old woman's mouth came the voice of a young woman. I felt a pain like a needle piecing my heart and tears ran down my cheeks.

Afterwards Syavouth said to me that the nun had told him and Vanda that if I became emotional during her singing it meant that her voice was mine when I had lived in Cambodia in a previous life.

This brought home to me why Cambodia draws me to its people and everything connected with it. I am powerless to stay away.

⌇

Also in September, I received an invitation from Austcare that thrilled and frightened me at the same time. They were looking for someone to be keynote speaker at their 1997 Refugee Week in Australia in October, and thought I would be suitable to make a speech about how armed conflict affects children. They would pay my fare and other associated costs.

It sounded pretty good to me until I heard that I would have to give my address at the National Press Club in Canberra. I broke out in a sweat at the thought. It had been the platform for so many greats and I had never given a speech before. However, I recognised it was a chance to draw attention to the orphanage and hopefully attract more financial support for it. We certainly needed more sponsors. Many had stopped paying their $25 a month because they thought Cambodia was too unstable and that the money wouldn't reach the children.

I agonised over preparing my speech, and when the day came to deliver it I was as nervous as a kitten and threw up in the ladies' bathroom minutes before I had to get up and speak. I had spent hours preparing my address, really putting my heart and soul into it. Once I got the hang of speaking, I relaxed, though. By the time I finished telling the stories of my children as they had told them to me, there wasn't a dry eye in the house. I saw that even some hard-nosed political journalists were trying inconspicuously to wipe away a tear or two.

However, I knew my speech was going to be shown on a television channel that aired in Cambodia. I had to be very careful what I said about Hun Sen and the coup. The children were very vulnerable, as I still had not been able to get any response from Hun Sen before I had left for Australia. At question time the journalists asked me heavy political questions. If I had answered them frankly I would probably never have been able to return to Cambodia. I danced around the questions, giving evasive responses. I had no intention of shooting myself in the foot on international television!

After this media exposure through Austcare, I was regularly asked to talk on television and radio. I discovered what a marvellous tool this could be to try to show Australians what the children's lives were like and what the future held for them. I signed up dozens of sponsors, and before I returned to Cambodia had a contract with Channel Seven for them to film the children for the television program *Witness*.

Another real highlight at the end of 1997 was meeting up with Lynne Folster, my friend from my days in Iran. She volunteered to be the foundation's new treasurer and it was reassuring to have such a trusted friend help me to take care of the kids. She had never had children either, and I knew how much she wanted them. This way, she could have dozens.

I knew how hard Lynne worked from our time together at the embassy and had no doubt about what an asset she would be. I wasn't disappointed.

Whenever I got too harebrained an idea, Lynne was able to pull me up in time. She told me I should delegate more and accept volunteers. She told me straight that there was no way I could do everything myself and that if I wanted the children to benefit and the foundation to grow, I had to let go of the reins a bit. I knew she was right and made a conscious effort to follow her wise advice.

I stayed on in Australia and had Christmas with my mother in Adelaide. Her health had suffered due to the worry I had caused her by staying in Cambodia after the coup, and so I wanted to spend some time with her.

⌒

In February 1998 I flew into Cambodia from Australia with the *Witness* camera crew, full of anticipation because Hun Sen had consented to meet with me. More than that, he had agreed that the meeting could be televised by the crew. I knew that only good could come of this.

However, I felt some trepidation while I waited outside Hun Sen's mansion in the small town of Takhmau, a few kilometres outside Phnom Penh. In the days after the coup I had on international television made no secret of my belief that Hun Sen was in the same category of leader as Pol Pot. I had condemned him for mounting the attack against Prince Ranariddh that had caused so many deaths. Also, on the way back to Cambodia I had stopped in Bangkok to pay my respects to Prince Ranariddh. I expected that Hun Sen's people would have kept him informed of all those who met with the prince, and that he would be aware my sympathies were still with FUNCINPEC.

At the meeting, Hun Sen said he had been briefed on my work with Cambodian children and that he was aware of the problems soldiers had caused at the orphanage. He said that he regretted that some soldiers had taken matters into their own hands during the beginning of the July 'event' (namely the coup). Hun Sen claimed some of these soldiers had been beyond his control for a time, but that I could rest assured the orphanage would be safe in the future.

I hesitated, and decided not to apologise for the comments he may have heard me make about him, and thanked him for his action through General Tea Banh to provide military police protection for the orphanage. Things were going so well that I thought it best to stay right away from any negative issues. I remembered a Cambodian saying, 'Don't wake sleeping tigers'. In my most respectful tone, I informed him that I had legally registered all the orphans, but understood that to comply with Cambodian laws fully, my foundation had to become a registered non-government organisation. I asked for his help in getting the papers I had lodged with the Ministry of Social Affairs approved so that I could accept more children. Hun Sen said he would look into it and that someone would contact me very soon. I left feeling somewhat differently about Hun Sen and more optimistic about the future of the orphanage and Cambodia generally.

Just a week after my talk with Hun Sen I was called into the Ministry of Social Affairs to sign a memorandum of understanding. After five minutes I left with the papers that allowed the foundation to operate as an NGO clutched in my hand.

I could have jumped over the moon! I leapt into my old car to go and tell the children the good news, but as I turned the radio on, was stopped dead in my tracks. The familiar melody of Michael Jackson's 'I'll Be There' was blasting on the local station. I felt goose bumps all over my body and knew without a doubt that Riddth's spirit was celebrating with me. I could almost hear him saying a phrase he had picked up in Sydney: 'Good on you, Mum.'

Although Prince Ranariddh and Princess Marie had been out of the country since July of the year before, I knew that they would hear about my meeting with Hun Sen and be disappointed to think I was collaborating with him and the CPP. But the fact was that for the orphanage to operate safely, it had to become a legally recognised NGO. And Hun Sen was the only person who could do this.

I was able to accept more children into the orphanage. Before I knew it, I had more than fifty orphans and had to stop until I could raise more money.

Six of the new children were from the Krean family, brothers and sisters whose parents had been killed during the fighting the year before. Their village couldn't feed all of them and they were in danger of being separated. Sukunthear, the eldest boy, aged fourteen, was father to his siblings, the youngest of whom was just three. Sukunthear had been petrified that they would be sent to distant relatives all over the country; I saw the relief on his face when he realised that they could stay together.

And how could I forget the day little Mik Samay came? Just before I had left Cambodia in October 1997, a man in his thirties came to the orphanage with his nine-year-old daughter. He was a soldier who had worked in Phnom Penh and had lost his wife in a minefield accident. He'd always been able to care for Samay since, being able to return home each evening. Now he'd been ordered to the border to fight and, unlike many soldiers, who elected to take their families to the front, had decided to leave her behind, hoping she would be safer with us.

I asked him if he wanted us to mind her for him, or was he leaving her with us permanently. This hardened soldier looked into my eyes, and said: 'She is all I have. Of course I'll return for her – if I'm alive.' Samay heard this, threw her arms around her father's neck and hugged him very tightly.

If he died in the fighting, she would never be informed. If he didn't walk through the gates to reclaim her, Samay would forever wonder what had happened to her dad. Did he die? How did he die? Did he simply stop loving her?

I couldn't watch them say goodbye to each other.

The files with the children's explanations of why they have come to the orphanage never fail to move me. All their stories are sadly familiar, telling of neglect, abuse, abandonment, slavery and violence.

Seila was about nine when his uncle brought him to my room at Sakal. The boy just sat very quietly while his story was translated.

Seila's father was a farmer who was killed when he stepped on a landmine while planting rice. Seila's mother had no way to feed her four boys; she gave them to her brother for him to take care of, before she went to Phnom Penh to become a prostitute and thus send money to provide for her children.

He told me that every month the money came from Phnom Penh to feed the children, and that there was even enough money to send Seila to school. But when he went to the village school, the other children had taunted him because everyone knew his mother was a prostitute. His uncle came home one day and found Seila trying to hang himself. He had taken the rope used to tie up the ox and climbed on a chair to throw it over a wooden rafter. He had the rope around his neck, and had just jumped off the chair when his uncle returned home and cut him down.

It was obvious that this man loved his sister's children, but he was afraid Seila would try to commit suicide again. Seila wouldn't go to school anymore and the children still called him names when they passed him in the village. Seila's uncle had tried to get the villagers to tell their children to stop treating him so badly but they didn't listen.

I agreed to take Seila on the spot. He had brought a little bag of his clothes that had been packed carefully by his uncle, who was sincere in his affection for Seila. He hugged his nephew and waved goodbye to us as we drove away.

Seila cried silently in the car and let me hold his hand, while I managed to drive and change gears with the other hand. The children greeted me with the curiosity they always showed when I arrived with someone new. They asked Seila all sorts of questions about what had happened to his family. When they asked him what had happened to his mother, Seila said that she was dead. He clearly thought that this way he could keep his shameful secret, and would not be tormented anymore.

Within two weeks, Seila was being rehabilitated from a suicidal child into one who was happily attending the local school, learning traditional dance, studying English at night classes and looking forward to attending the computer school that was being set up. What a transformation.

⌒

However, not all the children are success stories. In a group of over sixty orphans from backgrounds of hardship, it can only be expected that a few of them will have some serious behavioural problems.

The orphanage was home to me and when I was there I often forgot to take care of my wallet and other personal belongings. This was too much temptation for fourteen-year-old Phut. I had noticed that he was not as affectionate towards me as the others were. I filed this away in my mind, deciding to spend some special time with him to try to find out what was bothering him. I left this too late.

One day I left my wallet, containing a considerable amount of my own money, in the kitchen. When I went to get it, it was gone. I went home feeling very dejected. It had to be one of the children, but who?

The next morning Soth called to tell me that Phut had disappeared during the night, taking all his clothes and personal belongings. The other, older, children were very ashamed and apologised for him. Unfortunately, though, Phut had a life where the odds were stacked against him. I thought that perhaps if I had taken more notice of his behaviour and spent more one-on-one time with him, I could have prevented what happened. I did not see this theft as Phut's fault, but rather as the result of my failure to see that he was losing his battle with his problems.

However, I had to accept the fact that there were bound to be more situations like this. I vowed to try to be more perceptive in the future, and to spend more time with the children who seemed to be growing up too fast.

It is not feasible to hope Phut will return. His shame alone would prevent him from ever wanting to see me again. I wish it were otherwise.

As the children grow older it is not uncommon for some of them to grow to hate those who help them. Some feel stifled by the web of dependence that has been woven around them and will do anything to break out of it. Others, despite their resentment, stay out of fear of the unknown.

⌒

In March 1998, Prince Ranariddh and Princess Marie were allowed to return briefly to Phnom Pehn. It even looked as though the prince would be allowed to campaign as FUNCINPEC's leader in the forthcoming elections.

I knew that Princess Marie would want to see the children, so I took them in a bus to the Royal Hotel where she was staying. She told them she would always love them, but that she had asked me to take care of them for her.

In my meeting with her and Prince Ranariddh afterwards, nothing was said about my meeting with Hun Sen. I had been advised by Syavouth to take the precaution of writing a letter to Hun Sen to advise him that I was taking the children to see Princess Marie. In the letter, I said this was a personal gesture, as she was their original patron, not a politically motivated visit. I didn't want to annoy Hun Sen in any way now that things were going so well for us. I was so happy to be able to run the orphanage without the fear of the previous year, and I was encouraged by all that was happening in Cambodia as the elections approached.

I was accepted, along with dozens of others, as an official international observer by the National Election Committee (NEC), which would be monitoring the election process on 26 July. It was not lost on me that the date of the election was the first-year anniversary of Riddth's death.

Also, I spent a lot of time with Syavouth and Vanda. They had been newlyweds when Phnom Penh fell to the Khmer Rouge. Vanda delivered the first of their seven children at the end of their first year in a labour camp. Every day Syavouth saw his people become more like skeletons, and he knew that he and his family would have to escape to Thailand before they became too weak. They were in the jungle for days before they reached the border of Thailand. He killed whatever animal he could to feed them. One day he was cooking a small wild dog he had killed with his knife. He looked up to see a woman and her children, who were also trying to make it to the Thai border, staring at the cooking meat. She begged him for some, and he finally tore off a small piece and threw it on the ground, telling her to leave him alone. She picked up the dusty meat and left with her children. Syavouth said he still had nightmares about those days and wished he could see the woman and her children again. He said he would go down on his knees before them and beg their forgiveness.

Syavouth was now working hard on FUNCINPEC's election campaign. He was not being paid a salary by FUNCINPEC, which had hardly any money to spend on the campaign. But things improved for him before I went to Australia when I was able to pay him a small salary by putting him on the orphanage staff as my official translator, and counsellor for the children while I was away. At least he was able to feed himself and Vanda, and he certainly made my life easier.

The day of the elections came and I selected the village near the orphanage from which to do my observing. Many of the villagers called out greetings to me and gave me the victory sign. Everyone was dressed in their best and the whole day had a festive air about it.

When everyone had voted at the village school, the schoolyard started to empty, and the only ones left were some soldiers whose duty it was to see that the ballot boxes were kept in a locked room and not tampered with. However, observers were encouraged to stay at election points for the night as extra supervision. I wanted to finish the job and make sure the ballot boxes were not touched. I borrowed a soldier's camp bed and a mosquito net, and placed the bed right in front of the locked door where the ballot boxes were kept.

'If you want to meddle with the boxes, you will have to find men strong enough to lift me in my bed!' I joked with the villagers.

I wasn't surprised when the results showed Hun Sen and the CPP as the victors. I also knew that thousands of FUNCINPEC voters would scream corruption and intimidation by the CPP. But I had done my bit, and was satisfied that at least in my village there had been no fooling around with the votes.

⌒

I left in September to go to Australia to raise funds. Also, my eighty-four-year-old mother was very ill, and I wanted for once in my life to be of some comfort to her and to give Sandra some support.

The children kissed me goodbye with the expected tears, and promised they would pray to Buddha for my mother to get well. I knew from previous experience how much I would miss them and the extent to which they were now a permanent part of my life.

Dried Tears

Australia and Cambodia,
October 1998 – March 2000

I always found it hard to settle back into the comfortable life in Australia after spending long periods in Cambodia. Everything was so easy and uncomplicated. You turned a light switch on and you had light. You turned a tap on and you had water. Everything was as it should be. I missed the excitement and the unexpectedness of Cambodia.

At the supermarket one day the sharp contrast between Australia and Cambodia was brought home to me when a woman asked me a question.

'Excuse me, do you know where I can find the scented garbage bin liners?'

I wasn't able to answer her, I was laughing so much. *Scented* garbage bin liners. Riddth would have loved that one.

But I did overdose on movies, home-cooked meals, bubble baths, long chats with old friends, jazz clubs and driving on roads where my life was not in constant peril. It made a change arriving home from a night out and not having to pry my fingers off the steering wheel, surprised at once again having arrived home alive from venturing into Phnom Penh's traffic.

I spent some months in Adelaide caring for my mother, who was slowly recovering from another serious bout of depression. Sandra had been juggling the situation and I knew she welcomed my help. Although it was distressing to see Mum in the grip of her depression, there were times of intimacy with her which I will forever treasure.

I was dismayed when I saw on television the street riots in Phnom Penh, where government soldiers had fired on people demonstrating against the results of the elections. The sight of a monk being carried away, his saffron robes drenched with his blood, made me boil with hatred for the kind of men who could shoot their own religious leaders. But the riots were contained quickly and things went back to normal. I reminded myself that my children would not have been affected by this new outbreak of violence, as they never went into the city without my permission.

I had a challenge for this trip back to Australia. I wanted the children to have a computer school. I knew I could not rely on the government schools to give my children a decent education. The nation's literacy rate was less than 40 per cent. Teachers were either badly trained or not trained at all. The government salaries at the village school were as low as US$15 a month and were often paid several months late. This meant that the teachers had to insist that village families pay something for each child who attended the school. If I didn't pay the school, my children were threatened with being shut out of the classroom or officially failed whether or not they had passed.

Evidence of what happened to the uneducated was everywhere. I had seen for myself the *krouch chrorback*, or orange girls, as they were known, in the park near Sakal. Many of these girls were orphans who had left government orphanages at the age of eighteen and had no jobs to go to. They set themselves up on a woven mat with a plastic bag of sweet oranges, and called out to mostly teenage boys to enjoy an orange that they would peel for them. The cost of the orange increased depending on what part of the girl's body the boys wanted to touch. If the complete sex act were negotiated, the girl would take her customer to a cheap guest room nearby. Life was very dangerous for these young girls. They worked alone and had no protector. They were just one level up from the girls who travelled in pairs around the capital's restaurants and bars offering 'two for the price of one' deals. They were at the mercy of the worst kinds of drunks and sleazebags, Cambodians and foreigners alike.

One of Cambodia's problems is that visas are available on arrival at the airport, and no checks are ever done on the bona fides or characters of incoming tourists. Therefore, Cambodia is often a haven for sexual predators and other criminals. I hit the roof when I got wind that some of the older children had snuck out at night to go to a village party. They thought I was being unreasonably strict. However, they didn't read the daily newspapers that told of girls as young as eleven being abducted to be sold to men who wanted an untouched child they were sure was not carrying AIDS.

In Cambodia people were murdered every day, and half the time people never bothered to report these crimes to the police, because they knew no effort would be made to bring the guilty to justice. I read a story in the newspaper about a man who had returned to his parked car to find a seven-year-old boy stealing his side mirrors. He whipped out a knife and decapitated the boy in front of dozens of witnesses. Then he calmly drove away, knowing no-one would report the murder of an unwanted street child.

I was determined that my children would be given every opportunity not to number amongst these lost souls of Cambodia. The most I could hope for my kids when they left school were jobs as drivers, bodyguards, workers in garment factories, or as cooks or maids. I wanted more for them. Learning to use computers would give them the edge they needed to get good, well-paid jobs that would give them self-respect and independent futures.

I had promised them before I left that I would give them a computer school when I returned. They believed me, but I had no idea how I was going to achieve this. Still, bit by bit, the dream of a computer school took shape. During a visit to Chase Manhattan Bank in Sydney to see my old colleagues, I noticed that they were upgrading their computers. I asked what they were going to do with the old ones, and the rest is history. An Adelaide shipping company, Schenkers, told me if I could fill a container, they, together with P&O, would ship it to Cambodia free of charge. I was cooking with gas!

I would return to Cambodia to tell the children that, yes, their computer school was on its way. By the middle of 1999 the building to house it would have been renovated, the computers would be unpacked, I would have found a wonderful young Cambodian man to teach them, and lessons would be in full swing.

The new Australian ambassador, Dr Malcolm Leader, would officially open the school in October, and in no time the children would know more than I did. They absorbed everything the world of computers could offer them and I knew I would be able to help them find great jobs when they were ready to leave. I could hardly wait to start networking for the older ones, who would soon be ready for the big world outside the orphanage walls.

⟷

In January 1999, my visit to Australia was over and once again I was flying low over Cambodia's rice paddies. The scenes from the window were so familiar and dear to my eyes. I was in a hurry to get out to the orphanage to surprise the children, who didn't know my exact date of return.

While I was waiting for my luggage, I went to the ladies room. The toilet seat had been stolen, the top was missing from the cistern, there was no toilet paper and no water came from the tap when I turned it on. This was more like it. I really was home.

⟷

In April 1999, I was asked by the Ministry of Social Affairs to take some disabled children. I said I could only take children who were not mentally disabled and didn't need full-time nursing care. I told them I couldn't afford to employ more staff for special needs children. The ministry sent me to a government-run orphanage to see if there were disabled children there who I thought we could manage.

Here I found a collection of children with mental and physical problems that all the love and money in the world couldn't help. The staff were obviously working hard to keep the tiled floor clean, but it was impossible to keep up with the urinating of many of the young adults, whose nappies were just not big enough. There were children strapped into chairs, banging their heads against the wall. The blind, deaf, crippled, twisted and deranged were all in one room. I admired the young Cambodian women who faced this human misery every day.

There was one girl – I think she was a girl, but there was no way of knowing for sure – who consisted of only a head on a torso. She had no arms or legs, and the torso ended where the genitals would normally be. She was utterly dependent. But her face, and especially her eyes, said everything she was feeling. She didn't want to be alive. She could hear, I was told, and had 'normal' intelligence. How it would have hurt her to know that she was called 'The Football Girl' because of her shape.

I stepped over the children laid out on the floor waiting to be fed by the staff. And then I saw her. She was in a wheelchair and her legs were withered from what was obviously polio. The power of her eyes pulled me across the room. I had Syavouth with me to translate. Her name was Roth Hak Sary and she was almost eight years old.

She was intelligent enough to pick up immediately that I might be her ticket out of the hell she was living in. 'I am from Pailin, where there was a lot of fighting,' she said. 'My father was killed by a landmine, and my mother brought me here because she has a lot of children and I am too much trouble to look after. It's not my mother's fault. I cause a lot of work. It's not her fault,' Sary said. She was very anxious to defend her mother. I told Syavouth to ask her if she would like to live in a new place.

'If you come to Big Mum's orphanage you can go to the village school and play with normal children, you can learn English and how to use a sewing machine. You can learn to play music if you like and you can also learn computers,' Syavouth explained to her. 'Which one of these things would you like to do first?' he asked Sary.

She looked at him like he was a complete idiot and said, 'All of them, silly!'

I visited her often over the next couple of weeks while I was waiting for the transfer documents to be completed. I was soon able to tell her that we would pick her up at 2.00 p.m. the next day to take her to her new home.

When Syavouth and I drove up it was 2.05 p.m. Sary had got herself in her wheelchair right to the front gate and was sitting there with a small suitcase on her lap. When I lifted her out of the wheelchair to put her in the car, she looked at my watch and tapped it with her hand.

'You are five minutes late,' she complained.

Sary now practically runs the orphanage and never asks for help. She gets herself in and out of her wheelchair for meals and to bathe herself. I wanted to hug myself with joy when I heard her play in the orchestra with the other children. She is also learning computers with great zeal.

The children include her in all their games and the wheelchair is part of many of them. I worried when the road was impassable in the first wet season she was with us because the children couldn't push her wheelchair through the mud. But they sorted this out themselves, working out a roster system. The older boys and girls take it in turns carrying her piggy-back style for the kilometre and a half they have to walk to school.

These children are just so damned wonderful!

<hr>

In mid-April 1999, I joined in the festivities to mark the first time in more than thirty years that Cambodians were able to celebrate their New Year without war. There was actually no fighting anywhere in Cambodia. It seemed too good to be true. But it *was* true.

Everything was perfect. Of course, I always needed more sponsors, but all my plans were succeeding, and I started to believe that the bad times were well and truly over.

I was getting help from all kinds of volunteers. Rosanna White was a woman from Victoria, just a few years younger than me, who was to become as important to the children as I am. She lived with them for six months and did everything from teaching English and computers, to shovelling gravel and cowshit. It came as no surprise when she told me that the children had enriched her life so much that she couldn't bear to think of returning to her corporate job in Melbourne. She returned only to make arrangements so that she could come back to the children permanently.

Rosanna had been hit by the same thunderbolt that had struck me a few years before. I was going to be able to continue improving the orphanage with someone by my side who loved the children every bit as much as I did. I had thought I might feel a little jealousy, but I didn't. There are more than enough kids in Cambodia who need all the mothers they can get, and I welcomed her to my world with open arms.

⟿

Then I was hit by a seemingly impossible setback.

Princess Marie was back in Phnom Penh, as Prince Ranariddh was now the President of the National Assembly, an outcome of the 1998 elections. I hadn't spoken to her since March of the previous year. At that time she had seemed happy for me to be running the orphanage in the way I was. I now received a letter from her saying that after August 2000 my services were no longer required, as they wanted the land for another purpose. Others would take care of the orphans. This couldn't be happening.

I requested an audience with her and she accused me of taking over her project. She said she was not happy with many of the decisions I had made while she was out of the country. She was particularly furious that I had gone to Hun Sen and appeared with him on television. She did not seem to understand that I had requested the meeting because he was the only person who could stop the rebel soldiers from threatening to take over the orphanage land. I tried to explain that, in the absence of her or any of her staff, I had done the best I could. But she was very angry with me, and in Cambodia you don't argue with a princess. So I bowed my head and took her accusations.

I followed up the meeting with an abject written apology, including a print-out of the last annual report showing how much money I had raised attached. Princess Marie relayed a message to me that she could not maintain the level of financial care I seemed to need and that perhaps when August came, I should take the children with me. She did not offer any suggestions as to where I might go with over sixty children and ten staff members.

I had unwittingly made an enemy of the very family that I had originally come to Cambodia to work with. I was incredibly hurt and saddened by this turn of events, and for the next few months tried, through many channels, to get the princess to negotiate with me. This was to no avail.

I received a letter on Prince Ranariddh's letterhead in his capacity as President of the National Assembly, but signed by an assistant, asking me to leave my free accommodation. My experience told me that if the prince had not personally signed a letter, I could only assume he was unaware of its existence. I thought it was the work of Princess Marie. Quite correctly, only people who worked with the government were entitled to these free rooms, but I had remained there after the coup, simply because no-one had asked me to leave. Now she had. I could not live in Cambodia and pay rent, it was as simple as that. I ignored the letter.

Shortly after this I was called in to the Ministry of Foreign Affairs, where friends told me that I had been asked to submit my passport in the hope that if my visa was not current, I could be thrown out of the country. All this they told me confidentially. So I knew that I might not be granted another residence visa when my current one expired in May 2000.

I couldn't eat. I couldn't sleep. I was losing the orphanage land, my accommodation, and if I was not allowed to live in Cambodia, I would lose the children, and the privilege and joy of working with them. I was, in effect, about to lose my whole reason for living.

I believe there were other people behind Princess Marie's change of heart, and perhaps one day I will know the true story. I hope that in the future Princess Marie will understand why I took the actions I did and that we might once again have a friendly relationship. I will always have great admiration for the work she did in Thailand in the Cambodian refugee camps, and I know the children still honour her as their original patron, as do I.

I was well aware that the land the children occupied was coveted by many, and that Princess Marie would have been under pressure to find ways to get rid of me. Anyway, all the things she had accused me of, I could only plead guilty to. I did take over her project in her absence; I had no choice. I was often too aggressive in my desire to keep the orphanage going, and insensitive to Cambodian ways in achieving these ends. However,

I am sorry the princess could not see the hand of friendship I extended to her, and still do because I am convinced that, like me, she only wants what is best for the children. Unfortunately, so many forces were at work behind her back that she could not see me for the friend I wanted to be.

But I eventually decided that, again, the only person who could help me was Hun Sen. I knew that if he helped me, I would forever be in his debt.

When Hun Sen agreed to another Australian-televised audience in November 1999 to discuss the future of the orphanage, he surpassed all my expectations by giving the foundation ten hectares of government land with a free fifty-year lease with a right to renew.

This time I did say I was sorry for statements I had made at the time of the July 1997 'event'. I went on to say I would always respect the ruling government of Cambodia. And I meant what I said. I learn from my mistakes. In Cambodia I can't afford not to.

Hun Sen gave a gracious smile and said I did not have all the facts to hand at the time and that all this was behind us. He and I would now move forward to a new relationship.

If in late 1997 anyone had predicted I would ever feel any differently towards Hun Sen, I would have laughed in their face. But my views were changing somewhat. Although Hun Sen's actions in the past could never be overlooked or made light of, especially by those who had suffered personally, since my return to Cambodia I had seen signs of improvement. He had surrounded himself with a dedicated, hard-working team of highly educated Cambodian returnees who seemed to know what had to be done and were doing it.

The coup had taught me a lesson I needed to learn. Getting too involved in politics in Cambodia was not wise. I would have to learn to bend and sway with the bamboo stalk and swim with the tide wherever it flowed. Being too outspoken about my political preferences was flirting with danger. From now on, I would only do whatever needed to be done to improve the lot of my children.

Later in the audience with Hun Sen, while his aides were translating from documents, I mused that Cambodia was like a cork bobbing about in the surging waters of the Mekong River. When the river swells with the flood-waters of the rainy season, it becomes wild and overpowers the tiny cork, submerging it. But a cork cannot sink. And like that cork, no matter how disastrous things may be, Cambodia sooner or later drifts back to the surface to survive. The spirit of the people is unconquerable.

The icing on the cake of this audience with Hun Sen was yet to come.

'Madam, you are no longer a guest in my country,' said Hun Sen, beaming widely.

I didn't understand what he meant.

'I have the honour to inform you that I have applied to His Majesty King Sihanouk to sign a royal declaration that you be bestowed with Cambodian citizenship for your work with our country's children, and His Majesty has agreed. You are now a real Cambodian. Congratulations!'

If I had thought Hun Sen could have survived one of my bear hugs he would have got one. I spared him that, but he did not escape a kiss on the cheek.

This was an honour I would not take lightly.

⟞⟶

Now the real work would have to start. If I had achieved anything in the last six years, I was going to have to work even harder to be worthy of being so completely accepted by Cambodia. I knew that with the help of my tireless and gifted volunteers, sponsors old and new, and the support of my family and friends, I would find the strength and money I was going to need to make all the dreams for the children a reality.

In a few short years fate had swung me about like a pendulum, from a hedonistic life to a life in one of the most dangerous countries in the world. I had (and have) very little in the way of comforts that most people take for granted and my savings were dangerously low. Despite all this I was happier than I had ever been. A hedonist is one who selfishly seeks pleasure. I still do that as shamelessly as ever. I have simply found that sweet elusive pleasure in the children of Cambodia, whose unconditional love gives me everything I had been searching for.

I remember once hearing someone ask a man who was addicted to heroin what was so special about the drug. He couldn't answer. And often when I am asked, 'Why Cambodia?' I can't explain.

All I can say is that each time I fly out of Phnom Penh, I feel a flickering candle is being snuffed out in my soul. But when I return, and join the hustle and bustle at the airport, push for a place in the queues and fight to get my hands on a trolley cart for my luggage, I can feel my heart begin to chuckle. Within seconds the burnt-out candle once again burns brightly, filling me with strength, courage and love for the months of hard work ahead.

The year 2000 and beyond demands so much activity I can feel my fingers itching at the thought of all that has to be achieved. I sometimes feel like a salmon swimming against the stream when I look every day at my list of things to do. But this salmon is going to make it.

Head of the list is an operation for Roth Hak Sary. A French doctor examined her, and believes hip surgery will enable her to walk upright with the aid of callipers and sticks. At the moment she gets to and from her wheelchair on all fours and I have to stop myself from running to help her. She would hate that.

Wedding bells are in the air for Tek Lak, Riddth's best friend, who is studying sculpture in Thailand. He returned in 1999 and proposed to Phon Sophon, the oldest of the Phon family in the orphanage. She is now working as a housekeeper in Phnom Penh (she was just a little too old to start learning to use computers). They are so in love. Lak needs only another year to earn enough money to build a house for them to start their married life in and then bring up their own family.

The new land given to us by Hun Sen is crying out for farming volunteers to develop our pig, chicken, duck and fish farms, as well as our plans for growing vegetables, fruit, wood forest and flowers for profit. We must work towards being self-sufficient. My friends and volunteers have also talked about establishing a meditation area, and a beautiful fragrant garden where the children can walk and take their books to study. We want a playing field as well.

Cambodia's art is all but lost to the new generation. Eb Chea is a perfect example. He is in his seventies and one of the few music teachers alive and working. The situation is the same in sculpture, silver-smithing, lacquer-work, pottery, painting and weaving. I want to open a free mini fine arts school on the new land, not only for the orphans, but for children from the area who would return to their families at the end of the day. I envisage busloads of tourists coming to the centre to see the music and dance lessons in progress, to see the computer school and to buy the children's artwork.

I can see it all in my mind when I close my eyes. The trick is to see it when I open them.

I don't want to take in more than 100 children. When I have enough resources to take in thirty-five more I will close the doors. With over 100 children any orphanage takes on an institutional air, and we would lose that intimacy that is part of what we are. We are one big happy family, with all the joys, arguments and sorrows of one, and we want to keep it that way.

But the most daunting challenge ahead is the funding of an all-purpose building on the new land. Within weeks of having the lease signed I engaged the services of an Australian architect, and am lugging the plans for this new building with me all over Australia, trying to get corporate support. The children need to live under one roof. Living in military barracks is no way to live in Cambodia if you are an orphan. They need to feel secure under a roof where they sleep, eat and study together with their friends, and the staff, volunteers and their Big Mum are on the same property. The plans show how this can be achieved in true Cambodian architectural style, with imported building materials that will stand the test of time.

This dream to house 100 children and twenty staff and volunteers under one roof is going to cost around US$1 million, including furniture and fittings. My mouth dries up at the thought of one million anything, but I believe if I can create this home for the children in my dreams, it will happen in reality.

My pleas to the Australian government for funding have fallen on deaf ears. Their type of funding is for much larger projects, where thousands in the community benefit. The kids and me fall between the cracks.

However, through the nomination of a sponsor of the orphanage I was honoured with a Member of Australia award on Australia Day in January 2000.

I can't help thinking how fortunate I am that the A.M. award was given to me prior to the publication of this book. I wonder if I would have been crossed off the list after all was revealed about certain aspects of my life before the children found me and saved me. With this quite magnificent gold medal tucked away in a safe place, I can only hope that with the respect that comes with this kind of recognition, I can tempt more people to support the orphanage financially.

I almost feel sorry for all the Australian companies that are going to get telephone calls from me, asking to talk to them about the only Australian privately funded orphanage outside Australia. I'm not an easy person to say no to these days.

And another goal on my list, very close to the children's hearts, is a trip to Australia, so that the children can perform traditional Cambodian music and dance concerts all over the country. This is to show their appreciation and love of, and thanks to, the Australian people who have improved the quality of their lives since 1993.

When I am with the children it's as though they are the wind in the sails of my dreams, and they somehow will into being everything I wish for them. They deserve all that we can give them.